Partis

Partisan Ruptures

Self-Management, Market Reform
and the Spectre of Socialist Yugoslavia

Gal Kirn

Translated by Borut Praper
and Gal Kirn

First published by Založba Sophia, Ljubljana 2014 as *Partizanski prelomi in protislovja tržnega socializma v Jugoslaviji*

First English language edition published 2019 by Pluto Press
345 Archway Road, London N6 5AA

www.plutobooks.com

British Library Cataloguing in Publication Data
A catalogue record for this book is available from the British Library

ISBN   978 0 7453 3896 5   Hardback
ISBN   978 0 7453 3894 1   Paperback
ISBN   978 1 7868 0535 5   PDF eBook
ISBN   978 1 7868 0537 9   Kindle eBook
ISBN   978 1 7868 0536 2   EPUB eBook

This book is printed on paper suitable for recycling and made from fully managed and sustained forest sources. Logging, pulping and manufacturing processes are expected to conform to the environmental standards of the country of origin.

Typeset by Stanford DTP Services, Northampton, England

Simultaneously printed in the United Kingdom and United States of America

Contents

Illustrations

Tables

Figures

Preface

This book is a result of long-lasting research that I undertook at the end of my dissertation thesis, and which I expanded into my first monograph in Slovenian, entitled *Partizanski prelomi in protislovja tržnega social-izma* ([Partisan Ruptures and the Contradictions of Market Socialism], 2014). The English edition that you are holding in your hands is an updated and reviewed version that I translated with tremendous help from Borut Praper. In this edition I have added several sections with less locally-specific discussions that will guide readers through Yugoslav self-management, while also highlighting the radicality and experimental nature of Yugoslavia as an 'unfinished project' that continues to exert political influence despite its physical death in the 1990s. For this edition I wrote a new introduction and also Chapter 13 on socialist civil society is a result of new research. Regardless of the dominant narratives that have repeatedly demonised any return to revolution, socialism, and Yugoslavia as nostalgic at best and totalitarian at worst, I believe that the time has come when the Yugoslav project can once again shed some light on the crisis of the European project as well as becoming a vehicle for retrieving revolutionary resources for current struggles. This book does not view history as a closed process, but as a complex mixture of relations and determinations that can help prevent us from repeating certain mistakes, or, to paraphrase Beckett, help us to repeat them better. Despite numerous contradictions and internal tensions, Yugoslavia was one of the experiences on the left that can be identified as a *victory of the oppressed*. Instead of nurturing the culture of defeat and permanent crisis – the 'leftist melancholia' – it is high time for us to turn to consider the lasting ruptures and contributions to the global emancipatory movement. It is noteworthy that these victories were achieved despite major objective and subjective obstacles. Consider for a moment World War II in the heart of occupied Europe, with strong local collaborationist forces. How could one even consider and risk a partisan uprising in 1941 that would rely solely on its own forces, without any help from the Allies, who continued to support the Chetniks for a long period? Or, consider the isolation of Yugoslavia from the entire Eastern bloc in 1948? What is to be done? These events presented deep challenges to the mere existence of emancipatory movements and communist leadership. Despite all the odds, however, the oppressed were not only able to survive, but even to dream and realise another world. Another world was possible. And it still is today. And it will be possible to change the world in the future. Resisting the status quo takes tremendous powers of imagination and organisation. This is one of the important reasons why we should revisit Yugoslavia today: to insist – despite all odds and the obscurantism that surrounds us – on our alternative trajectories, to imagine and organise without succumbing to cynicism and individual micropolitics.

Let me express my deepest thanks to the individuals, collectives, and institutions that helped me develop my thoughts on this journey. First of all, the project started within the Scientific Research Centre of the Slovenian Academy of Sciences and Arts and at the University of Nova Gorica, where I finished my dissertation under the supervision of prof. Rado Riha. At the time, I also participated in numerous reading seminars at the Workers and Punks' University and benefited from the theoretical exchange with Ozren Pupovac, Slobodan Karamanić, Lev Centrih, Marko Kržan, Jernej Habjan, Stipe Čurković, Ankica Čakardić, Chiara Bonfiglioli, Mirt Komel, and Domagoj Mihajlević. During my scholarship at the Jan van Eyck Academie I held heated discussions with Panagiotis Sotiris, Peter Thomas, Nathaniel Boyd, Samo Tomšič, Sara Farris, Alberto Toscano, Katja Diefenbach, Dubravka Sekulić, Ernst van den Hemel, Pietro Bianchi, and many others. My deepest theoretical debt in the return to socialist Yugoslavia goes to Darko Suvin, Catherine Samary, Rastko Močnik, and Boris Buden, whose works left a deep impression that can be felt in parts of the book. Furthermore, I would like to mention Michael Lebowitz, who commented on the specific chapters in the book and provided strategic feedback that improved the manuscript. I have also had a few fascinating debates on the comparison between early Chavez's Venezuela and early Yugoslavia with Nestor Lopez and Carlos Gonzalos Villa. I am also grateful to Tanja Velagić from the publishing house Sophia, who helped me improve the Slovenian version of the book. I would also like to thank the previously mentioned translator Borut Praper, for whose tremendous work and comments I am extremely grateful, while for the language editing, I would like to thank Sunčan Stone, Monika Fritz, and George MacBeth. I am also grateful for the opportunity to edit and work on the translation during my Open Topic fellowship at TU Dresden, where I was hosted by prof. Christian

Prunitsch (Slavonic Studies). Last but not least, I would like to thank JAK (Slovenian Book Agency) for financially supporting the translation of my book and I would like to thank Pluto Press, especially David Shulman and Neda Tehrani for their assistance and feedback during the process. Finally, I would like to thank my parents Srečo and Nada, my brother Bor, and my partner Niloufar Tajeri for their affective and theoretical support, without which my work would never have seen the light of day.

Introduction: Beyond the Spectrum of Partisan and Socialist Yugoslavia

[…] after having overthrown totalitarian rule the societies of former Eastern Europe don't enter directly into the world of developed capitalism and Western democracy, but rather must undergo first the process of transition to this final condition, which poses as normality, that is as the universal norm of historical development in general. The process of transition is accordingly understood as the process of normalization. So everything that happens during this process automatically gains the teleological meaning intrinsically tied to the transitional narrative. This also includes the logic that before things get better – normal, capitalist, democratic, etc – they must first get worse in comparison to the former situation, concretely to the state of actual socialism. But the problem is that the transition process can turn into a real disaster. This is precisely what happened in former Yugoslavia: the collapse of the state, civil wars with horrible destruction, ethnic cleansing, atrocities, human losses, economic breakdown, political chaos.

Boris Buden, 'The Post-Yugoslavian
Condition of Institutional Critique' (2007)

To look back at Yugoslavia, socialism, and the People's Liberation Struggle during World War II in the mid-2000s, and to see in these experiences something that was worth revisiting politically or theoretically, was seen as a pure intellectual exercise, an academic curiosity, or even a nostalgic return to an irretrievable and long buried past. Post-socialism was presented as the transitional phase en route to the final stage of history – neoliberal capitalism – so why would anyone need to look backwards upon the failed projects and catastrophes of the twentieth century? This brings me to a clear starting premise linked to a research object that has not only undergone a physical death, but has also been diagnosed as a symbolically dead project. *History* had truly ended, for Yugoslavia and socialism. This did not mean merely that socialist Yugoslavia no longer existed, but also that the utopian promise and major political principles on which the new Yugoslavia was based – antifascist solidarity, abolition of class society through social ownership and workers' self-management, the equality of nations – were absent from the theoretical and political imagination of the post-socialist transition. Symbolic death carries a much more tragic dimension than physical death, since it claims that this object can never again be recuperated or resurrected. In other words, the symbolic death of socialist Yugoslavia means that her emancipatory ideas and experiences have been relegated to the dustbin of history for eternity. On the one hand, post-socialist ideology forces us to abandon the history and politics of socialism and self-management, as the general frame and system that achieved and guaranteed long-term and relative prosperity for large segments of the population, while on the other hand, post-socialism also forces us to bid farewell to Yugoslavia, the political entity that was organised as a federation in which various collectives, peoples, nations, nationalities, and (non)religions that underwent brutal civil wars in World War II could live together in peace. The historical death of socialist Yugoslavia was followed by the emergence of seven new nation-states and one ethnical state within a federative state: Slovenia, Croatia, Bosnia and Herzegovina (and within it, Republika Srpska), Montenegro, Serbia, Kosovo, and North Macedonia. Authoritarian capitalism within mono-ethnical and mono-religious communities became the indisputable horizon of their future.

Such a constellation pre-emptively strikes against any emancipatory thoughts or actions, which is the reasoning behind the interventionist nature of this book. The book will tackle a theoretical-political problem: firstly, it will attempt to unravel a (research) object thoroughly infused with negative connotations (a totalitarian state, communist crimes, dictator Tito, ethnic hatred, Balkanisation), while secondly it will approach this object by applying a theoretical means – a Marxist/historical materialist analysis – that were, within the post-Yugoslav context, not only taken out of the university curricula, but were also burnt and sent to a recycling plant in the papermills of the 1990s (Lešaja 2012).[1] The 'unbearable lightness' of the post-socialist eradication of its own recent past should not be challenged by the blind embrace of anything related to the socialist past, whether a part of the Yugoslav political or Marxist legacy. Instead, the following chapters present both failures and errors in the political and theoretical legacy, as well as detailing inspiring political ruptures and fascinating passages in the history of legal communism and self-management. In short, the main goal of this book is to present a critical and dialectical journey through partisan ruptures and their exhaustion in socialist Yugoslavia.

Even though critical reservations are necessary in relation to the (socialist) past, one should be even more critical towards the current situation of the triumphalism of the (neo)liberal and nationalist doxa. Repeating Marx's gesture, Walter Benjamin was aware that any (historical) materialist analysis needs to take an 'un-royal' road to truth and depart from the dominant ideology:

> For the materialist method the division of the true from the false is not the point of departure but the goal. That is, in other words, it takes the subject matter shot through with error, *doxa*, as its starting point. The divisions with which it begins – it is a dividing method right from the start – are divisions within this extremely mixed object itself; and the realization of this object can never be mixed and uncritical enough. Starting with the claim of presenting the object truthfully, it would minimize its chances; and it increases them significantly the more it drops this claim in its pursuit and prepares itself to realize that 'the object in itself' is not [the object] 'in truth'. (1974: 1160–61)

Thus, intervening in a specific theoretical-political context necessitates a critical evaluation of the current ideological panorama of 'post-socialism'. The initial question is how can one – *in a materialist way* – return and rethink a Yugoslavia that is marked by numerous posts: post-socialist, post-Yugoslav, and post-Marxist? Ozren Pupovac critically examined the central problematic, under the name 'post-socialism', that encompasses the situation and final horizon of all former socialist countries:

> How does post-socialism begin? The troubles of the post-socialist beginning begin already at the level of nomination … The beginning of post-socialism, its historical inception, immediately presents itself as an end, a beginning in and through an end: the end of socialism, the end of communism. This end is an exhilarating one: the end of a perceived disaster, the liberation from the torments and horrors of a 'deadly illusion' to which Cold War ideology attributed the criminalising name of "totalitarianism". But is this projection of an end, this negativity, all there is? Is post-socialism simply an announcement of something that has ended, something that has passed? Because, one might as well also ask: What is it that begins, properly speaking, after

the end? Is there something that post-socialism can claim as its own beyond the simple fact of the negation of its anteriority? (2010: 107).

Post-socialism has become the mainstream doxa, but I suggest we call it by its real name: 'national-liberalism'. The latter has not only held the keys to the interpretation of recent history but has also become the hegemonic ideological backbone for the implementation of authoritarian capitalism. Its major coordinates were based on an openly negative modality, which entails a substitution of the prefix 'post-' with the prefix 'anti-'. The real negative starting point for the dominant doxa is based on *anti*-Yugoslav(ism), *anti*-Marxism, and *anti*-socialism/-communism. Needless to say, the transitional discourse, or the 'transitology' (Kirn 2017), has taken an openly apologetic stance towards the transition to capitalism with a nationalist face. If one takes Benjamin's warning seriously, one needs to point out the most symptomatic blind spots of the dominant ideological formation. Only then can one fully understand how all critical thinking and emancipatory actions have come to be seen as youthful naivety, nostalgia, or even a claim for a totalitarian future.

There are at least *three* major symptomatic facts that the ruling ideology silenced during the transition process: *firstly*, through its socialist industrialisation, social infrastructure, and social ownership Yugoslav self-management brought major material improvements to the everyday life of the majority of people; *secondly*, in the name of the nation and its 'liberation' from socialism and Yugoslavia, the social wealth and social ownership was at first nationalised and then privatised (a dispossession of the productive means and social infrastructure); and *thirdly* – and more awkwardly for transitologists – the transition to capitalism and liberal democracy was conducted after democratic elections in which the victorious political parties promoted and led the ethnic wars. The initial quote by Boris Buden (2007) lucidly argues that the post-Yugoslavian case demonstrates where the transition process went terribly wrong and turned into a disaster. The apologists attributed the failure of the transition to a variety of causes: from the backward rural environment and the prolonged economic crisis to the lack of democratic culture and remnants of a totalitarian past. Those who spoke of 'Yugoslav totalitarianism' (see Dyker and Vejvoda 1994) actually made it 'responsible for repressing ethnic issues'. The same people also came up with the conspiracy theory stating that 'post-Yugoslav nationalism' was merely a 'continuation of Yugoslav socialism by other means, conducted essentially by the same agencies and actors'. (Jovanović 2012: 151). The process of converting the old communists into new political elites was accompanied by this bizarre confusion as regards the causes and effects and on a deeper level it functioned as a sort of redemption for the guilt that the transitional elites felt for the wars. In juxtaposition to the apologetic, (self)orientalising, and ethno-methodologist standpoint of transitional ideology Nikola Dedić articulated the intimate nexus between capitalist transition and nationalism within the post-Yugoslav context:

> Nationalism is not a phenomenon that is separate from the 'logic of transition'. On the contrary, nationalism made room for the establishment of neoliberalism, and genocide is a radical consequence of the privatization that began in the 1990s. Afterwards, with the empowerment of 'democratic' transitional governments and privatization laws (which most of the former Yugoslav states adopted in the late 1990s and early 2000s), genocide was finally legalized. Genocide, ethnic cleansing, and *nationalism*, therefore, *served* as the basis for the *accumulation of surplus value*, and paved the way for the integration of the former Yugoslav societies into the system of global capitalism. (2016: 184, emphasis mine).

Even if Dedić concluded with the instrumental relation between nationalism and the 'accumulation of surplus value', this rich passage directs us to the concept that is relevant for a concise understanding of the transition from socialism to capitalism, namely to Karl Marx's 'primitive/original accumulation of capital'.

Primitive Accumulation of Memory: Historical Revisionism and National Liberalism

Marx used the concept of 'primitive accumulation of capital' towards the end of *Capital* (vol. I) in his historical-political analysis of the beginnings of capitalism. The latter is marked by an encounter between capital and labour that has a very different rationality to Robinson Crusoe's bourgeois myth. Marx critically addressed the bourgeois narrative of the mythical origins of capitalism that divides society into diligent, creative, and deserving capitalists (embodied by the figure of Robinson) and the lazy, poor, racialised workers, whose only contribution can be found in the sale of their labour power which only takes place if the workers are necessitated by capital. Thus, the myth of Robinson as an early capitalist figure lacks a set of historical preconditions that had to take place for capitalism to occur. According to Marx the emergence of capitalism was not linked to economic skills, but to non-economic constraints that combined expropriations and enclosures, as well as disciplining the potential labour force through state violence, wars, and colonialism. The concept of primitive accumulation of capital is not useful merely for the historical evaluation of the origins of the capitalist mode of production that points to an impure start of the hegemony of capitalism over other modes of production, for it also shows in what way the economic instance was over-determined by other instances (ideological, political, legal). Furthermore, Marx's concept does not merely trace a long-gone 'primitive' mode of capitalism, but points to its structural features. One is able to detect the repetitive 'primitive' patterns of capital accumulation within each cycle of systemic crisis and further enclosures. An extremely violent process can be expected by anything and anyone who finds themselves in the way of capital expansion.

This concept could be, with a few alterations, also used to understand the post-socialist transition.[2] Evidently, the entire range of extra-economic policies and pressures, from market reform and denationalisation laws to austerity politics and foreign credits, were needed in order to execute the transition, however, I would like to add another twist. Numerous critical approaches to the post-socialist transition reveal a division between the theorists of the ideological critique (critique of historical revisionism and liberalism as the dominant ideology)[3] and those who criticise political economy (neoliberal capitalism). If the ideology critique tends to overwrite the analysis with its critique of nationalism (and wars) and focuses on the analysis of the *state* agency, then the critique of political economy observes nationalism as a secondary phenomenon, something that was practically absent in times of socialism, and focuses on the agency of *capital*. Instead of settling for a mutually exclusive alternative, the concept of 'primitive accumulation of capital' evaluates both poles of the transition process at the same time and makes it possible for us to fully understand the temporality and structural causality of the early transition process. If post-socialism is a transitory social formation dominated by capitalist elements, one should acknowledge that during the wars, it was the state and ideology (the politico-ideological instance) that guided the historical processes and determined reality, and with this, the economic transition. Furthermore, due to the state of the exception process it was easier to conduct the economic transition to capitalism. War can be seen as the ultimate 'spending' (waste and ruination) of the resources, infrastructure, wealth, and people accumulated and born in socialism. War and the transition to capitalism entailed great amounts of violence that were necessary to dismantle socialist forms of management and belief, full and stable employment (private labour power market), the sell-out of the accumulated and socialised means of (re)production and infrastructure (privatisation).[4] This process resulted in the deaths of approximately 140,000 people, the marginalisation of entire social groups and minorities, class stratification, increasing pauperisation, and intensive migration that has not stopped ever since. The post-socialist transition was structured as a 'modernisation' campaign and conducted in compliance with foreign investment agencies and European Union prerogatives (Živković 2015). However, one should not forget that the post-socialist transition was effectively organised from within, and was a consequence of the internal fractures of self-management that I explain in greater detail in the last chapters of this book.

In order to return to the 'primitive accumulation of capital' I will add that this process unfolded with a long-term *counter*-revolutionary transformation of the ideological apparatuses that targeted the memory of socialism and the events surrounding World War II. This is a process that I call the 'primitive accumulation of memory' by the state. As previously pointed out, some right-wing historical revisionists have argued that Yugoslavia was totalitarian and, in that way, the Yugoslav people experienced a 'double occupation': at first by fascism/Nazism (e.g. Germans, Italians) and then by Titoism/communism (Soviets, Yugoslavs). This situation was resolved by the final hero: the *nation*, which was affirmed during the ethnic wars of the 1990s. Prior to the 1990s nations were victims subjugated to the cruelty of external forces – be it communism, fascism, Tito, Stalin, Europe, big powers, neighbouring states – however, since the 1990s the nations live in freedom and independence.

In this constellation the historical memory of socialism and World War II had to undergo major changes and everything socialist Yugoslavia stood for had to be ideologically dismantled. Historical and political revisionism thus organised ideological campaigns that 'reinvented traditions', which defined nations as eternal, together with the presupposed pre-modern substance and religion (Salecl 1994). The new–old double bind materialised into the following: Croat–Catholic, Serbian–Orthodox, Bosnian–Muslim, Slovenian–Catholic, and 'reinvented' the specific traditions (Hobsbawm and Ranger, 1983: 1).

Within the post-socialist context, the invisible hand of the nation was presented as the eternal ether of a distant past, specific for each individual nation. The sequence of the late 1980s and 1990s worked on the 'structure of feeling' (Williams 1961) that imposed memorial continuity, and largely succeeded in re-interpreting the recent and distant history in light of methodological unity of the nation. Nationalist 'modernisation' took place despite being a theoretically outdated and sublated epistemological project, which was deconstructed and criticised by various critical feminists, post-colonialists and Marxist theorists since the 1970s.[5]

The process of 'inventing tradition' is not understood merely through the capacity to adapt and substitute the 'real' tradition as suggested by Hobsbawm but can be placed in correlation with Marx's concept of the 'primitive accumulation of capital'. This is the connection that I call the 'primitive accumulation of memory' by the state which can be seen in the saturation of nationalist memory and invented traditions. This additionally explains the creation of the strong nexus between the nation-state and capital in the former republics of Yugoslavia. The primitive accumulation of *capital* was executed in the name of the nation and expropriated people of their means of social ownership; as such it can be seen as internally linked to the memorial accumulation of the *state*. The violent beginning of the new states did not have to be shrouded in silence and concealed (cf. Žižek 2008a), as violence became the dominant language and practice within the post-Yugoslav context.

The 'accumulation of memory' by the state was deployed through *symbolic* violence with respect to the past and was tied to the physical destruction of partisan monuments and books, renaming streets and schools and erasing ideas that evoked the non-aligned, modernist, partisan, and socialist figures and times. This intensified through ethnic and legal cleansing of people who failed to comply with the ideas and the newly imagined borders of the great new nation-states. The easiest way of getting rid of partisan-socialist Yugoslavia was to consider it 'totalitarian', which drew a parallel between fascism and communism (Traverso 2017). This tale fulfilled the fantasies of both liberal and nationalist critics of Yugoslavia. However, already at first glance the totalitarian lenses presented a major misfit with the reality: firstly, the partisan struggle in Yugoslavia waged a successful struggle against fascism in World War II (defeated Hitler), and secondly, as a socialist state it was able to achieve a considerable degree of political autonomy and 'defeat' Stalin in 1948. If we apply the totalitarian paradigm to the Yugoslav context, then we have to conclude that it was partisan Tito and statesman Tito who – in real historical terms – defeated both totalitarianisms. This may seem a banal historical fact, but as the Yugoslavian legacy has been portrayed in an extremely black and white fashion during the last two decades, one needs to repeat both banal historical facts and point out the specificity of the Yugoslav path through various everyday practices, as well as explaining political and cultural critiques of the workers' self-management model with extremely complex political and economic logic (Kirn 2015).[6] Instead of the image of totalitarianism, partisan/socialist Yugoslavia was the name given to a transnational and federal idea, which was constituted through a revolution that started in multinational and antifascist solidarity. One could even claim that it was precisely because of the uniqueness of the partisan event, its relative autonomy, and the economic prosperity of socialist Yugoslavia that the recent regressive recourse to post-Yugoslavian revisionism, wars, and iconoclasm towards the recent past was so dramatic.

In the comparative perspective one should note that, despite resulting in wars, post-Yugoslav revisionism was not so different in its discursive and commemorative forms from the revisionist process in the European context. The first 'heroic' steps towards memorial regression could be traced to the (West) German revisionist historian Ernst Nolte and the *nouveaux philosophes* that dominated the French debates. The rise of neoliberalism can be understood as a double attack on the welfare state, and a neoconservative assault on the emancipatory narratives of the past (Buden 2009). Dominico Losurdo (2015) traced the ways in which the right-wing revisionists, from Furet to Nolte, demonised the legacy of the European and non-European revolutionary and Enlightenment past. In political events, the commemorative shift that most openly rehabilitated fascism dates to 1985 when the West German prime minister Helmut Kohl organised a visit and remembrance gathering at the Bitburg cemetery with the US president Ronald Reagan. While commemorating the Normandy invasion, they decided to also pay respect to 2000 German soldiers at Bitburg, which is also the final resting place of 50 SS soldiers. It did not matter that Nolte and co., were academically defeated in the *Historikstreik* of the late 1980s, as – with the German reunification and the fall of socialism – this revisionist historiography was soon translated into one of the most potent narratives of new nation-states in the former East and the recent musealisations of the socialist European past. Historical revisionism materialised in a range of cultural and academic institutions: museums, research centres, and magazines, as well as monument parks, documentary films, and commissions, all of which attempted to evidence the history of totalitarian – this time communist and partisan – violence.[7] In the post-Yugoslav transition, right-wing historical revisionism was translated into ethnic wars and cleansing of the revolutionary and antifascist past. Even though separated by their ethnic communities, the new agents of the post-Yugoslav transition collectively embarked on a clear course of historical *regression*: in moving from the federalism, multiethnicity, and transnationality of Yugoslavia to the ethnically exclusive concept of the new states, they also moved from the somewhat just redistribution of surplus value and the legal empowerment of workers to more brutal forms of extraction and hierarchical social organisation that imposed stark class divisions, pauperisation, and a peripheral position within the European economy.

The memorial accumulation of the new state and its new historians negated the established historical tenets (Hobsbawm 1992, Deutsch 1996, Anderson 2010) that modern nations did not exist before the nineteenth century 'spring of nations' (1848). Moreover, primitive memorial accumulation dug deep into the past in order to retrieve its 'symbolic capital'. Thus, the new historians and political elites helped to cultivate national myths and personal fortunes by *speculating on history instead of the future*. In more concrete terms, this memorial speculation operated across a diverse range of phantasmatic events: the Serbian nationalist ideology was launched on the 600th anniversary of the battle on the field of Kosovo with all its traumas (1389); the great Croatia appropriated the Middle Age Kingdom of Croatia; while Bosnia operated according to the legacy of the Middle Age Kingdom and the Ottoman empire. The Slovenian nationalist ideology plunged even further into the past, to the early medieval Carinthian Kingdom and realised the millennial dream of the first independent state. It was only through such speculative forces that one could draw continuity with the present times. The climax of memorial speculation was achieved in North Macedonia, which set off on the course of reviving the glory and the lineage of Alexander the Great. It did not matter that Alexander the Great was born in the Greek part of Macedonia, nor did it matter that he did not speak any Macedonian, what mattered was that the national origins were speculated far into the past in the midst of its precarious and unsecure present and future.

Musing on the absurdities of the primitive memorial accumulation of the new nation-state can easily become an ironic as well as an arrogant exercise that displays merely the 'spirit' of the ruling classes of the new nation-states. However, rather than bitterly dwelling on this distraction of the distant origins one should detect a more tragic reversal played by the resurrected ghosts of twentieth century history. All new national-ist ideologies had particular stakes on the World War II period and as Walter Benjamin warned us: *'even the dead* will not be safe from the enemy if he wins. And this enemy has not ceased to be victorious.' (1968: 255, emphasis mine). Benjamin spoke of the ruling class and the threat of fascism in the 1930s, which was realised through the horrors of World War II, and was in the post-festum of Auschwitz concluded with a warning of 'never again'. This moral norm, which was also an official ideology of socialist Yugoslavia, was completely discarded within the context of the 1990s. Furthermore, it is noteworthy that the post-Yugoslav context rehabilitated the defeated fascists from World War II who, in some places, even got baptised as the true patriots of the respective nations. These defeated ghosts were the local fascist collaborators: the Chetniks, Ustashe, Home Guards, and others. The slogans of these true 'patriots' and the ideas of great nations were openly displayed on the pedestal of new wars; moreover, the politics of ethnically cleansed and internation-ally recognised areas reigned victorious also in the Dayton peace treaty. The true 'patriots' were recognised as the real victims of the totalitarian/ partisan past, and some were even publicly or privately commemorated with memorial inscriptions, monuments, revised textbooks, TV series, Wikipedia inscriptions, and museum exhibitions. In short, right-wing historical revisionism succeeded in imagining new 'sites of memory' (victims of totalitarian crimes, rehabilitation of fascist collaborators) that in turn produced a new set of practices which strengthened the ideolog-ical cohesion of the new nation-states (Kirn 2019).

However, post-socialism did not know only right-wing historical revi-sionism. A positive narrative on the socialist past appeared as resistance to nationalism and ethnic wars. Many researchers called it 'Yugonos-talgia': a discourse that ideologically rejected the contours of the small nation-states and promoted the (after)life of Yugoslavia. Nostalgia is typically defined as the yearning for the past that had never existed and is as such marked by the obsessive fixation on the past as a way of resisting the present. Yugonostalgia is a narrative that idealises everything connected to the partisan times and socialist Yugoslavia, which is often united under the grand personality of Tito.[8] The constant reference to the great leadership of Tito is a positive appropriation of the 'totalitarian' notion of the 'cult of personality' and in many ways contributes to the commodification of the past through memorabilia, networks of bars, pilgrimage spaces, and dates to celebrate. Broadly speaking, Yugonostalgia can be measured along the effects of passivising individuals, however Tanja Petrović (2013) contributed a solid historical-anthropological study that found emancipatory dimensions within the nostalgic practices. Nostalgic individuals emerged with a critique of nationalism that can be seen in the post-conflict areas as something that provides a cohesive point amongst the youth, the history of the older generation, and the various ways of confronting the present. Despite the certain validity of this argumentation – nostalgia can be progressive – a more general strand of Yugonostalgia has already been reconciled with the new national present. The most visible Yugo-nostalgic rituals are connected to the official commemorations of heroic partisan battles during World War II. The discourse surrounding the commemorations perceives the partisan struggle merely as evidence of sovereignty of a specific nation. The revolutionary dimensions of the People's Liberation Struggle are forgotten and remain a mere sentimental *Goodbye to Tito*. The more the cultural discourses idealise the good old times, the more they confirm the *Goodbye to Tito*, which drives the final nail into the coffin of communism.

Despite its critique of nationalist excesses, Yugonostalgia – in a more structural sense – functions as the other side of the anti-totalitarian ideology. It is a reaction to the anti-totalitarian ideology, but it also succumbs to nurturing a very atemporal image of Yugoslavia that reduces the complexity of the Yugoslav past, and perhaps even contributes to the passivation. Yugonostalgia and the anti-totalitarian ideology share a discursive set of rules of what can be visible and said about the Yugoslav past. These two narratives ascribe a certain presupposed origin, goal, and subject to the historical process: there is a well-defined idealised 'origin' (Nation or Yugoslavia), 'goal' (Nation or Yugoslavia), and 'subject' (Nation or Tito).[9] If the first narrative deals with the legitimisation of the present by demonising or forgetting the partisan/Yugoslav past (and glorifying the nationalist past/present), the Yugo-nostalgic account remains stranded in its partisan and 'glorious' Yugoslav past.

Even though these accounts differ in their political conclusions, they share the same teleological structure that affirms the necessity in history, insofar as the predestined origin, goal, and subject function as the fixed and sacred core of the ideological, political, and memorial project.[10]

With the recent strengthening of the capitalist crisis that triggered a general move towards extreme right-wing populism across Europe in the wake of the 'refugee crisis', the narrative of open rehabilitation of fascism and local collaborationism is yet again on the rise across the entire territory of former Yugoslavia. The direct rehabilitation of local fascism assumes various forms: from the popularisation of fascist songs and celebrating the Hague war criminals as heroes – regardless of whether they have been released, convicted or have died – through to the erection of monuments to war criminals from the recent wars and fascist collaborators from World War II and setting up paramilitary groups that will defend the homeland against migrants and the left. This is undoubtedly a grim landscape for the post-Yugoslav culture and the politics of memory, which does not trigger any political enthusiasm, hope, or inspiration for the immediate future. This is why it is so important to resurrect the militant figures of the past and mobilise the revolutionary resources, while at the same time remaining aware of a trap of simple nostalgic commodification. Critical theory, emancipatory politics, and art need to become more combative in their claim to repeat the partisan rupture. This does not mean that we should blindly *repeat* what is clearly not here anymore, that is we cannot simply walk through the forests and imagine that we are partisans and that this is Yugoslavia and its heroic past. *On the contrary, affirming the Yugoslavian revolution means repeating the partisan and communist gesture, i.e. continuing with the communist politics that strived for a new encounter of emancipatory thought and political practice in new circumstances.* One needs to rethink Yugoslavian socialism and understand that its contradictory developments implied a form of thinking about Yugoslavia from its interiority that was linked to the affirmation of the partisan ruptures as well as to the uncompromising criticism of the revolutionary and post-revolutionary socialist transition.

The Breakdown of the Chapters

This book will take you on a journey through the major lessons of the rise and demise of project Yugoslavia, which represented a veritable rupture for radical thought and the politics of the international workers' movement. The book is divided into two parts: the first part consists of six chapters that discuss the rise of socialist Yugoslavia, conceptualised here through three 'partisan ruptures'. *Chapter 1* is theoretical and argues for a new reading of the 'partisan figure' and explains how to understand the 'partisan rupture'. Drawing on the conceptual legacy of Louis Althusser I define a 'rupture' as something that goes beyond the status quo and radically transforms the existing state of affairs. The rupture is primarily contingent; thus, it cannot be explained merely through simple historical causality; secondly, it is not irreversible; and thirdly, it is not a miraculous one-time event. I argue that the rupture is merely the beginning of a revolutionary process that has strong consequences. Finally, this chapter also offers a refutation of Carl Schmitt's 'partisan figure' that is determined by its 'telluric'/ethnical inscription. *Chapter 2* offers a short historical analysis of the material conditions in the pre-war Kingdom of Yugoslavia, the wave of repressions and exploitations of the working people, focusing on the Yugoslav communists, namely how and why they became the most important force in organising the resistance. *Chapter 3* will deploy the aforementioned conceptual means of a 'rupture' in order to understand how the Yugoslav partisans managed to launch such a successful antifascist struggle that also turned into a genuine social revolution. Against all odds and without much external support, the People's Liberation Struggle performed a long-lasting rupture that imagined a new Yugoslavia (federative and socially just) that was based on antifascist solidarity of the people within the struggle and the liberated territories. The partisan 'leap into the void' took place without any initial support or international recognition from the Allies, pointing towards political autonomy as early as 1943. This is crucial for the understanding of the subsequent partisan ruptures that followed after the war, which I argue should be understood as a continuation of the partisan politics by other means. *Chapter 4* will sketch the most pressing challenges of new Yugoslavia in light of the Trieste question, the civil war in Greece, and the failed attempt to form a Balkan socialist federation. The political enthusiasm for the reconstruction and revolutionary process brought the Yugoslav leadership and new Yugoslavia to the brink of collapse and international isolation, both from the East (the break with Stalin occurred in 1948) as well as from the West. The next two chapters focus on the lasting political capacity of the partisan-communist leadership and the strong popular support that was crucial for the undertaking of the two ruptures that followed: externally, Yugoslavia moved into a completely new arena and helped create the *Non-Aligned Movement* (*Chapter 5*) and ruptured with the Cold War bloc politics; then internally, as a critique of Stalinist 'socialism' and state nationalisation of the means of production, Yugoslav communists developed their own brand of socialism, i.e. *self-management* (*Chapter 6*). Despite the various contradictions – the workers' self-management (councils) were launched from above, the non-aligned movement presented a political compromise between extremely different economic and political state formations – I argue that the new Yugoslavia cannot be understood without the radicality of the three partisan ruptures: the *People's Liberation Struggle*, *self-management*, and the *Non-Aligned Movement*, despite the ranging levels of intensity and the different global and local effects. The first six chapters underline the affirmation of the partisan ruptures, which show Yugoslavia as a successful social revolution in the (South) European periphery (sequence 1936–1949: Spain, Greece, and Yugoslavia), a part of the forgotten history of the oppressed, while some of its consequences can be seen resonating with the anti-colonial revolutions that took place during the second part of the twentieth century.

In the second part of the book I critically dissect the developments, ambivalences, and contradictions of the socialist transition and the self-management model. *Chapter 7* offers a short theoretical journey through the recent Yugoslav studies and points out some of the major research foci. I define socialism as a transitional form that contains capitalist as well as communist elements and can be understood with the help of Michael Lebowitz's term 'contested reproduction'. The chapters will focus on various historical periods between 1950 and 1990, but the main emphasis of this part of the book can be found in the argument that the major transition to post-socialism took place through the market reform that strengthened the capitalist elements in the period between 1965 and 1972.[11] *Chapter 8* offers a short historical overview of the first and predominantly successful phase of workers' self-management that was marked by high economic growth, socialist industrialisation, the expansion of the social infrastructure, and political consolidation. The shift from nationalisation to the socialisation of the means of (re) production in the 1960s reveals a contradictory Yugoslav appropriation of Lenin's slogan 'withering away of the state'. The latter was conceived and materialised mainly through the decentralisation policy, which fought the centralising tendency of the existing socialism by gradually weakening the federal authority, while also expanding into a gigantic social self-management apparatus that accumulated on various levels and through new political institutions. *Chapter 9* provides the reader with an overview of the main characteristics of the market reform and the period that some authors refer to as 'market socialism'. The reform was devised to further democratisation and decentralisation by empowering workers in their workplaces and broadening self-management rights and institutions. One could observe the gradual establishment of the new power coalition of technocrats and the republican powers from the richer regions.

Chapters 10, 11, and *12* present the major analytical frame as well as the results of the Marxian investigation into 'market socialism' which was performed with the dissection of the proto-capitalist tendency within the enterprise (division of workers from the management over the issue of surplus value), the competition between the enterprises and regions (separation of working collectives over the issue of value distribution on the macrolevel), and the ideological critique of liberalism (the main ideological force of the reform) and finally, the nascent nationalism that took hold at the end of the sequence and as a response to the events of June 1968. These chapters exert a critique of self-management after the market reform (1965–72) and launch the hypothesis *that this historical sequence indicated the transition to post-socialism. The latter saw the strengthening of the (proto)capitalist tendency and attested to the exhaustion of the partisan ruptures that can be noticed on the social, ideological, political, and economic level.* The analysis reveals the most contradictory movements within this sequence during the following moments and processes: firstly, the class relations within the new regime were highlighted in the antagonism between the working class and the ruling class (labour strikes) on the one hand, and the temporary reconciliation between the technocrats and bureaucrats that formed the new ruling class on the other; secondly, if the market reform extended the self-management rights alongside the economic stagnation, it also contributed to ever higher unemployment, and escalated the socioeconomic differences between the various regions. The social contract between working people and their formal representatives was gradually exhausted (protests, wildcat strikes), and the core model of inter-republican solidarity – the basis of post-war Yugoslavia – was dismantled and most of the capacities were invested into new commercial banks. The concrete analysis in these chapters addresses the dynamics of the new political coalitions and subjects as well as 'external' factors: the entry into the global financial markets, establishment of commercial banks, and the criteria of economic rationality. *Chapter 12* is an ideological critique that points out how the former political figure of the working people gave space to the signifiers of market, man and even the nation. Juxtaposed to the revolutionary subjectivity of the events of June 1968, the rise in nationalist ideology formally articulated an openly anti-communist and anti-Yugoslav platform (MASPOK) for the first time since the end of the war, which was met by a wave of political repressions. In *Chapter 13* I focus on the logical conclusion of the post-socialist and market logic that peaked during the tumultuous years of the 1980s. This chapter takes the reader on a short journey through Slovenian 'civil society'. Slovenia was long seen as the most advanced of all republics and as an exemplary case for the transition to liberal capitalism. Rather than presenting a liberal teleology in the necessary destruction of socialism and Yugoslavia, this chapter presents the internal contradictions within the plural civil society agents and their subsequent 'nationalisation' during the second part of the 1980s. If the first part of the book provides an affirmative overview of the partisan ruptures, the second part of the book (Chapters 7–13) can be seen as an exhaustion of the partisan ruptures and a fresh contribution to the understanding of the internal and external causes that led to the failure of Yugoslav self-management.

Today seems to bring additional helplessness in the wake of the continuing neoliberal austerity, the strong tide of authoritarianism, and the looming climate catastrophe. But then, it never was easy. Consider a single precious lesson of the Yugoslav partisan struggle. The rupture took place in the worst possible circumstances: genocide, extermination policies, civil war, and fascist occupation, in addition to which those who participated in the partisan uprising had no external help and no allied organisation that possessed weapons in larger quantities. However, despite these objective limitations and the subjective despair of many in occupied Europe, the partisan resistance took place, based solely on its own forces and political will on the one hand, and the global theoretical and utopian image of a different world on the other hand. It moved the masses without referring to only the identitarian homogenic ethnical body which, in times of war, is a fascinating fact and legacy for future. What would the partisan rupture have been without its strong consequences in socialism and the new federative Yugoslavia? It would have remained a partisan resistance with its durability limited to the period of war. How are we to continue the revolutionary process, and are the new reproductive forms more emancipatory than the old? How and where do the dangers of the revolutionary process lie? Where and how can they be exhausted? It is the encounter between socialism and communism, revolutionary practice and theory, that can fuel new militant subjectivities, which will practice not only the idea of communism, but also fuel the critique and affirmation of socialism. Some of these challenges and questions, that were answered by socialist Yugoslavia, are highlighted in this book.

1

On Partisan Rupture as a Revolutionary Process: Tito Versus Schmitt

> Every real revolution is actually the most direct form of self-management. Our revolution was just such a revolution.
>
> Edvard Kardelj, *Reminiscences*, 1977

This chapter is a theoretical intervention, which reads Yugoslavia as a revolutionary project that consisted of three partisan ruptures. The key thesis focuses on the beginnings of the *new Yugoslavia* that emerged from World War II. New Yugoslavia cannot be regarded either as a continuation of the old Yugoslavia nor as a representative of the Eastern Bloc, whose liberation and socialist tradition were 'bestowed' upon it by the Soviet Union and in some cases, local partisan resistance formations. In Yugoslavia, the People's Liberation Struggle (the PLS) was not only a resistance movement against the fascist occupation and local collaboration, but rather the beginning of something radically new, bringing about a resolute rupture with the old order of the Kingdom of Yugoslavia. In the 'impossible circumstances' that were present in 1941, when any kind of resistance appeared futile and the 'enemy' that occupied Europe seemed invincible, nobody, it seemed, could even conceive the organisation of a resistance on the symbolical, military, or political level.

According to the philosophical–political thesis, the first partisan rupture of the PLS did not conclude with the end of the war. Instead it was a rupture that had 'long-term consequences'[1] for the way of thinking as well as for the political organisation. It continued, with somewhat different means, as the rupture with Stalin (1948), which resulted in the workers' self-management and in the rupture with the Stalinist road to socialism. Furthermore, it was also followed by the rupture with the bloc division and the establishment of the Non-Aligned Movement, which catapulted Yugoslavia from total isolation onto the global scene. The PLS rupture thus far overreached the Yugoslav context, contributing significantly to the social revolutions of the working classes and the anti-imperialist struggles of the second half of the twentieth century. To a certain degree, Yugoslavia can be perceived as a successful case of the anti-imperialist as well as anti-fascist struggle. Yugoslavia represented the victorious part of the forgotten underground history of the (South) European periphery that started with the revolution in Spain (1936–49), continued in Yugoslavia (1941–45), and ended with the defeat of the partisans in Greece (1941–49). Minehan (2006) wrote a fascinating study about this sequence, which represents the struggles against fascism and the civil wars between 1936 and 1949. We should add that this sequence is overdetermined by the social revolution that was taking place in these peripheral conjunctures. In my understanding, this was the last major revolutionary sequence in Europe in the twentieth century, characterised by the intervention of the local ruling class and the global superpowers that carried out counter-revolutionary politics.

The philosophical-political intervention of this chapter departs from the recent political-philosophical debates, through what I here term 'partisan ruptures' with the help of Althusser's concept of 'rupture'. Althusser is, in the history of Marxism, not deemed a theoretician who contributes a great deal to the thought of revolution. Indeed, he became much more famous for writing about ideology and state apparatuses (structure), for his critique of humanism, and for his structuralist understanding of capital. There are evidently very conjunctural and political texts that deal with Lenin and the October Revolution (conjuncture). Althusser put forwards a concept of 'overdetermination' that went beyond a theory of 'the weakest link' and provided a more appropriate explanation of the revolutionary situation in October. He criticised the more vulgar Marxist (and the Second International) thesis, based on the strict economic determinism that predicted the following historical development: revolution would first take place in the industrialised centres of the West. Althusser pointed out how this line of argumentation remained predominantly teleological. Although he was not specifically interested in the studies concerning the revolutionary dynamics of socialist transitions or the Yugoslav partisan revolution in particular, I argue that his most productive theses on rupture can be useful for reconsidering the radicality of the partisan rupture in the Yugoslav context, which spread beyond World War II, as we will see in the chapters yet to come.

Thoughts on Rupture: Althusser and Machiavelli

Besides reconsidering the October Revolution through the prism of 'overdetermination', we should mention another more radical shift in

Althusser's political thought, based on the concept of 'rupture' which took place already in the early 1970s. Instead of turning to the Marxist classics, Althusser returned to the Florentine thinker Machiavelli, who helped him point out one of the innermost 'limits' of Marx: the theory of the politics of 'rupture' and 'state' from the *point of view of reproduction*.[2] Instead of looking towards Marx or Lenin as the key theoreticians of the modern concept of revolution, Althusser turned to Machiavelli, who had worked and written in the extreme circumstances of political division and wild macro conflicts between the pontificate, France, the Holy Roman Empire of the German Nation, and the city-states on the one hand, and class conflicts between *popolo grosso* and *popolo minuto* on the other hand. These extreme circumstances and impossible conditions for the emergence of anything new were of key importance for Machiavelli's theoretical invention as well as for answering the question of transcending the existing coordinates and starting to think and act politically without resorting to the classic 'guidance' to the ruler or to an apology of the theological doctrine of 'divine providence'. According to Althusser, Machiavelli was the one who stumbled upon something that seemed practically and – until Machiavelli – even theoretically impossible: the establishment of Italy as an entirely new political entity.[3] The novelty or the beginning of the new politics was Machiavelli's central problem, by far transcending the clichéd syntagm of 'the end justifying the means' and the realist definition of politics as a residue of the Machiavellian legacy. In contrast, Althusser correctly demonstrated that the politics of a new beginning, of a rupture that transcends the coordinates of the existing – which in turn, even if merely provisionally, suspends the objective circumstances of the possible – is immanent to the realistic thought. Machiavelli undermined the existing traditions and performed a double rupture: one regarding the theorisation of the concrete field of politics, and the other within the social formation – a cut that leads us beyond the concrete situation. For Althusser, Machiavelli was a thinker of the 'materialism of the encounter',

> [...] thought by way of politics, and which, as such, does not take anything for granted. It is in the political void that the encounter must come about, and that national unity must 'take hold'. But this political void is first a philosophical void ... No Cause that precedes its effects is to be found in it, no Principle of morality or theology. (Althusser 2006: 113).

To think of a political void in impossible circumstances is not merely an exercise in thinking or a utopic thought experiment.[4] Through Machiavelli, Althusser extracted the main essence of the thought of a void,[5] which emerges and speaks from the position of the 'non-accomplished fact' rather than the already accomplished fact. This non-accomplished fact concerns the new position of politics and revolutionary temporality, thus significantly distinguishing Machiavelli's conception from the prevailing traditions of theology in that period. The theology of temporality of that time was rooted in the Aristotelian universe and the doctrine of 'divine providence', where the position of politics was strongly intertwined with religion. Another aspect of the prevailing 'thought' in politics during that era was embodied in a type of moral humanism, performed by Renaissance thinkers, particularly through the genre of 'advising the prince', which interlaced the position of politics with morality. Both prevailing traditions – theology as well as moral philosophy – always assigned the position of the 'accomplished fact' that had been given in advance to the origin and goal of power, thus attesting to the inevitability of the 'end' of development. In order to consider politics in this way, we do not need to think politically, but merely take a wide and final turn at the bastion of religion and morality. Althusser's Machiavelli speaks about a different kind of politics that he placed at the beginning, without any original foundations that could be deduced from the moral norms or divine providence. According to Althusser, this new politics is defined as a revolutionary encounter, 'aleatory in its effects, in that nothing in the elements of the encounter prefigures, before the actual encounter' (2006: 193). Thus, with regard to the politics of rupture, we speak about self-reference or the substantiation of the revolutionary encounter in itself, which results in an elementary equation $politics = politics$.[6] This tautological formula deals with politics in its interiority, from within and through its rupture, which pierces the presupposed morality, religion, and even the historically objective imperatives. The politics of rupture is contingent, which means that it has its own temporal modality and it does not follow any other imperatives, not even the economic one. One needs to act as if the rupture has already occurred, which indicates a specific revolutionary temporality (a concrete example of this can be seen in the next chapter, see also Žižek 2008: 460). Therefore, the politics of rupture is impossible to foresee or predict merely on the basis of the existing social circumstances or the clichéd apocalyptic prophecies: the worse the situation, the better for the revolution.[7] As I intend to demonstrate, this does not mean that the social in itself is structured as a contingency, which would reflect in a somewhat weaker version of the chaos theory. Instead, the focus will be on the point and the mechanisms that drive the contingent rupture in the moment when it becomes necessary, i.e. when it produces material consequences.

The Althusserian consideration of novelty in politics does not remain at the level of utopia that supports politics as an exercise in thought and normativisation of the Event. Instead, it measures the materiality of rupture, which influences the broader objective social circumstances. Machiavelli himself transcended purely 'utopian ideas' (Habermas 1973) and rather backed a new political figure – Cesare Borgia – in impossible circumstances. With his political ingenuity, Machiavelli was the first to suggest the political project of a unified Italy that stood against internal divisions and external imperial interests. Machiavelli's solitude in thought and politics does not mean that he remained merely on the theoretical level, lonely and misunderstood in his time. He drew an important lesson for politics from this solitude of thought: the key problems of politics are revealed and settled within the political practice itself – or, in other words, they cannot be solved in the kingdom of ideas.[8] Every revolutionary politics advances theoretically as well as in practice – through political work, which is the only way to ensure that even the most meticulous plans and ideas about the new community do not remain merely abstract, without any effects.[9] This thesis is characteristic of Althusser already in his early period, when he considered politics (and theory itself) beyond the strict division into political theory and political practice.[10]

The politics of rupture primarily addresses self-foundation – namely, the beginning of something new, supported by nothing but the rupture itself. Althusser claimed that the most important matters come after the rupture: a genuine revolutionary encounter has long-term consequences.[11] Instead of a dichotomy between political organisation and political theory, the consideration of the consequences of rupture aims to place theoretical inventions in specific historical spaces within the political practice itself – and vice versa when establishing how the mere theorisation of the new is materially connected with political struggles. Revolutionary theory and practice can never exist without each other, and they can also not be understood in a purely instrumental-linear manner: we need an idea that can be implemented in practice; or, conversely, we can wait for a revolution and then reflect upon it. These positions can be used as caricatures of the anti-intellectual and aristocrat philosophers' standpoints but will not be able to provide us with the complex relationship between theoretical and political practice. The politics of rupture follows the path of theoretical and political struggles, as it is impossible to speak of revolutionary politics otherwise. The subsequent analysis will focus primarily on the partisan rupture, which affected, with varying intensity, the political, ideological, and economic formations of the later socialist transition. This thesis tries to demythologise the 'purity' of the PLS, which appeals to the revolutionary immaculacy, as it is only interested in the impact that the PLS had on the emerging political forms.

In the current theoretical discussions that focus on the revolutionary rupture and politics of emancipation, various theoreticians no longer refer to the concept of revolution or the possibility of future socialism. Quite the opposite: many new radical theoreticians underline the 'ultimate' exhaustion and inoperability of these concepts. They prefer discussing the more tangible hegemonic populist struggles on the one hand and 'pure politics'/'the idea of communism' on the other hand.[12] Despite the important contributions of the radical theories of politics, a part of these theories is sworn to Laclau and Mouffe's project of 'radical democracy' that strives for an increasingly open and democratic society through the 'chain of equivalence' and the accumulation of various struggles that result in the diverse co-existence of all positions and groups; on the other hand Badiou's paradigm of the Event refers to a clean cut that completely severs the historical time.

Just like Althusser's rupture, Badiou's 'event' also focuses on the fundamental overthrow[13] that changes the world; an event that is by definition always infrequent and short-term. If Althusser might have agreed with Badiou's criticism of the teleology of time and the return to communism, he would definitely not agree with him regarding the non-thought of the transition into communism: the blind spot of socialism. Within the multitude of Marxist theories, significant contradictions occur regarding the pivotal questions. On the one hand we witness teleological conceptions of the end of history; while, on the other hand, messianic conceptions of revolutionary time frequently become popular. The latter are more suggestive of the theory of apocalypse or catastrophism, where – with or without the messiah – a new world is supposed to begin after the catastrophe. The choice is therefore either between teleology and the preliminary submission to the law of the capital, or the messiah of the catastrophe that starts from a blank slate, from which mankind will be born (Toscano 2013).[14]

Therefore, we cannot consider revolutionary rupture as a unique (messianic) event or as pure contingency, but rather as a process of basic social transformation. In order to truly unfold, this process has to penetrate the class relations, which is to say the productive relations, and other forms of domination. Revolutionary rupture can thus no longer be deemed as a mere rupture that interrupts time on a single occasion, but rather as a revolutionary process that produces and continues the material consequences of rupture.[15] This revolutionary process should not be sought and understood simply in terms of economic movement and modernisation. The vulgar Marxists and socialist ideologues replied to the issues of the capitalist contradiction by equating revolution with economic modernisation, i.e. a constant growth of production and competition within capitalism.[16]

Nevertheless, Althusser self-critically shifted from the theoretical to a more political conceptualisation of rupture already in the beginning of the 1970s – when he began to read Machiavelli more closely.[17] The new conception considers rupture not as a final and irreversible fact, but as a non-accomplished fact. In other words, rupture exists only in its duality: firstly, in the thought of its radical interiority and self-foundation; and secondly, in its material results and influences that unfold and form the new coordinates of material reality. In light of this, one can understand the naive theses constructed by representatives of the socialist authority, who claimed that the class struggle had already ended and that this allows us to surrender ourselves to the flow of history under the patronage of the infallible party. Following the 'end of history', we can hear more often about the teleology of the 'invisible hand of the market' that will allegedly lead to freer, more democratic, and more open societies.

Althusser initially developed the central lesson of the complex nature of rupture from the field of science. He referred to it as 'epistemological rupture',[18] which is related to the way that new scientific discoveries are made and how they are developed further:

> It is not born out of nothing, but out of a process of labour ... It is born out of the unpredictable, incredibly complex and paradoxical – but, in its contingency, necessary – conjunction of ideological, political, scientific (related to other sciences), philosophical and other 'elements',

which at some moment 'discover', but after the event, that they needed each other. (1976: 112).

If we apply the same conclusion to the political conception of rupture, we can observe that the rupture is not irreversible and does not simply end after the (revolutionary) event, but rather continues indefinitely. In other words, the emerging political form should never become completely consolidated into an institutional form that would cover up the revolutionary rupture with the state and its ideology.[19] Hence, this makes Machiavelli a predecessor to Robespierre and radical Jacobinism that had strongly influenced revolutionary thought and practice over the last two centuries. In this respect, I would also agree with Andrew Levine who wrote – in his interpretation of the French Revolution – that revolution was not merely an event 'but a process of internal transformation: a long and difficult process of unforeseeable vicissitudes and indefinite duration. Revolutionary government is a continuing and integral part of this process' (1978: 543–57).[20]

Continuation of the Rupture

The theory and politics of rupture cannot circumvent the questions about political subjectivity and the location of the revolution. Who carried out the socialist revolution and where did it happen? Did the politics of rupture already belong to the Communist Party and their connection with the space of workers (factories) beforehand, or should we be talking about a contingent encounter between the working masses, their self-organisation, and the political organisation – the Party? Was this a culmination of labour strikes and riots by the masses in predominantly urban areas, or a revolutionary strategy aimed at the connections between the agricultural and worker's population, between the underdeveloped and developed areas? We could quickly resent Althusser for his conventional academic Marxist topoi, as he never managed to break away from the privileged position and subject of politics – the vanguardist French Communist Party, whose member he remained for the rest of his life. We can follow his deliberations on revolutionary politics only indirectly – for example in the declarative statements on 'the primacy of class struggle' or the necessity of 'adopting a position'. However, even more frequently, we encounter his insistence on the political 'overdetermination' of all conjunctures. Only with Althusser's return to Machiavelli is it possible to speak about a potential, yet still immature, theorisation of political subjectivity, and the position of revolutionary politics.

If revolution is a process that starts with a rupture and often ends prematurely, a few minimum conditions have to be fulfilled in order for it to become a more permanent encounter. We can find Althusser's key thesis in the fragments that refer to the solid encounter of fortune as objective circumstances and of *virtù* as the political ability of the agent.[21] The encounter may lead to a longer duration, meaning that fortune as well as *virtù* will both undergo a transformative process. In more concrete terms, Althusser does not consider the position of political subjectivity to be necessarily assumed by a king, parliament, party, or some existing and privileged political entity. Moreover, the position of political subjectivity is determined only by the transformation during or after the rupture: '*A man of nothing who has started out from nothing starting out from an unassignable place*: these are, for Machiavelli, the conditions for regeneration' (Althusser 2006: 172). Althusser insists on considering the position of the new prince as being open to anybody, thereby fundamentally transforming the meaning of 'hereditary' prince. The new prince is no longer connected to the social or hereditary status: the natural and objective circumstances do not predetermine the fate (fortune) of the new prince. Ever since Gramsci, the figure of the prince has been completely de-individualised (Gramsci 1957), and instead of a history of great winners and conquerors, we speak about the history of people, which stays open for the emerging political subjectivity, whether it be social movements, the working class, proletariat, the Party, class coalitions, and so forth. In comparison with Gramsci's Party, Althusser does not cite any privileged cases of organisational forms. Instead, he appeals to the power and movement of the masses.[22] The duality of rupture demands a process of transformation on the part of political subjectivity, defined here as the desubstantialisation of subjectivity. The latter requires the dissolution of all presumed characteristics that adhere to the representatives of the existing order. Desubstantialisation shatters the protocols of the established political activity, meaning that in the moment of the rupture, the new prince becomes 'blind' for his past ideological predicates and identifications.

Jacques Rancière has something similar in mind when he proclaims the 'de-identification' of the political subject as the key trait of the new politics.[23] 'De-identification' means that the political agent's previous identity (in view of guild, gender, nation, class), in a fundamental discord with the existing police order, de-identifies or desubstantial-ises itself. This procedure relies on the political ability (*virtù*) of the new subjectivity, which manages (or fails) to mobilise and discipline the popular masses through a transformative process. For a long time, Lukács's definition, which considers the subjectivation of the prole-tariat as the transition from a class 'in itself' to a class 'for itself', has remained one of the most pervasive theories of political subjectivation in Marxism. The class consciousness of the part of society that is devoid of all means and will abolish all class relations is of key importance in this supposition (Lukács 1971). The proletariat occupies the key position that brings together the various Marxist currents: from the economic teleology and the urgency of the revolution due to unbearable circumstances to the eschatological narrations about the coming of the proletariat. Althusser maintains a position that is not easily included in these Marxist currents and definitely differs from Lukács's position. Once Althusser considers that a revolutionary encounter does not pre-suppose a single privileged subject it becomes clear that this progress in history does not presuppose the necessity of the revolutionary success of the proletariat.[24] The dialectics of encounter and radical contingency that unfolds within the political process does not give us any guarantees for 'success'. The sole guarantee of success lies, at the very best, in the longstanding, difficult, and frequently contradictory political part of the masses and political organisation, which cannot be limited to the hope that the better side of history will progress, or to technocratic planned economic development.

When Althusser insists on the primacy of rupture and the desubstan-tialisation procedure, he declares war on the subject of the prince; the new prince is secondary. His attack on the 'cult of personality' and the criticism of the humanist thesis, which is the mirror image of the per-sonality cult, should be seen in this light. One vital question emerges in the politics of rupture and in all theories of transition: *who or what makes history*? If we cannot answer this question in accordance with economic teleology, the humanist answer, however, suggests activity. In humanism, history is made by humans (Althusser 2005). Humanism puts the new prince in the position of the primary agent of human practice and the construction of the world; on the other hand, Althusser's position implies the prince's secondary position. When we proceed from the primacy of encounter over subject, this results in the separation of substance or de-identification of the prince with the prefigured categories of nation, race, civilisation. This process also enables us to draw a strong dividing line against the fascist politics, which ascribes a presupposed identity of a pure nation, pure race, and pure religion and introduces the categories of 'enemies' and 'friends'.[25] Certain considerations of 'pure politics' share the Schmittian moment that actually criticises the institutions of liberal democracy and even calls for a discontinuation and breakdown of the liberal (democratic) legal order. In this sense, we can speak about the radicalism of fascism, which inscribes substance into its politics: in the name of the superior race and nation, a new civilisation and a new order of death shall emerge. This politics of hatred encompasses a logic that differs utterly from the one addressed by a revolutionary politics (of the proletariat), which calls for a de-identification process. The new politics is committed to the revolutionary perspective of a non-accomplished fact that, through rupture, builds a new community, which abolishes the relations of exploitation and dominance.[26] The continuation of the revolutionary process is therefore not merely a formal gesture of disruption, but a long-term process of establishing egalitarian relations within the new social formation. Instead of defending an authentic community of a national state machine that reconciles and neutralises class interests, we must, at this point, deal with the movement of negation, which abolishes the relations of exploitation and dominance. By practicing negative politics and rupture, another kind of exclusion is presumed: i.e. the exclusion of the politics of exploitation and dominance, which can lead, in the event of tension between classes and threats to the colonial constellation or capitalist investments to a civil war, an anti-colonialist war, an armed rebellion, or even revolutionary terror.[27] Despite the process of desubstantialisation, the new prince does not remain desubstantialised forever, i.e. he does not remain an ever floating empty signifier that is without any kind of identity: if a permanent encounter with long-term consequences occurs, we are likely to witness a transition into a new social formation that will develop new political forms. If they are not capable of continuing or repeating the rupture, these political forms may easily succumb to corruption, disintegration, and exhaustion of the revolutionary politics. The long duration of the new politics fails if it is incapable of maintaining the contingency (of rupture) in the centre of its actions. The inclusion of contingency in the core of the new political authority requires the communist organisation to distance itself from the state, meaning that the Party – although it assumes power – does not become merely one of the components of the state apparatus.[28] This means that in the new situation, the 'new prince' will not act without conflicts, as the new political form is not an isolated utopian island. Instead, he will constantly face the basic political quandary: in what way should the rupture continue and how should he form new connections between himself, the political organisation, the masses, and the political ideas? Therefore, the new political organisation does not merely point to an open and contingent position of power,[29] but needs to restore the encounter between the universal political principles (equality, justice) and social emancipatory movements.[30]

The political process does not progress only on the part of the new prince, but also on the part of fortune – i.e. those historical circumstances that we encountered in the moment of rupture. Althusser says that the new prince is 'a man of nothing who has started out from nothing starting out from an unassignable place'.[31] The fact that he can start anywhere implies a process of 'delocalisation', and let us say with Fanon 'decolonisation' of the existing fortune, meaning that we also need to tackle the issue of the status of space, its use, appropriation, occupation, or even destruction.[32] Delocalisation/decolonisation is a process that encompasses the transformation of the political space and emphasises the capability of politics to expand outside the presupposed spaces of public politics. Thus, the classic gathering spaces – agorae, parliaments, governments, and all those established institutions of democratic imagery that have strict procedural rules of governing in common – are joined by a plethora of less visible spaces that managed to establish recognised spaces of politics. The twentieth century's revolutionary experiences also show that the politics of rupture occurred outside of the established spaces of public politics. Apart from anticolonial struggles it was feminist struggles that loosened the paradigm of the inevitable connection between public spaces and politics in the most significant way. This occurred due to the lack of recognition of women in political bodies, as well as the subsequent suppositions that stemmed from the motto 'the personal is political', – issues that were at a later stage politicised by feminist theory and struggles through the viewpoint of reproduction (for recent research, see Bhattacharya 2017). Through this the relationship between the visible and the invisible, as well as the general perception of the space of politics, experienced a colossal shift. Delocalisation can be seen in the politicisation of everyday practices in all those spaces that are (still) designated as private or corporate. The key focus of politics shifts toward the spheres of *work* (factories, trade unions, workers' parties), *family* (feminist movements, subcultural movements, gender emancipation), the *military apparatus* (Soviets, guerrilla movements), *universities* (student movements), *colonies* (anti-colonial movements), as well as other marginal and cultural institutions.

Regardless of the underground and increasingly stronger current of delocalisation – something that Deleuze and Guattari called 'deterritorialisation' – it is still possible to claim that the majority of twentieth-century revolutionary movements intended to take over the public as well as state authority. The invisible and unrecognised parts of society with their spaces of politics aimed at the appropriation as well as occupation of the apparatuses of power. Radical political practice and theory often encountered the most difficulties in the area of state and politics of the Party, in which it failed to develop a conceptual apparatus and long-term political alternatives. In accordance with the vulgar definition of the state as 'a tool in the hands of the working class', the socialist revolutions were followed by a synthesis of the Party's authority and the authority of the state. This process was (also) used to stifle the revolutionary process.[33] Regardless of the relevance and necessity of the critique of the state as the ultimate instance of the political and the restriction of the parliamentary horizon, I do not consider the politics of rupture as unequivocally anti-state. Not only is this trait typical of the official libertarian ideology and neoliberalism, but in a 'leftist' politics the position of the 'beautiful soul' of utopianism and anti-institutionalism is also quite frequent. As Paul le Blanc astutely wrote when he revisited Lenin, a revolutionary leap is not something that occurs instantaneously in a pure form as the immediate and ultimate abolition of capital and the state, as the political forces never operate at their maximum. Instead, the politics of rupture develops strategies that fight the battle within the existing forms as well as establishing new political forms that are herein referred to as anti-apparatus forms.

The delocalisation current is associated with relocalisation; or, to put it differently, the new and the old spaces of politics are always an open field of the ideological, economic, and political struggle. Delocalisation should therefore not be equated with the concept of exodus or Negri's ontological-natural transition of the multitude into the communist reality.[34] Instead, delocalisation should be considered as immanent to the process of political subjectivation that takes place within the system and makes room for the emergence of an anti-apparatus. A provisional conclusion would thus be that the politics of rupture is successful only when both the desubstantialisation of the new prince (which activates the people's political ability – *virtù* – by organising new political forms) and the delocalisation of fortune (a transformation of the old circumstances and the emergence of the spaces of the anti-apparatus) take place simultaneously. The strenuous political work only begins once the rupture has occurred: decolonised subject, decolonised political space. Moreover, the rupture functions as a permanent implementation of a non-accomplished fact: the revolutionary process.

Tito's No to Schmitt: On the Incompatibility of the Partisan Figures

Let me conclude with a short refutation of Schmitt's theorisation of partisan politics that has become popular in recent years. What would be Tito's answer to Carl Schmitt? Why turn to Schmitt, if we can instead enter into conversation with Che Guevara, Ho Chi Minh, Frantz Fanon, or Angela Davis? Why make popular a figure who expressed nothing but cynicism over anti-colonial and liberation struggles? Due to recent attempts to mobilise Schmitt in the populist left struggle and left thinking, I have decided to take part in this discussion.[35] It might come as a surprise that one of the more elaborate theories of partisan subjectivity was created by a fascist thinker. Furthermore, Schmitt's general definition of politics is restricted to a more formal understanding of a new sovereign's decision, which is very convenient for taking shortcuts in the political arena. There are thus several reasons for an attack against Schmitt's position. Firstly, there are merely a few theoretical works that consistently focus on the partisan politics, and for this reason alone the partisan figure deserves a more detailed conceptualisation.[36] Secondly, my intention is to remove the partisan figure from both the nostalgic outlook on the immaculate beginnings of the PLS and Schmitt's famous nationalist reappropriation of the partisan figure: the fascist enemies have to be beaten also in their own territory, although retrospectively.

It is interesting that we can barely find any mention of the Yugoslav People's Liberation Struggle in Schmitt's book – in fact, there is a single footnote, stating that during World War II a struggle took place between Tito's and the monarchic partisans.[37] However, this historical inaccuracy – or simply a deception – is not the book's main blind spot. Namely, Schmitt's analyses do not contain any thematisations between colonialism and Nazism, as he ignores a broad range of class-related and geopolitical conflicts in the middle of the twentieth century.[38] Schmitt remains blind to the critique of Nazism as a radical continuation of colonialism and to the recognition of the very core of the partisan movement, which (also) involves an anti-colonial moment. As I have already pointed out, the Yugoslav People's Liberation Struggle was a name for a revolutionary project that severed the bindings of European colonialism, asserting the Balkans as an area of negative phantasm and colonial interests.

Schmitt's argument in favour of the partisan figure contradicts his previous works, in which he firmly defended the concept of sovereignty and the primacy of the state of emergency during the establishment of state authority. His theory of the partisan figure does not exhibit merely a critique of liberal democratic institutions: the partisan figure allows him to sever the umbilical cord of the Westphalian state sovereignty, which allegedly no longer corresponded to the new international reality of the twentieth century. The partisan political and military strategy shook the ground beneath the (inter)state sovereignty and the state monopoly on the physical force: namely, the partisans as a political force undermined the international state legal order at the point where enemies are seen as other states (Schmitt 2004: 14).[39] If international law recognises clearly-defined state borders, partisan warfare does not necessarily observe them. Moreover, partisans became the greatest threat to the sovereign order because they failed to settle for an easy integration into the state apparatuses.[40]

According to Schmitt, the main characteristics of the partisan figure include the following: dedication to the struggle, mobility, irregular military forces, and the telluric character of the struggle. Schmitt's definition is partially accurate, as he correctly points out the novelty of the partisan struggle as one that subverts the conventional framework of the war between two or more countries. I also agree with his definition of two otherwise secondary characteristics of the partisan struggle: the mobility of the struggle and the irregularity of the military forces. Schmitt does not elaborate further on these two moments. I can only add that the irregularity of the partisan struggle results from the shortage of material resources and the availability of fighting men and women that primarily depends on the seasons, the situation during offensives, and the support of the local population. The thesis of the mobility of the partisan operations is also not disputable, as the partisan units attempt – in light of their deficient weaponry and inferior numbers – to surprise the occupiers by means of various tactics: impeding the occupiers' strike forces, in particular by destroying their infrastructure, while simultaneously organising a decent, even uncompromising resistance in case of open confrontations with the enemy forces. The typology of the military actions varies – from diversions, infiltrations, and sabotage, to assassinations and lightning-quick actions – which points at the peculiarities involved in the partisan warfare that ceased to be restricted merely to the partisan struggle a long time ago.

The next characteristic is perhaps more surprising, as Schmitt underlined the partisans' political and even revolutionary dedication. It is also interesting that Schmitt referred to Mao Tse-Tung as the main protagonist of his theory. What were the reasons behind Schmitt's choice? As Toscano has correctly ascertained (2008: 430), Schmitt's key goal was to destroy the bipolarity of the world, thus opening three extensive areas of civilisations. This vision of a new world is profoundly depoliticised and in accordance with the Huntingtonian orientalistic-culturalist vision found in his *Clash of Civilisations*. It is interesting that Mao's China is supposed to play an important role in this new multipolarity (ibid., 426).[41] Schmitt keeps looking for the enemies of the bipolar world and for eternal conflicts (Žižek 1999: 28),[42] which culminates in a depoliticised vision of the world and the re-establishment of the authority of the major sovereign states. Paradoxically, the figure of the partisan (Mao) and his revolutionary dedication fall back to the model of sovereignty and a multipolar civilisational order.

However, the key problem of Schmitt's partisan figure lies in the last characteristic: the supposed 'telluric character' of the struggle points at an important foundation of its position, which, in turn, reveals a very important feature. Namely, the telluric character 'overdetermines' all other elements – including the revolutionary dedication of the partisan struggle. The partisan's adherence and attachment to the land points out the exceedingly conservative character of Schmitt's deliberations, referred to as a '*counter*-revolutionary position' by Toscano.[43] The telluric nature of partisans thus remains intimately associated with their native soil, for which they are ready to fight to their bitter end. This sort of emphasis neutralises or even denies the political and revolutionary engagement of the national liberation struggles, which have defined the revolutionary political theory and practice in the twentieth century. The definition of 'earth' transforms radically in the partisan struggles. To put this differently: new political communities that did not exist before the struggle or have since been built on new foundations can only arise through this struggle. Contrary to this, Schmitt's conception of the telluric is placed into the imagery of a new race or nation, while the broader transformative dynamics and the inclusion of the partisan figure into the anti-imperialist, anti-fascist, or anti-colonial struggle remain absent.

The points at which Schmitt's supposedly formal theory turns to focus on history and presents a few key examples of partisan struggles, provide for even more obvious evidence of the privileged position he accords to the telluric. Schmitt likes to discuss the Spanish guerrilla warfare against Napoleon and Mao's global struggle for extensive areas that we have already mentioned. He does not theorise about the possibility that tensions can arise between the telluric and the political engagement; however, this can be applied for a more precise upgrade of the partisan figure. It is precisely this internal tension between the telluric and the revolutionary that severs the partisan figure in two: we are *either* dealing with a strictly-defined national partisan struggle,[44] *or* we are discussing a revolutionary partisan struggle. This does not mean that a revolutionary struggle cannot contain telluric moments, nor that a partisan struggle cannot also be a national struggle. It only means that for the analysis at hand, the awareness of the other aspect – i.e. the place and time in which the revolutionary struggle 'overdetermines' the telluric dimension – is more important. As a rule, the telluric-national dimension applies to the struggle against the oppression of national and ethnic minorities, and against foreign occupiers. The differentiation of the partisan figure from the revolutionary and national struggle is beneficial if we can evaluate whether a certain partisan struggle also practices more universal and revolutionary politics besides its national-telluric dimensions. These moments can only be determined by analysing the political actions and demands and by establishing whether the struggle has indeed transformed the existing social relations, or whether it has remained within the framework of the (national) reaction to occupation and horizon of a liberal state. Has the struggle resulted in liberation or a compromise with the existing regime? Has the partisan movement in question ended up in the position of the old political structures and been reintegrated into the political system, or has a wider transformative process been at work? When partisan movements preserve their merely telluric and national dimensions, they can readily succumb to 'phobic nationalism'.[45] The Yugoslav partisans – the movement as well as the leadership of this revolutionary project – were well aware of this fact. To have insisted solely on the telluric moment would not have resulted in Tito's victory. Furthermore, it would also not have had much in common with the idea and policy of international solidarity or the creation of a new egalitarian world. The scope of Schmitt's ideas has much more to do with the politics of the substantialisation of the enemy and the exclusion of the Other than with the watershed achievements that could be noticed in Spain, Yugoslavia, Greece, and other anti-colonial struggles following the end of World War II.[46]

Benjamin Noys is right in opposing Schmitt's apparent support for the revolutionary dedication of the partisans. He established that Schmitt's argument in favour of the telluric is much closer to the telluric elements of Fichte's formulations that 'are displaced by a proletarian internationalism that has no respect for the "nomos of the earth"' (Noys 2019).[47] Schmitt thus concludes that the core of the partisan struggle lies in the defence of the telluric, while the partisans must by no means become a 'manipulated cog in the wheel of world-revolutionary aggression' (ibid., 52). Our thesis on Schmitt's oscillation between the telluric and the revolutionary is even more intense at this point, as Schmitt is clearly leaning towards the telluric. Instead of the telluric differentiation between enemies and friends, the partisan struggle can also be defined, in Toscano's words, as: 'practices of antagonism that do not substantialize friendship and enmity' (2008: 250), but instead attempt 'to revisit the idea of solidarity, which combines the reference to an abstract principle, collective action and a widening circle of allegiances' (ibid., 251). In political reality, the ideal partisan figure does not exist, or it is at the very outset characterised by the collective dimension of the partisan struggle. The latter consists of a multitude of individuals – fighting women and men, supporters, and groups of exceedingly diverse political convictions and individual motivations. All of these actors are resolved to take a position that also has consequences for the (re)definition of *the nomos* in a given situation.

The concretisation and the historical circumstances of the emergence of the Yugoslav People's Liberation Struggle will be discussed in the following two chapters, which are more historical-political and adhere to the aforementioned theoretical guidelines: firstly, that a rupture with long-term effects took place in Yugoslavia during World War II; and secondly that the strategy of the liberation struggle 'solved' the national as well as the class question. This is why we can speak of a revolution and the emergence of the Second Yugoslavia, qualitatively different from the First. In short, Tito's answer to Schmitt's telluric image of the national partisan was a resolute *no*. Instead, Tito embarked on a path of international struggle alongside the oppressed and colonised nations, which will become even clearer after World War II.

2

A Brief Outline of the End of the Kingdom of Yugoslavia and the Partisan Beginnings of World War II

The Kingdom of Serbs, Croats, and Slovenes (the Kingdom of SHS) was established after the end of World War I with the dissolution of the Austro-Hungarian Monarchy and the Ottoman Empire and in light of the regional dominance of the Kingdom of Serbia, which had been a part of the so-called Little Entente and therefore on the victorious side in the war. For the bourgeois elites and the representatives of the three nations that lived in the Balkans, the Kingdom of SHS represented a historical achievement, which can be interpreted as a part of the bourgeois struggle for national liberation that had begun with the Balkan Wars in the years leading up to World War I. The Kingdom of SHS was a monarchy ruled by the Karađorđević Royal Family. As such, it should be understood as a temporary class compromise of the contemporaneous ruling stratum – the bourgeois representatives of the national parties and the Serbian aristocracy (Čalić 2010). As soon as we examine the Kingdom of SHS 'from below', it becomes clear that the working masses did not gain any social or economic rights in this new entity and that they were formally – only for a very short time – not represented. The Kingdom of SHS was therefore not only shaken by the open political tensions between the various parts of the bourgeoisie, but in particular by labour strikes and peasant uprisings that hinted at the increasingly evident economic contradictions.

From the global perspective, the Kingdom of SHS was notably underdeveloped, with significant illiteracy levels (over 80 per cent of the peasant population). In the context of the European economy, this placed it on the very periphery to which foreign capital investments would flow in the subsequent years. The spirit of the October Revolution crossed the borders of the Kingdom of SHS in at least two important political experiences. Firstly, it is significant that as early as in the beginning of 1919, all local social democratic parties (with a membership of 130,000 people, see Tomić and Stojaković 2013) merged into what would eventually be called the Communist Party of Yugoslavia. At the first local elections, the latter gained enormous support in larger cities, for example in Niš and Skopje. It also became the majority party in Belgrade and Zagreb. The democratically elected communist mayors were not allowed to assume their offices and take over city governance. Moreover, in 1920 the Communist Party of Yugoslavia (the CPY) became the third strongest party with 13 per cent of all votes, which triggered a red alert amongst the aristocracy and the bourgeois political parties. It is clear that the anti-communist fears were very much alive also due to the brief autonomist experiments in the territory of the Kingdom of SHS at the end of World War I, which involved a few socialist elements. Both, the Republic of Prekmurje (in the east of present-day Slovenia) and the Banat Republic (in Vojvodina/Romania), were exceedingly mixed areas in terms of ethnicities. At the time, the precise locations of the new national borders were still subject to interpretation, and the communist revolution in Hungary was spreading.[1]

The first political debates in parliament immediately revealed that not even all of the key bourgeois political parties were able to find common ground in relation to the system in the Kingdom of SHS. The first constitution – the St. Vitus' Day Constitution – was implemented in 1921, and it specified a clear political orientation of the new entity. This Constitution was characterised by the centralist and unitarian conception of Yugoslavia, based on the idea of integral Yugoslavism. A Yugoslav melting pot, leading to the merger of the three tribes within the Kingdom of SHS, was a fantasy of the Royal Family.[2] This ethnic-tribal 'trinity' would fuse into a single Yugoslav nation. However, this idea was not funded on solid grounds and in practice resulted in constant repression of a number of nations, nationalities, and a permanent political conflict, even in the bourgeois arena. The unitarianism of the trinity eclipsed the autonomist[3] and clericalist visions of the Monarchy, supported in particular by the Croatian Peasant Party and the Slovenian Clerical Party, the representatives of the Croatian and Slovenian interests. The third alternative vision, favouring a radical transformation of the Kingdom of SHS, was communist. As already mentioned, this vision initially rode the wave of communist revolutions at the end of World War I. 1920 was characterised by a massive railway strike and a genuine peasant uprising in Croatia. The labour strikes and rebellions were violently suppressed (Tomić and Stojaković, 2013). At the same time, the police and the former authorities prevented the communists who had won the local elections in cities from taking over their positions of power. Thus, the communist leaders were arrested in some cities, and their authority was severely impeded in others. In 1920, with the so-called 'obznana' (announcement), the ruling class prohibited the activities of the Communist Party and severely restricted the 'democratic' political space as well as – in particular – the actions of the working classes. The workers lost their political representation, while the members of the Party had no choice but to start operating illegally. Some of them fled the country, others were imprisoned, and at various times certain leaders and activists would even be executed (Petranović, 1988). The internal political conflicts and economic contradictions kept deteriorating until the end of the 1920s. Assassinations of MPs and political activists were a matter of everyday political repression, and the 'murder of Stjepan Radić, leader of the Croatian Peasant Party (HSS – *Hrvatska seljačka stranka*), that prompted King Alexander Karađorđević to declare a royal dictatorship' (Pavlaković 2016: 19) on 6 January 1929 was the most symptomatic. At that time, the Kingdom of SHS was renamed into the Kingdom of Yugoslavia – i.e. the First Yugoslavia. In the new state, the level of censorship was severe, while political freedoms were additionally restricted to the political struggle of the two Yugoslav bourgeois parties that were recognised by the aristocracy.[4] In these circumstances, the Kingdom did not merely end up on the outskirts of the capitalist system, which was subject to rampant exploitation, but instead – as Lev Centrih correctly concluded – Yugoslavia 'assumed the position of the periphery, where fascist regimes prevailed'.[5] In the mid-1930s, the ruling class within the Kingdom of Yugoslavia became increasingly dependent on Germany and Italy in the economic sense, while it based its 'authentic' political ideas on the theories of fascist corporatism. This was especially true of the Catholic conservative circles. At the time, Yugoslavia functioned as a semi-fascist dictatorship, in which the working and peasant masses were brutally exploited. Due to the increasingly prominent protests of peasants and workers, the severe political repression became ever stronger.[6] Long prison sentences, forced relocations, and death penalties for communist leaders and protest organisers constituted a part of everyday politics. Concentration camps for political opponents – mainly communists and nationalists – existed in Yugoslavia already in 1935.[7]

Throughout the 1920s, the CPY was pushed underground due to its illegal status. Due to the separation between the activists and operatives within the Kingdom of SHS and those who operated in exile, and in light of the activities of the various factions, the CPY could in no way agree on a single vision with regard to the future of Yugoslavia. Ever since its establishment in 1919, the Communist Party was beset by the internal conflicts between the centralists and internationalists; those who wanted to use Yugoslavia in order to establish a Balkan socialist federation, and those who were leaning towards federalism in Yugoslavia (Petranović 1988). Therefore, the only vision that actually existed for a long time was the importance of the class struggle and Balkan internationalism, while the question of the nations and specifics pertaining to Yugoslavia itself remained marginal. In the circumstances of the increasingly intense class struggle, the dictatorship, and the worsening oppression against the nations and nationalities, the support of the socialist and communist forces gradually increased. These forces were therefore becoming more and more visible and active, also because of the international struggle against fascism. In 1935, the CPY leadership decided to no longer support the breakup of Yugoslavia. Instead, it gradually focused on the possibility of a federal regime and a more prudent resolution of the national issue, which it had ignored for far too long due to the dictate of the Comintern and its interests. In this year, the Party membership increased to 3000 members. However, their persecution was intense, and almost a thousand members and most leaders were arrested by March 1936. 1937 was probably the most critical year for the CPY. In this year the Communist Party of Croatia and the Communist Party of Slovenia were established, and this indicated the political and organisational shift towards the federalist principle as well as the emphasis on the national liberation and the joint Popular Front efforts against fascism.[8] The Party leadership was taken over by someone belonging to the new generation of leaders, who had stayed out of the factional struggles for a long time: Josip Broz Tito (Pirjevec 2011), who was appointed as the active General Secretary of the CPY. A year later, in 1938, Tito managed to avoid Stalin's extensive purges in Moscow and gradually became a de facto general secretary without being confirmed by Moscow (for details see Gužvica forthcoming). At the time he coordinated the Party's activities from Paris.[9]

While the communist parties in Yugoslavia and elsewhere were undergoing a process of reorganisation, an enormous and coordinated action took place, ensuring solidarity with the international brigades in the Spanish Civil War, which were joined by many communists and anti-fascists. At the time, the Party's central leadership, headed by Tito, was located in Paris, from where it coordinated the Spanish volunteers as well as the political programme and actions in its native Yugoslavia.[10] The Spanish Revolution and Civil War certainly represented the most important political event for the Yugoslav communist movement, as they both influenced the new theoretical and political conception of the partisan struggle and the imagery of the people's liberation that brought together the class and national struggles. Many survivors of the Spanish conflict gained precious experience that was used in the partisan struggle in Yugoslavia a few years later. On 23 October 1937, Tito gave a directive to all CPY regional committees, stating that Spain was

> [...] the central question of all international politics. The struggle of the heroic Spanish people is not just a struggle which will result in the victory or defeat of democracy only in Spain, rather it is the beginning of an armed conflict between fascism and democracy over the world. (Pavlaković 2016: 29).

Despite the fact that the dictatorship in Yugoslavia attempted to prevent any involvement of its citizens in Spain, the CPY managed to successfully coordinate an action in which they brought 1665 volunteers (including fourteen women) to Spain, all of whom would fight on the republican side. During the war, most of the Yugoslav volunteers fought in different battalions, however at some point the majority of them formed and assumed command of the 129th international brigade. More than half of the volunteers died in action, while at least some 300 of them returned to Yugoslavia following their captivity in Gurs and other camps in France. All of them joined the partisans and were amongst the first political and military organisers. Most of them were in charge of the most important military detachments once the partisan resistance had been properly organised.

Pavlaković's study correctly assessed the role Spain played for the Yugoslav communists and for the specificity of the liberation struggle. Spain was important for both Croats and Slovenians, as

> The CPY characterised the Spanish Popular Front as a defender of democracy and of the national rights of Basques and Catalans. Although the origins of the national question in Spain differed greatly

from the situation in Yugoslavia, there were many similarities between the Basque and Catalan struggles for national rights with those of Yugoslavia's own ethnic groups. During the Spanish Civil War, the Republic gave the Basques and Catalans significant autonomy that was in sharp contrast to the centralised state envisioned by the Nationalists. This federal concept of the state had many parallels with the CPY's political platform, which was frequently emphasised in communist publications. It was during this period that Tito oversaw the creation of the Communist Parties of Slovenia and Croatia, which further strengthened the CPY's claim that they fought for national liberation from the *Greater Serbian* bourgeoisie. (Ibid. 30).

In 1939, in light of the experiences from Spain and as a critical reflection on the Kingdom of Yugoslavia and the historical conditions, Edvard Kardelj, who would later become the major ideologue of Yugoslav self-management, published his most widely-known book on the national question, entitled *The Development of the Slovenian National Question*. This work brought together a new articulation of class and nation that was realised and continued in the partisan struggle during World War II. Apart from the theoretical assessment, the Yugoslav leadership also took a critical note of certain vital experiences in the tragic defeat. Unlike the warfare in Spain,[11] Tito and his entourage decided already early in the war not to fight frontally or in urban centres, but instead decided to organise guerrilla partisan warfare: 'Tito rejected the classic form of a revolutionary uprising, organised and spreading in the cities: instead, he would lead a partisan war' (Nađ 1979: 7).

Despite the much more active involvement of the CPY in Yugoslavia at the end of the 1930s, the Party leadership's return to Yugoslavia, and the experiences in Spain, we need to be aware that in 1940 the CPY only had a few thousand members, while the League of Communist Youth had a few thousand members more: its membership consisted mostly of students and cultural workers from the big cities. As we have already mentioned, these modest numbers were compensated by a very well-organised network of cells and local organisations, which were, on one hand used to operating illegally, and exceedingly dedicated and determined in their belief in a different world on the other. This major organisational network proved to be of the highest importance once the invasion and the fascist occupation began.

The Invasion of Yugoslavia began on 6 April 1941 and ended on 17 April with the total surrender of the Yugoslav government to the Axis powers. The Yugoslav army disarmed voluntarily, and the Royal Court and the majority of the government emigrated to London, where they acted as legal representatives of the Kingdom of Yugoslavia that in reality no longer existed. During the war, the government-in-exile would gradually lose the people's support, while the situation in Yugoslavia was worsening: the peoples and nations of Yugoslavia were subjected to atrocities performed over them by the occupiers. The occupying forces divided Yugoslavia into the following occupation zones: Italian (parts of Slovenia, Croatia, Montenegro, and western Macedonia), German (parts of Slovenia, Croatia, Serbia, Bosnia and Herzegovina), Hungarian (a part of Slovenia, minor parts of Croatia and Serbia), Bulgarian (parts of Serbia and Macedonia), and Albanian (Kosovo) (Tomasevich 2001: 175–228). Apart from these occupation regimes, the quisling fascist Independent State of Croatia (*Nezavisna država Hrvatska*, the NDH) was also established. In reality, this was an Italian–German protectorate, and the authority of the Croatian nation was only asserted within a permitted framework.[12] An exceedingly strong Ustasha movement existed in the NDH: as the most extreme part of this fascist entity, the Ustashe actively participated in all of the genocidal policies and offensives against the anti-fascist movement as well as managing the largest Croatian concentration camp of Jasenovac. A part of the Monarchy's old political elite – in particular the bourgeois and conservative clerical forces including the Catholic Church leadership – started openly collaborating with the Nazis and fascists, serving the occupation regime as informers, translators, guards, executioners, denunciators of the partisans, and so forth: in short, as national traitors, as they were later called by the anti-fascist organisations.

From the very beginning, the occupation regimes implemented a policy of racial and ethnic cleansing, subjecting the members of the resistance movement as well as the civilian population to brutal terror. The violence against civilians was sometimes justified as 'retaliatory measures' due to the activities of 'the bandits'. The local population would be sent to forced labour; their homes would be burned down; and many were exterminated en masse in the concentration camps. All of this was a part of the systematic extrajudicial executions and the normal Nazi sovereign regime, in which the local collaborators played an important role. During fascist terror in Yugoslavia, hundreds of thousands of members of the Roma, Jewish, and homosexual communities, as well as partisans, anti-fascists, and generally members of various Slavic nationalities lost their lives due to their racial/ethnical belonging or (alleged) political opposition to fascism (Tomasevich 2001: 580–610).[13]

The beginning of the war was completely chaotic: the Yugoslav army capitulated, many of those who had not been politically active until then had no wish of joining the resistance straight away, and some people were unsure as to whom they should join. In the aftermath of the invasion, a significant number of competitive political and military formations, which declared themselves as truly patriotic, started operating autonomously – or they, at least on the declarative level, fought against the occupiers. We must not forget that in the countryside, mobilisation into military formations would often take place by force and in fear, and therefore the situation was not immediately clear. Apart from the partisans, the White Guard, and the Ustashe, Draža Mihailović's Chetniks were at the forefront when it came to organising the countryside and the peasant population. Mihailović would soon become the Royal Minister of the army and thus an extended arm of the King and the government-in-exile in London. Chetniks were predominantly active in Serbia and parts of the NDH, and until mid-1943 they kept receiving significant material support from the British and American Allies. Despite the currently popular historical revisionism,[14] which attempts to show the Chetniks in a positive and almost heroic light, the historical facts indicate that soon after the onset of the organised resistance, Chetniks started collaborating with the German and Italian forces. As of the end of 1943 and especially during the last year of the war, Chetniks would occasionally openly use the Nazis weapons and transport.[15] Officially, the political goal of the Chetnik movement was to restore the monarchic Greater Serbia in Yugoslavia, while its military operations focused in particular on the struggle against the partisans, whom the Chetniks had renounced as early as at the end of the autumn of 1941 in Užice. Furthermore, the Chetniks were not much better than the Ustashe in their actions against the local population in Bosnia, where mass killings and rape took place. The Chetniks fought openly on the side of the Nazis during the main offensives of 1942 and 1943, which were aimed at destroying the Supreme Headquarters of the People's Liberation Struggle headed by Tito and eradicating the majority of the partisan forces in Bosnia.[16] Half way through 1943, following the Battle of Sutjeska, the partisans completely defeated the majority of Chetnik detachments. The Chetnik movement never recovered from this defeat.

Quite a few recognised collaborating formations, which organised themselves against the PLS and assisted in upholding the order in the occupation zones, existed in the territory of Yugoslavia. Politically, these forces can be defined as anti-revolutionary and fascist, with the local specifics of patriotism and clericalism. In Slovenia, the White Guard or the anti-communist militia – which mostly mobilised the clerical-fascist youth, a part of the peasant population, and the conservative camp – was the best organised. Until the capitulation of Italy, it was sponsored by the Italian fascists. However, in 1943 the Home Guard, which swore its allegiance to Hitler, was formed.[17] The Albanian SS units, called *Skanderbeg*, operated in Kosovo and Macedonia, while the more bourgeois Albanian forces established their resistance in the *Balli Kombëtar* organisation, which would later collaborate with the Nazis as well as with the Chetniks in order to prevent the partisan resistance forming in Kosovo (Magaš 1993: 32–4). The Muslim *Handschar* SS division was formed in Bosnia and took part in military operations, while a strong Ustashe movement operated in the NDH. Smaller groups were also in existence – for example the Serbian State Guard (the so-called *Nedićevci* or *Nedić's Men*), the Serbian Volunteer Corps (also known as *Ljotićevci* or *Ljotić's Men*), and others who remained loyal to the Royal Family – however, these smaller formations never gained any significant military importance.

The local collaborators would mainly represent the class interests of the old political class and the ideology of extreme nationalists, who were (with the exception of the Chetniks) excluded from the government and the optics regarding the trinity of the Kingdom of Yugoslavia. All fascist collaborators supported ethnically-cleansed territories, radicalising the logic of the national particularisms dating back to pre-war Yugoslavia. Nevertheless, it remained a delicate question as to how the collaborators would justify their subservience to their fascist overlords, who pursued denationalisation policies that were in complete opposition with the collaborators' own national allegiance. How could they portray their activities as truly patriotic when they swore allegiance to fascism? Let us not forget that the pre-war anti-Bolshevism was an ideological platform organised by the clericalist circles in conjuncture with pan-European fascism. These unappeasable oppositions and the fusion of local fascism with the occupying forces led directly to the civil war, in which people from the same regions and villages fought each other.

Moreover, sometimes the political dividing lines would be drawn within a single family. The fascist terror and the civil war ultimately resulted in a high number of fatalities and a vast displaced population within Yugoslavia, as well as paving the way towards the mass resistance against fascism. The illegal communist organisation was the best 'prepared' for the war and the fascist occupation, even though it started out weak in numbers. However, not even this can explain the social moment, rupture, and revolution, all of which took place during the course of war. The following chapter will focus on the reasons why the PLS presented a clear rupture with the old Yugoslavia.

3
Partisan Rupture I:
The People's Liberation Struggle

Once we delve into the prevailing discussions on World War II and the National Liberation Struggle in the post-Yugoslav context, we face two rather poor alternatives: one can either side with the rightists who promote the open rehabilitation of (local) fascism (see Kirn, forthcoming); or, within a more liberal discourse, one can hear the arguments that may indeed favour the National Liberation Struggle, but merely refer to the nationalistic aspect of the partisan struggle. In other words, the latter perceive the partisan struggle as a part of the national history and the struggle for the national statehood, while overlooking the most inventive and pivotal element within this struggle: the dialectics between the working classes and nations, the social revolution, national liberation, and the more far-reaching anti-imperialist struggle. The struggle over the ideological and political meanings of the National Liberation Struggle involves additional confusion, as the concepts of 'the nation' and 'the people' are often merged into a single phrase: *the nation*.[1] In order to emphasise the revolutionary side of the struggle, Ozren Pupovac recently promoted the term People's Liberation Struggle (the PLS), which also gives the political subject in the term a more open character. It is also noteworthy that the term and strategy of the PLS simultaneously implies and puts into practice this very separation and re-articulation of the struggles for the liberation of the dominated people and oppressed nations.

This chapter follows the hypothesis that the PLS did not abolish the two sides of the liberation, which would result in the 'national reconciliation' that is the dominant liberal policy of memory; but rather, that the PLS was constantly affected by a variety of intensities and by the diverse conceptions of the 'revolutionary people'.[2] The national question was never secondary; but as pointed out above, the image of the 'partisan' introduced a criterion that goes beyond the specific ethnic adherence. The PLS became a political space open to male as well as female members of all nations and nationalities, which means that it was, from the outset, built on the international anti-fascist foundations. In Pupovac's opinion, the PLS practiced a political principle which not only related to 'a single people or a single nation, but rather to all nations and peoples within the repressive monarchic regime as well as to all the people beset by domination, whether on the basis of class, gender, nationality or religion'.[3] The partisan movement represents a rupture, placed in the position of an 'unrealised fact', which did not exist and was impossible to predict in the contemporaneous situation and in the kingdom that had capitulated. The Yugoslav PLS represents one of the few examples of anti-fascist politics (if not the only successful one) that developed a positive programme. The issue of the PLS does not concern merely the military victory over the foreign occupying forces or the proclamation of the end of the Kingdom of Yugoslavia's dictatorship. What is of key importance is the phenomenon of the 'long duration' of the PLS, which does not only praise the winter sessions or spotlessness of the Anti-Fascist Council for the National Liberation of Yugoslavia, but rather focuses on the long-term effects of the new cultural and political forms of the mass people's democracy, continued after the war by the socialist revolution and the Federal People's Republic of Yugoslavia.

Desubstantialisation of the Partisan Figure and Delocalisation/Decolonisation of the Struggle

In this section I will address the most important aspects that gave rise to the 'long duration' of the PLS and show what were its major long-term effects. Firstly, I will be working with parts of the Althusserian conceptual apparatus from the previous chapter, which understands the PLS as the revolutionary encounter between the political capacity (*virtù*) and the wartime fortune of the partisans, resulting in the desubstantialisation of the previous identifications and delocalisation of politics; secondly, I would like to define the PLS as a unique encounter between the masses, revolutionary ideas, and the anti-fascist organisation. At the beginning of the war, the partisan struggle had to rely on its own forces, as it did not enjoy strong external support: the considerable material support, provided by the (Western) Allies, was intended primarily for the Chetniks. However, despite the impossible situation, the male and female fighters of the PLS did not wait pragmatically. Instead, they risked the entire existence of all those who resisted the occupation.[4] The resolute faith in a different world and the unwavering discipline of the communists, proletarian brigades, and the Supreme Headquarters certainly contributed greatly to the long duration of the partisan rupture. However, at the same time we cannot overlook the tenacity and determination of the masses and the people's discipline, which gradually seeped into all segments of society. Without the people's support and inventiveness, the PLS would never have existed nor persisted. In the cultivation and development of political agility and people's discipline I would like to locate what Althusser abstractly termed *virtù*: the partisan *virtù* is therefore the cultural and political capacity, the inventiveness of the people, and the people's reliance on their own forces. The PLS is not merely the official socialist ideology, constructing the myth of epic battles:[5] its essential part can be found in the less visible dimensions of the people's support and political endeavours. Instead of praising the great leader Tito and the image of partisan shock troops, the PLS is much more suitably described with the image of the *collective partisan movement*.

The processes of *desubstantialisation* and *delocalisation* of the struggle played a key role in the continuation of the consequences of the partisan rupture. The essence of the desubstantialisation of the partisan struggle lies in the fact that despite the all-present fascist politics and the ethnic moment, the partisans did not succumb to arguing in favour of ethnic communities. Instead, they had the national emancipation policy in mind. In his extensive study, Miklavž Komelj (2008) analysed a number of partisan discussions and artworks that refrained from equating fascism and Nazism with Germanism or Italianism. Partisans did not consider the Italian or German nation as the external enemy, but instead focused on the fascist occupiers, which confirms Carl Schmitt's departure critique and his insistence on the 'telluric' (see Chapter 1). Furthermore, the partisans also fought against the local 'patriotic' collaborators. If we based our criterion for the distinction between friends and foes solely on Schmitt's telluric-ethnic foundation, we would find it impossible to avoid the revolutionary dimensions of the civil war that took place between the two politically exclusive principles: international anti-fascist solidarity and people's authority on the one hand, and the regime of death and nationalist hatred, taking place in the name of a pure race/nation, on the other hand (Komelj 2008: 30).[6] The main mottoes and goals of the Liberation Front appealed to the aforementioned struggle against the occupiers among the ruins of imperialism and the call to the fight 'against our own traitorous capitalist elite'. Unlike the ethnic model of politics, the partisans opened a completely *new horizon for Yugoslavia*, as Komelj argues,

> the Yugoslav partisan Movement was … the first mass people's uprising in occupied Europe and should as such be considered as one of the large-scale revolutionary movements of the twentieth century … the Yugoslav revolution was the largest revolutionary uprising after the Spanish Civil War. (Ibid., 24).

In juxtaposition to the moral pragmatism of those who waited for the Allies and contrary to the principle of ethnic hatred, the PLS represented the only political force open to all nations and nationalities, men and women. In reality, the partisans can be seen as the only 'Yugoslav' and gender-mixed armed group that operated within Yugoslavia. Moreover, the Yugoslav partisans operated and cooperated beyond the 'ethnic' borders, aiding in the formation of other partisan detachments.[7] In late 1943, the detachments of the Italian Army that refused to serve the Nazis changed sides and joined the 'Garibaldi partisan Division' – over 5000 Italian soldiers became partisans and fought against the Nazi occupation.[8]

In order to understand the novelty of the partisan figure, which was introduced into the Yugoslav context, one needs to point out the evident fact that the partisans did not operate on the basis of a (single) ethnic identity.[9] The partisan struggle became a movement with political implications, a movement open to male and female members of all nations and nationalities, which made it a unique phenomenon. In the eyes of the partisans, one's adherence to the international anti-fascist struggle was the main criterion, which went against the mainstream journalistic and political definition of a partisan as someone connected to a party. Also, if we refer to the Merriam–Webster Dictionary, it defines a 'partisan' as 'a firm adherent to a party, faction, cause or person, especially one exhibiting blind, prejudiced and unreasoning allegiance'. The second part of the sentence works as an ideological supplement that assigns a very concrete feature to partisans: the absence of any regulative idea, faculty of reasoning; a partisan exhibits blind and unreasoning allegiance. This sombre representation delegitimises the figure of the partisan from the outset and implies fanaticism, thus eternally resigning the partisan to the realm of irrational politics. Not only does the revolt and resistance against the fascist occupation in such harsh circumstances demand political courage, but it also departs from the abstract and very rational maxim: *we have a right and reason to revolt*, to paraphrase Badiou (2005). Each and every Yugoslav partisan had to take an oath, which on 26 September 1941 Tito himself drafted:

> We, the people's partisans of Yugoslavia, have taken up arms to wage a relentless struggle against the bloodthirsty enemies who have enslaved our country and are exterminating our peoples. In the name of liberty and justice for our people, we swear that we shall be orderly, persevering and fearless, that we shall spare neither blood nor life in fighting the fascist invaders and all traitors to the people until they are completely annihilated. (Tito 1966: 31).

The subject is 'we, the people's partisans of Yugoslavia', which already points to the collective dimension of the partisans – rather than starting with 'I' (and stating one's name, as was the case in the army of the Kingdom of Yugoslavia), the partisan oath opened with a proclamation that goes beyond an individual partisan and calls for a fighting collective. This call is voiced by the people and addresses all antifascists within Yugoslavia. The partisan oath used in Slovenia declares the wartime allegiances even more politically and explicitly. It reads as follows:

> I – a partisan of the People's Liberation Army of the Slovenian nation, who fights on the side of the Soviet Union's Red Army of workers and peasants and all other nations that struggle for freedom … for brotherhood and peace among nations and the people, for a better future of the working people … against the fascist oppressors and barbarians; and that I will not leave the ranks of the partisans … until the ultimate victory over the fascist occupiers and the complete liberation of the Slovenian nation … To the fight for freedom! (In Lešnik and Tomc 1995: 84)[10]

This oath did not merely highlight the Red Army as the main ally of the Slovenian partisans, but also mentioned the nascent political subject of the 'working people' (cf. Pupovac 2008). This announced a very different political imagery, a kind of synthesis between the working class, the peasants, and the people. The oath ended on a more poetic appeal, stating that freedom was only attainable through fighting. Partisan is thus the name that stands for both the collective struggle and the new beginning, for the modality that made an immense sacrifice in the name of liberation. The partisan figure is therefore not male and militaristic, but rather a symbol of a collective transformation. This collective embodied the partisan principle that was directed against the World War II principle of ethnic hatred.

Once we start discussing the process of the desubstantialisation of the partisan figure, we immediately come across the process of the delocalisation of the PLS. If the PLS members were not only members of ethnically-cleansed communities (e.g. Slovenians), then the PLS affirmed itself as a framework in which the former symbolic meanings dissolved, redefining the concepts of territory, country, and state and with it a question of belonging. Desubstantialisation triggered the process of rebuilding something that was supposedly eternal and unchanging: *the national character*. Article No. 4 of the Slovenian Liberation Front programme addressed this issue head-on, as it called upon the people to change their human nature as well as everything that had formerly functioned as a natural fact:

> With the fight for liberation and the activation of the Slovenian masses, the Liberation Front will transform the Slovenian national character. The Slovenian people, fighting for their national and human rights, are creating a new model of active Slovenianism.[11]

The commitment to the new model of 'active Slovenianism' represented a change to the pre-existing situation, going beyond the prevailing stereotype of servitude and instead practicing the principles of solidarity, brotherhood, and comradeship between the members of the various religious, national, as well as (inter)class alliances. The partisan movement did not merely aspire to liberate the country from its occupiers, but strove to radically transform Slovenia, Yugoslavia, as well as the entire world. The partisan movement worked in accordance with what Deleuze and Guattari refer to as 'deterritorialisation' – i.e. constantly moving and attempting to liberate the occupied territories. Furthermore, the modality of 'deterritorialisation' and the principle of comradeship are openly critical of the presupposed link between the population, territory, and the state that today sees partisans as a proto form of a nation-state. I would argue against this national reading of the partisan past, which also refrains from seeing any real political alternatives – the gems of the future alternative world – in it. Thus, despite their precarious and unstable existence, the partisan-liberated territories practiced forms of self-government, while their deterritorialising principle was re-territorialised. One could speak of the realisation of the partisan imaginary and the materialisation of solidarity in the liberated territories with their set of political, cultural, and social institutions. This 'dual power' structure and alternative spatiality came into existence in the autumn of 1941 and expanded exponentially until the autumn of 1943. The liberated areas were predominantly located in the countryside and contributed to the accelerated revolutionising of the rural population.

If we understand the logic of delocalisation in more concrete spatial terms, then we can speak of the PLS unfolding in both the occupied as well as the liberated territories. Large cities in particular possessed excellently-organised illegal networks of activities and organisations.[12] Delocalisation is thus inherent to the more general politics of decolonisation of the whole space. The trust between the numerous members was quintessential, since the fascist secret police constantly pursued the organisers of the illegal networks in larger cities. In Ljubljana, for example, the latter extended from an illegal radio station (*Kričač*) and printing presses (*Podmornica*[13]), poster-graphic design workshops and gathering spaces for reading, to the production and supply of food and clothing, as well as to the provision of care for the children of the partisans and the internees and prisoners.[14] Komelj's thesis was that in Ljubljana, for example, a form of dual power – a city within the city – became apparent, and thus partisan organisations could be established deep in the hostile territory.[15] The partisan logic of delocalising the PLS entailed the politicisation of all the towns and areas that would by no means be thought of as political before the war: *the illiterate population in rural regions*. Although the importance of illegal activities and the political infrastructure in the cities should not be diminished, the key role in the PLS was nevertheless played by the countryside, which was otherwise traditionally conservative. This was where the vast majority of military operations and people's organisation of the political and cultural life took place during World War II. Due to the political and cultural education, the countryside became even more progressive than the cities by the end of the war (ibid., 58–9).[16]

The attainment of general literacy in impossible circumstances was enabled by the innovative and self-organised cultural groups, the Communist Youth of Yugoslavia, and especially the women's organisations (the Women's Anti-Fascist Front).[17] The PLS took place outside of the bourgeois apparatus of the state and local village and church organisations, thus making the new model of the people's authorities experimental: it quite often followed the rule of 'find a way, comrade' (cf Dean 2019).

Delocalisation means, primarily, that the resistance steered clear of the existing institutions as well as those established by the occupying forces and established a parallel network of authority. Furthermore, the partisan movement, as the name itself implies, involved constant movement through the occupied territories. The PLS was driven by its own dynamics towards a de-territorialising movement beyond the established occupation borders and the pre-war system. This de-territorialised movement was subsequently re-territorialised in each of the liberated territories as well as in the newly-established Councils and Committees of the National Liberation. As we have previously mentioned, the Supreme Plenum became the highest executive body of the Liberation Front in Slovenia. On 1 November 1941 it adopted the *Basic Points*, which also included the further logic of re-territorialisation. Thus, we should underline the demand for the unification of all Slovenians and the aspiration for the fellowship of all Yugoslav nations. However, all of this would be impossible without the consistent introduction of people's democracy and the takeover of power following the people's liberation. This was a revolutionary demand, carried out in the liberated territories already during the war. Besides its military organisations, the PLS had a very diverse political structure, consisting of the Slovenian People's Liberation Committees, the Executive Board, and the Secretariat, as well as a network of provincial, district, regional, and field committees at least since 1943. The Liberation organisation also comprised the central committees that represented the various vocations, as well as the institutions and Secretaries of the Committee of the Communist Party of Slovenia. The activists of all four founding groups of the Liberation Front were operating within the network of committees in the territory of Slovenia. This organisation was also preserved after the Dolomites Declaration, when the avant-garde role in the PLS was taken over by the Communist Party of Slovenia. If we cannot simply equate the Liberation Front with the Communist Party of Slovenia, it is also true that the Party organisation itself kept changing and constantly growing during the war.

The Anti-Fascist Council of the People's Liberation of Yugoslavia: A New Yugoslavia

At the level of the Yugoslav Resistance Movement the first important political shift took place with the assembly of all the Committees of Deputies of the PLS on 26 November 1942 in Jajce. At this assembly they founded the central and mobile platform which characterised the entire wartime period: *The Anti-Fascist Council for the People's Liberation of Yugoslavia* (AVNOJ). This Council was created as a result of the meeting between the local anti-fascist organisations, communist ideas, and the people. AVNOJ was also the key political instance that launched ideas and homogenised the various ideological positions, disciplining them in the common anti-fascist struggle. This struggle remained open to everyone who was prepared to fight fascism and take part in this struggle.

AVNOJ and the Supreme Headquarters became the central hub that at least partially steered the regional or national resistance movements, although they could not oversee the political and military actions at the local level due to the slow communication between the partisan units. The PLS's Regional and Field Committees remained largely autonomous because of the enemy offensives and distances between them. Battalions, companies, and organisations – in short, the communities involved in the resistance – had to demonstrate a profound political and military inventiveness in order to successfully supply food and other necessities. One of the first examples of such self-organisation of the people can be found in the Republic of Užice, which was the first significant liberated territory in occupied Europe between September and November 1941. In practice this territory underwent some elements of a socialist revolution (the takeover of factories) as well as witnessing the very beginnings of the people's authorities that organised the political, military, cultural, and economic matters.[18] Such communities kept forming and extinguishing in other pockets of resistance as well as in the liberated territories all across Yugoslavia. Some of these territories managed to remain free from 1943 until the very end of the war.

1943 represented a turning point in World War II also for Yugoslavia, as the partisan movement and the Supreme Command in the territory of Bosnia, survived all of the large-scale Nazi offensives launched throughout that spring and summer. The majority of the Chetnik Army was defeated, Italy capitulated, and the international support started shifting towards the partisans.[19] At the Yalta Conference the imperialist interests and political calculations with regard to the post-war European order were openly discussed, and Yugoslavia was a part of the Western as well as Eastern spheres of interest.[20] Despite the unsteady support and imperialist calculations, the Second Meeting of AVNOJ took place in the liberated territories around Livno between 21 and 29 November 1943. At this meeting the deputies of the partisan movement from all across Yugoslavia decided on the future of the new political entity. The deputies – men as well as women – adopted the AVNOJ Declaration, which contained the revolutionary points and represented the most significant political breakthrough of World War II. These points dealt with internal and external actors and autonomously proclaimed the independence of the anti-fascist resistance and the future system of Yugoslavia. The Declaration announced a revolutionary act, which cut off, in his absence, the King as the sovereign of the old Kingdom of Yugoslavia. Who says kings cannot be beheaded without bloodshed? If anyone did, the Yugoslav partisans proved this was possible: the King's return and the regime of the new Yugoslavia would be decided by the people at a post-war people's referendum.[21] The principles of the remaining points of the Declaration were no less revolutionary:[22] a federal and 'new Yugoslavia' was established, which recognised the equality of all its nations and nationalities as well as their 'right to self-determination';[23] members were elected for the National AVNOJ Committee, which was declared to represent the revolutionary government, assisted, in terms of organisation, by AVNOJ and its national, regional, and local committees of the PLS; and, last but not least, Tito became a marshal and the supreme commander of the partisan movement.

With its revolutionary principles, the AVNOJ Declaration placed international recognition at risk, even though this was a strategic and cunning move, as it drew back the curtain and revealed a battlefield where the Allies calculated their choices between the Chetniks and the partisans as well as between the subsequent spheres of influence. With the decision that the 'government-in-exile' and the King would be abolished and by establishing AVNOJ as the 'supreme executive and legislative body', the partisans made the Allies face an uncompromising choice. Instead of waiting for further negotiations and calculations, the partisans declared independence and reliance on their own, people's forces. A few days later, at the Allied conference in Tehran, the partisan movement was confirmed as the only Allied and anti-fascist force in the territory of Yugoslavia.[24] The AVNOJ gesture and its subsequent international recognition attest to the fact that this recognition was fought for (in blood) rather than inherited from the past sovereignty. This pivotal gesture attested to the political autonomy of the Yugoslav partisans and the people's organisation in the liberation of their territories as well as in their subsequent path towards socialism.[25]

The New Partisan Subject: Revolutionary People and Cultural Revolution

The AVNOJ Declaration cannot be interpreted as an affirmation of a sovereign state – which did not exist at all – but rather as a confirmation of the resisting partisan community, who were building the political anti-apparatus. As Ozren Pupovac worded it, the AVNOJ Declaration established the Yugoslav 'non-state ... with the primary contradictory unity of the state apparatus and those political manifestations that are actually anti-apparatus, forms of mass people's organisation and direct democracy' (Pupovac 2006: 10). In the context of this anti-apparatus, the definition and practice of the revolutionary peoples, which were different from the people in the bourgeois revolutions, were being established. In the more recent radical political theory, the critique of the bourgeois conception of 'homogenous' people was presented especially by Ernesto Laclau and Jacques Rancière. They believe the people are internally heterogeneous, and construct a 'political universality' through a transformative process (Laclau 2005: 240). The people possess an inherent discord, disagreement with the dominant sovereign order, and therefore represent an anti-state element. To put it differently and accordingly to the partisan moment 'revolutionary people' resist easy appropriation into the parliamentary democracy model (a legal conception[26]); they cannot be subjected to the regime of empirical censuses and homogenous majority (public opinion analyses and statistics), even though a large number of fighting men and women joined the PLS towards the end of the war.[27] Thus the partisan movement – instead of the state-forming and homogeneous people, who were abolished after the first and one-time confirmation of the 'general will' in the legislative body of a liberal state – established a political subjectivity that the state apparatus simply could not appropriate.[28] This also became apparent in the post-war period, when the socialist political community was being established.

The conception of a 'revolutionary people' largely corresponds to the context of the Yugoslav anti-fascist struggle, in which the former institutions and conceptions of the bourgeois people fused with the clean race of the new fascist apparatuses, while the new conception of the people was established through the people's, most widely and directly democratic, forms of authority. In this regard I can only agree with Komelj's thesis that the 'political subjectivity, forged in the PLS, transcended the national limitations because this fight was founded on the planetary socio-transformative perspective' (Komelj 2008: 24). We are therefore not talking about a synthesis of the people and the nation, but rather about a crucial differentiation, which in turn indicates that this conception of people involves a radical incongruity and can thus not be reduced to the homogenous subject of ethnicity.

The incompatibility and incomparability of the opposing camps' political principles explains the brutal dimensions of the civil war in Yugoslavia as well as indicating the tensions between the political factors within the PLS. Due to the heterogeneity of the revolutionary people, AVNOJ and the Supreme Headquarters headed by Tito did not encompass everyone. Instead, the broad people's support and emancipation were politically constructed by other large-scale people's organisations. Most of the work on culturally and politically mobilising the broader masses was performed by: the Women's Anti-Fascist Front (the AFŽ)[29] and the Young Communist League of Yugoslavia.[30] Not only did the Communist Youth of Yugoslavia help recruit new fighters for the PLS, it also kept developing its underground network and took part in military operations. Even though it functioned as the youth section of the Communist Party, it enjoyed significant autonomy, as it organised numerous educational and supply activities, similarly to the AFŽ.

The AFŽ's founding event took place in the liberated territory, in Bosanski Petrovac, on 6 December 1942 and gathered a few thousand women activists. The AFŽ did not only fight for the recognition of voting and political rights, but was also engaged in the profound cultural, social, and political transformation of pre-war Yugoslavia. Women were fully-armed fighters, partisan doctors, political commissars, cultural workers, and so forth, and they were also in charge of the social-familial reproduction of the struggle. The different roles taken on by the fighting women were a vital part of the partisan struggle. At a closer glance – even with a critical outlook on the subsequent normalisation of (partisan) women within the socialist context – it can be said that the figure of the partisan woman is 'more' revolutionary and ahead of time than its male counterpart (Vitorelli 2015). Women, who were traditionally subject to a traditionalist and patriarchal context, were now seen as fighters and educators of men (and women). During the war they were engaged in just as many, and indeed more, activities than men. Besides raising the awareness of the anti-fascist struggle, the AFŽ also educated and empowered all women. Already during the war, these women criticised the traditional division of labour, which often resulted in conflicts with the patriarchal system in the more conservative environments. However, with their dedication and hard work the female fighters challenged the previous balance of power: let me stress that over two million women took part in the PLS. Even though they were mostly in charge of food, patient care (in hospitals), and cultural activities, they were also included in the political as well as military activities. Prominent female partisans organised their own military battalions, which were not always approved of by the male fighters.[31] I can conclude that these two organisations made a decisive contribution to the establishment of the political and cultural-educational institutions of the new people's authorities, thus participating in the creation of 'heterogeneous' people and the implementation of the direct people's democracy principle (Pupovac 2006:17).

For the first time in history, the new institutions of the people's authority were directly engaged and gave voice to numerous individuals who had previously not been heard or even visible.[32] In this regard the issue of the relationship between the anti-fascist politics and culture was especially important. We could say that the partisans benefitted from practicing Benjamin's lesson (2008): they successfully resisted the aestheticisation of politics (fascism) by politicising culture. They surpassed the Home Guard propaganda in all aspects, substantively as well as formally, and I can only agree with Komelj that this was because partisan art went beyond propaganda, despite its openly political agenda. The PLS became the first pivotal period in history when masses of anonymous, lesser-known or more renowned cultural workers and artists entered the historical stage in order to create the symbolic networks of resistance. At this point we can mention the true process of a cultural revolution, as convincingly described by Komelj:

> It was not necessary for the masses who spoke out to utter revolutionary mottoes. They became involved in the revolutionary process merely by voicing their opinion in its context. The liberation struggle also entailed the liberation of expression: the right to public speech

was now assumed by people to whom it had previously been denied. (Komelj 2008: 104–105).

Illegal cultural activities were constantly taking place throughout the occupied territories, however the organisational centre was always located and established in the liberated territories, where new cultural institutions were being erected in the absence of conventional ones. The importance of cultural work was strengthened in the first liberated zone – the Republic of Užice, which was proclaimed on 24 September 1941 and persisted for more than two months. Thanks to the solid material conditions, the first running Tesla hydro-power plant provided electricity for the production of ammunition, textiles, as well as for a printing house. Numerous intellectuals and cultural workers were involved in organisational tasks. The partisan press flourished, and it is noteworthy that one of the first issues of *Borba* (early November 1941), the newspaper of the Communist Party, was accompanied by an extensive cultural edition and a special collection of international *Antifascist Songs*. Miletić and Radovanović (2017) underlined the vital importance of the first 'art unit' that consisted of cultural workers and artists, tasked with organising the printing, cultural, and political events, as well as producing artworks in the 'partisan atelier', staging theatre performances that were collectively directed, organising choir rehearsals, composing anti-fascist partisan songs, and so on. Milutin Čolić, one of the unit's surviving members, remembers the 'artist unit' in Užice:

In the beginning, there were only twenty of us soldiers – artists. It was a very unusual and unique experience: for example, one evening the group would go to defend the hills around Užice in order to suppress a Chetnik attack; while the next evening we would put down our guns and step onto the stage, where we would recite the words of Čapek, Mušić, or Goethe. There was this one evening when a rehearsal for Goethe's *Egmont* got disrupted by the first German offensive (1981: 313).

One of Komelj's theses is that the crucial importance of partisan art was that its actions were carried out in impossible circumstances: how can something emerge where nothing exists, in the absence of any canon or institutions. Komelj's response is biblical: in the beginning there was the partisan word that became a weapon, and it was from this impossible situation that it managed to bring to life the most creative symbolical part of the resistance and thus mobilise the masses that the PLS could not be imagined without. To put it poetically, the partisan cultural workers, men as well as women, gave up their warm homes and work in bourgeois institutions, in order to choose the path of cultural silence, hunger in the liberated territories, as well as cultural expression forged in tears and blood. Their words became weapons of mass creation, forming the symbolical connective tissue of the community in resistance. Even Komelj's interpretation, which is avant-garde, contains, on the one hand, the division into the considerations about the politicisation of art, without which the PLS would not be possible; and, on the other hand, the debates on the new autonomy of art, which established the foundations for art in the new world. This points towards the radical antinomy between the abolishment of art and its reestablishment in revolutionary circumstances.[33] The effects of these mass cultural activities, contributing to the construction of the 'new world', were of extreme importance. This avant-garde interpretation of the role of partisan art has to keep the antinomy at bay, as if only the aesthetic-autonomist position is emphasised, this could swiftly succumb to the ideology of the cultural rather than political formation of a 'small nation'.

Despite the slight romanticisation evident in Komelj's account, one should acknowledge that the partisan cultural legacy was not merely propagandistic, as interpreted by many later theorisations in socialist Yugoslavia. Of course, partisan art was political, as it 'inseparably associated its own freedom with the people's liberation' (Komelj 2008:31). However, an entire array of artworks and quite simply the very existence of partisan art ran counter to the paraphrase of old dictum of Cicero 'inter arma silent musae'. This is not to say that no aesthetic projects and efforts were launched during World War II – though some of the most intense propaganda campaigns were indeed aimed at mobilising the public to fight. However, this was nothing new. Modern media and arts have been used for the purposes of propaganda ever since the second part of the nineteenth century, and even more so during World War I. What intensified was the subjugation of art to war technology. This point needs to addressed also when we assess the initially 'progressive' artistic movements, such as Italian futurism. The latter was fascinated with the imperialist war and became a key aesthetical part of the emerging fascist order. Italian futurism combined the horizons of national will and technological imperialism (Boynik 2018: 13–15). It drew from certain elements of the avant-garde art and its call for the death of the (existing) arts in order to twist the new emerging art into a new political project for fascism. Marinetti and fascism replied to Cicero's ancient formula of war being the time during which the muses were silent, with the use of a saying by another Emperor of the Holy Roman Empire, Ferdinand I, which Benjamin paraphrased as 'Fiat ars, pereat mundus', which means 'Let art flourish and the world pass away' (Benjamin 2008: 55). In the eyes of fascist art and (later) Marinetti, mankind's experience of 'its own annihilation' became 'a supreme aesthetic pleasure' (ibid. 42), with which all art was subordinated to war in which it also culminated. The fascination with the acceleration and technology of war was thus not related to the historical emergence of industrialisation, but rather to the intimate links between those forces and the new role that art played in them. Contrary to the fascist subordination of art to war, Benjamin famously postulated the communist notion of politicising aesthetics (ibid.). One could argue that this last call can be attributed to his partisan position against fascism, which went beyond the two major approaches to war and art: partisan art neither glorified war and mankind's annihilation, nor did it limit itself to (the capitalist, or Soviet) state propaganda in order to mobilise the masses for the war. Instead, partisan art presented itself as an alternative that argued for a new role of art.

What made the partisans so culturally productive? What stands behind the thousands of poems that have been written and the numerous songs that have been composed and sung? Why have so many collected volumes of poetry been printed in editions of thousands? For example, the Supreme Command of the partisan resistance supported the printing of thousands of copies of avant-garde partisan poetry by Karel Destovnik Kajuh and Matej Bor. It also promoted collected volumes that consisted of anonymous and established poets, both dead and alive. It is still perplexing why partisans were so diligent and spent so much time on designing, editing, and printing thousands of copies of poetry collections. These collections were not only written by distinguished national poets, but also included collective volumes that combined anonymous partisan poems, folk songs of resistance, as well as established revolutionary songs.[34]

The extensive and impressive body of partisan art and the sheer numbers of art groups attest to the intense awareness and seriousness when it came to dealing with symbolical creation and the imaginary of the liberation struggle. The partisan struggle can therefore be seen as a carrier of a space of 'compossibility' (Badiou, 2005), a radical encounter between partisan art and politics. Partisan art was neither simple propaganda, nor a mere ornament of the struggle. Instead it imagined and radically strengthened the military and political struggle for liberation.

Partisan Reproduction:
Between a Survival Strategy and a Gift Economy

Towards the end of 1943, the People's Liberation Struggle entered a more revolutionary period, as many territories were liberated following the capitulation of Italy – some of which remained free until the very end of the war. People's Liberation Committees, which practiced the people's authority and held numerous discussions on the organisation of cultural and social life, were established within these liberated territories.[35] However, these revolutionary processes did not imply the realisation of a socialist revolution aimed at taking over the factories and carrying out an agrarian reform, and apart from extremely rare exceptions (i.e., the property of fascist occupiers and collaborators), the policy of expropriation had been neither announced nor implemented.[36] The following question needs to be addressed at this point: how were these autonomous and liberated political units (liberated territories) organised in terms of provisions such as food and the other material means needed for the basic partisan reproduction? How was it possible to sustain something as complex as a partisan hospital?

The research into partisan reproduction – into the very basis of the local economy – is extremely deficient in terms of theory and history. To my knowledge, in Slovenia only Metod Mikuž and, in the case of the coastal region, Fran Juriševič have focused on this issue in any detail whatsoever (Mikuž 1969; Juriševič 1975). In his study, Mikuž analysed a variety of historical materials, records, and interviews that convincingly revealed the primary tendency of the partisan economics as well as criticised the thesis of the socialist (economic) revolution during the war. His analysis indicates that the Supreme Headquarters and the Slovenian leadership of the Liberation Front – the same can also be said for the entire Yugoslav leadership throughout most of the war – stood resolutely against the expropriation or confiscation of produce, livestock, and land – as long as this was not critical for the survival of the fighting men, women, and the accompanying wounded and other personnel. Such actions would nevertheless occasionally occur, however, the partisan leadership quickly implemented extremely severe measures against those who stole, arbitrarily confiscated property, or profited from the situation in any way. Such offences were punishable by death – and in order to strengthen the partisan ethics and discipline, death sentences would in fact be carried out during the war, even against the partisans themselves.

Even though the leaders of the partisan movement as well as many antifascist groups and activists were dedicated to communist ideas, they refused to undertake a socialist revolution during the war. This strategy resulted from a concrete analysis of the situation at hand: the aversion towards the communist ideology in rural areas (anti-Bolshevism), which was present in the ideological state apparatuses in the former Kingdom of Yugoslavia as well as in the fascist occupation regime and the church already before the war, was an important factor that made the rural population fear Bolshevism. The latter was seen as a godless and anti-family ideology, allegedly aimed at indiscriminately raiding property.[37] Bearing these ideological battles in mind, the new political institutions of the People's Liberation Struggle placed a special emphasis on acquiring the trust and support of the popular masses.

For the major part of the war, the partisan's economics were not subjected to a socialist plan. Instead, they can be described as elementary wartime solidarity economics, encompassing the elements of survival economics, trust in the promise of a better future (gift economics),[38] as well as the confiscation of the occupiers' and collaborators' materiel and property.[39] The new people's government was in charge of the material reproduction of the partisan forces, which entailed the purchase and transportation of food, the supply of ammunition and other military equipment, medical care, as well as the material infrastructure for artists and cultural activities. The economic activities were exceedingly rudimentary: people would be given ration stamps, and in the liberated territories the people's authorities would often attempt improvised distribution. They were assisted by the Women's Anti-Fascist Front, the Communist Youth of Yugoslavia, and the local population, all of whom invested vast quantities of selfless voluntary work in the survival or 'gift' liberation economics.[40] The individual companies and battalions were left to their own devices and the people's support.[41] The various levels of the economic self-organisation of collectives could be assessed from the testimonies of partisans with regard to the war and the liberated territories. Many partisans mentioned the constant hunger, particularly during the winter months, and in this respect, it was vital that they could rely on the assistance of the local farmers.

Apart from the aforementioned survival strategies, the first outlines of a more consistent economic policy of the Liberation Front should be sought in the collection and provision of funds and other resources needed for the 1943 struggle. Metod Mikuž established that three types of collection prevailed in Slovenia: firstly, the collection of the so-called 'People's Liberation Struggle tax', which was paid by anyone who could afford it; secondly, the National Committees would issue bonds that the people's authority would pay out once the war ended;[42] and thirdly, the confiscation of the occupiers' and collaborators' materials. Of course, the establishment of the partisan gift or solidarity economics had its own problems: it would often encounter resistance from the rural population, especially during the winter and in times of general wartime exhaustion and hunger, when partisans needed to feed vast numbers of fighting men and women towards the end of the war. Occasionally, partisans had to acquire livestock and produce by force, and in this regard we cannot ignore the remark that the leadership of the Liberation Front was unable to oversee all actions carried out in the field.[43] However, we can conclude that the partisan economics remained exceedingly dependent on the external help provided by the Allies. In short, we can define it as a self-organised people's economic policy that combined self-initiative with the resourcefulness of the partisans and those who supported them.

At the End of the War: Revenge and Revolutionary Violence

Towards the end of the war, the new people's authorities and the idea of a new Yugoslavia started becoming much clearer in terms of its political, cultural, and economic outlines. Most importantly, in the autumn of 1944 the Yugoslav People's Liberation Struggle liberated vast territories, encompassing the rural regions of the Independent State of Croatia, Dalmatia, a large part of Serbia, and parts of Slovenia. Meanwhile, the Nazis and their collaborators concentrated their forces along the main roads and railway lines, as well as at certain vital points where the Srem Front was established – which, among other things, allowed the Nazis to retreat into the heart of Europe. In the political sense, this was a period in which the state apparatus and bureaucracy of the collaborators and occupiers started disintegrating, and the local people's authorities were being set-up intensively. As the support for the government-in-exile and the King's authority dwindled greatly, the simultaneous triple government was rapidly coming to an end. The political force focused on the development of a new Yugoslavia was becoming increasingly stronger.

In spite of the victory against fascism and the outstanding people's support for the People's Liberation Struggle and the communists, the future of the new Yugoslavia remained rather uncertain. In Europe, World War II ended in the territory of Yugoslavia, in Slovenia, a week after Germany capitulated: on 15 May 1945, when the last military conflict between the partisans and the Nazi forces, supported by Slovenian collaborators, took place near the town of Mežica (the Battle of Poljana). An extensive variety of fascist supporters ranging from Serbian and Montenegrin Chetniks, Croatian Ustashe, members of the Slovenian Home Guard, SS troops, and other members of the Nazi armies gathered on their way to Austria. The fascist forces had already been defeated, but most native collaborators managed to flee from the partisan army and surrendered to the British forces near the town of Bleiburg (Pliberk). As underlined by the historian Jozo Tomasevich, the Ustashe commanding officers and the collaborating military units informed the British forces that they were prepared to fight the communists in any potential future conflicts (Tomasevich 2001:114). Despite the fact that the British forces were aware of their role in the fascist collaboration and that during the last two years the Western Allies supported the partisans, the native traitors nevertheless hoped that the British forces would issue permissions for their emigration or make use of them in the anti-communist struggle (Hornberger, 1995). Naturally, it was naive to expect that the British forces would overlook the long years of collaboration with the fascist forces. In light of the total military defeat of fascism,[44] the war criminals knew they would not be greeted warmly by the People's Liberation Struggle. Furthermore, the British forces had no intention of interfering with the internal regime in new Yugoslavia; while the Tito–Šubašić Agreements, which defined the cooperation between the government-in-exile and AVNOJ, had already been in force for a while, none of the Western Allies had any intention of supporting the (local) fascists. While waiting for further measures near Bleiburg, the majority of the collaboration leadership managed to flee to other parts of Europe, Spain (e.g. the Ustashe leader Ante Pavelić), or Argentina, where they would never answer for their crimes. However, most of the collaborators' units remained in the prisoner-of-war camps near Bleiburg.

After the war, the British forces captured a number of collaborators from the Southern and Eastern Fronts in Austria, including the Yugoslav collaborators. Great Britain reached an agreement with the Soviet Union and began Operation Keelhaul (Epstein 1973).[45] In accordance with this agreement, the collaborators were repatriated to Eastern Europe, the Soviet Union, and Yugoslavia. Hornberger (2005) described the confusion and desperation of the collaborators, as they became aware that they would be sent back. Many officers knew they would face certain or even terrible death, thus quite a few of them committed suicide; however, the British soldiers kept sending the prisoners of war to their respective homelands. With this the British forces washed their hands of the affair; but this certainly does not make them any less responsible for what happened next.

During the first weeks after the liberation, the atmosphere in Yugoslavia was characterised by chaos, joy, sadness, and post-war violence, as fighting would occasionally still break out against smaller Ustashe units and Chetniks, who were still hiding in the woods. Personal vengeance and retaliation against the national traitors also took place, and the situation became all the more tense once the British repatriated approximately 25-30,000 prisoners of war (Booker 1997). Together with some 50,000 fascist collaborationists captured on the territory of Slovenia in the last week of war, the number amounted to some 80,000 prisoners of war. The period at the end and immediately after the end of World War II was marked by war and post-war executions and revolutionary violence, which the new conservative historiography often underlines as the only indicator of the People's Liberation Struggle and the totalitarian nature of the coming regime. Regardless of the dark nature of these post-war killings, we should bring to attention the context as well as the issue as to how the fascists and native traitors should have been treated. Naturally, the Security Intelligence Service, whose goal had been to terminate the collaborator's leadership, had operated already during the People's Liberation Struggle. In wartime circumstances, the collaborators together with the Nazis not only brutally murdered partisans and war prisoners, but also practiced reprisal measures that involved the executions of civilians for each killed German soldier – all of this with the aim of crushing the resistance and the people's support of it.

However, this took place in a wartime situation. Different measures could have been implemented in the post-war period, when the representatives of the People's Liberation Struggle were setting the foundations for the new people's government. Should the collaborators – especially those who had not been high-ranking officers – take part in the construction of the new Yugoslavia that they had fought against throughout the war? The partisan leadership speculated that this could be a risky move, as the approximately 80,000 fascist fighters could – were they to acquire weapons – quite easily trigger a new civil war or at least sabotage the processes of post-war reconstruction. How should the prisoners be treated? Was this the time for personal vendettas, massacres, or mass imprisonment? Gradual forgiveness and reconciliation? Reintegration into the community or expulsion – but where to? Regardless of the horrors that the fascist collaborators had caused during World War II and irrespective of these complicated issues with numerous and diverse answers, extrajudicial executions were certainly not the right option and should be condemned. However, it was clear that the returning collaborators would not be welcomed with open arms in Yugoslavia, as noted by the Croatian historian Jozo Tomasevich:

> Considering the nature of the struggle among the various competing forces during the Second World War in Yugoslavia, the Ustashe atrocities against the Serbian population in the territory of the Independent State of Croatia and against all pro-partisan Croats, the fact that the Ustashe adhered to the Nazis to the bitter end, and finally the fact that the Ustashe leadership wanted to put its troops at the disposal of the Western Allies for possible use against Yugoslav and other Communists, no mercy on the part of the Yugoslav partisans toward these troops could have been expected. (Tomasevich 2001: 113–14).

Regardless of the accuracy of this rational evaluation, I hereby argue for a clear condemnation of this unequivocal response, as this was not the only way to treat the local fascists. The post-war killings were a mixture of political liquidations and personal vendettas. Yet, irrespective of the individual attempts, it is very difficult to point a finger at merely one group of people responsible for this, as a number of different and contradictory clues exist. Officially, the Supreme Headquarters headed by Tito demanded that all suspects be brought in front of the people's and military courts. On 14 May – that is, even before the end of the war in Yugoslavia – Tito sent a telegram to all partisan units, in which he, among other things, ordered that

> We must decisively and quickly do everything in our powers to prevent the killing of the prisoners of war as well as those arrested by military units, state authorities, or individuals. Should people who must answer for war crimes be among those taken into custody or imprisoned, they should be immediately turned over to military courts, where they shall be tried. (In Ramet and Matić 2007: 274).[46]

In the case of post-war killings, this order was largely ignored, as many war prisoners were subject to personal revenge as well as to the more systematic executions.[47] The partisan army imprisoned some of the captives returned from Austria in the camps located in the vicinity of Maribor, only to send them to various prisons later on.[48] However, most of the captives were subject to extrajudicial executions, carried out by the secret police (the Department for the Protection of People) and parts of the 3rd Corps of the Yugoslav III. partisan army. We now know that 12,575 Slovenian fascist collaborators were killed in the vicinity of Kočevski Rog (Čepič, Guštin, and Troha, 2017: 436). The independent analyses roughly agree that all together between 30,000 and 35,000 all-Yugoslav fascists collaborators were killed after the war, others were imprisoned, some amnestied, some fled. The analyses of the (extreme) right-wing spectrum tend to inflate this number to 80,000 or even 120,000 casualties of what they call the 'totalitarian' crime (Job 2002).

Regardless of my strong belief in the politics and achievements of the People's Liberation Struggle, the post-war massacres were (post)war crimes and represent a dark moment in the Yugoslav Civil War. Furthermore, the killings marred the otherwise exceedingly humane way in which the partisans treated their prisoners of war.[49] The post-war executions represented a mixture of political motivation and revolutionary terror on the one hand, and, on the other hand, a vengeful politics that unfolded almost as if in a trance and in the course of retaliatory raids conducted by certain individuals and groups. Mass killings were the simplest solution: the ultimate bloody retaliation against the representatives of the old Yugoslavia and Nazi collaboration. However, the new political authorities should have opted for a politically smarter solution and more ethical action even though it would have been much harder to implement: they should have organised more judicial processes and allowed the youth to either start over or emigrate.

The end of the civil war represented a particularly traumatic moment in the history of socialist Yugoslavia. Instead of tackling this issue head on, the new socialist Yugoslavia swept most of these negative events under the rug. If it were not for a few critical films and stories that surfaced in the 1950s and 1960s, the state would have continued to conceal it all. Because the topic had for so long not been spoken about, its gradual exposure from the mid-1980s onwards has been one of the key points for anti-communist and nationalist purposes. Moreover, the new nationalists would make use of the post-war massacres in order to rehabilitate the local fascists by inflating the numbers of fatalities (to hundreds of thousands of corpses dumped in caves). By the end of the 1980s, this topic became the key perpetuator behind the spread of nationalist phobia and the introduction to new wars. The very idea of comparing Jasenovac to Bleiburg and reinterpreting the ethnic dimensions of the World War II conflict completely disregarded the dividing line between fascism and anti-fascism as well as the historical sequence of events. Bleiburg – a town in Austria in which none of the post-war killings actually took place – has become one of the major pro-fascist memorial sites in Europe. Since the early 1990s, the Croatian Catholic Church has organised an annual commemoration in this town, and the event itself has become officially registered as a church event. In reality, this is an event attended by the main pro-Ustashe civil groups and visited by approximately 20,000 people from across Europe, who celebrate and network around this new memorial site.[50]

Today, fascist collaboration and historical revisionism undoubtedly deserve to be resolutely criticised. However, this criticism should nevertheless not diminish the responsibility for the extrajudicial violence at the end of the liberation struggle, and its problematisation. The ruling ideology of the national reconciliation normalised and equalised all the casualties as the national victims of the civil war, while neglecting the context of the anti-fascist struggle.[51] The forensic counting of fascist bones was accompanied by the denial of the responsibility for the fascist crimes, and thus the post-war massacres have become a deep grave for the socialist authorities and the partisan heritage. Instead of re-actualising the anti-fascist struggle and the emancipatory dimensions of the People's Liberation Struggle, the fascist skeletons returned to the battlefields and raised the nationalistic flags in the name of ethnically-cleansed communities during the 1990s. A new history was being created, as the old one was being deleted.[52]

However, let us return to the new post-war Yugoslavia, which was – as it has already been pointed out – based on the universalist foundations of international solidarity and emancipation. It was born from ruins and hunger, and human casualties can be added to this infrastructural catastrophe as well: over a million dead, and an additional million displaced or emigrated.[53] Yugoslavia had to face great internal and external challenges, while the Cold War kept drawing closer and closer. How did the nascent political government cope with this situation, and to what degree did it keep building on the partisan rupture with the pre-war Kingdom of Yugoslavia?

4

Split with Stalin:
A New Road to Socialism?

The partisan Yugoslavia was inaugurated in late November 1943 with the declaration of the Anti-Fascist Council for the People's Liberation of Yugoslavia, which announced the federative and revolutionary character of the new entity. As mentioned in the previous chapter, this was a political act that was based on the strength and experiences of the partisan movement. In strictly legal terms, partisan Yugoslavia did not exist until it was internationally recognised, which only happened one year later. Until that moment in time it should be viewed as a transitory form that united the representatives of the People's Liberation Struggle (Tito) and the representatives of the Yugoslav government-in-exile (old Yugoslavia), which was done upon Churchill's insistence. A series of agreements between Tito and Šubašić, who was a prime minister of the government-in-exile, were reached in 1944 – with the most important one signed on 1 November. This is the date on which the interim government led by Tito was internationally recognised, and Šubašić was appointed its first foreign minister. The new political entity was known as the Democratic Federative Yugoslavia and it postponed the decision on the future form of the government (and a possible return of King Peter II) to the first post-war elections. Most importantly, the previous military representatives of the Yugoslav government-in-exile, Mihailović's Chetniks, now lost their formal support, while King Peter II called for everyone to join Tito's partisans in the liberation struggle. This was a major diplomatic victory for Tito and the People's Liberation Struggle: it indicated that political autonomy from Moscow would be retained, the staunchly anti-communist position of Churchill changed, and the Chetniks were stripped of their support. This influenced the post-war constitution of Yugoslavia. The Tito–Šubašić agreement also stipulated that both the local fascist collaborators and Chetnik formations lost all political grounds for further operations or any kind of speculation in the post-war Yugoslavia. Historical evidence shows that the collaborationist formations refused to give in, or join forces with the partisans, and instead decided to fight on the side of the Nazi army that was retreating towards Austria until the end of the war.

The People's Liberation Struggle (the PLS) epitomised the successful and heroic resistance that liberated its people from occupation with its own forces, as well as promising a very different Yugoslavia: one democratic, federal, and socialist. In Chapter 2 I mentioned that World War II started with a few thousand members of the Communist Party of Yugoslavia (the CPY), of which many died during the war – however, by the end of the war CPY's membership soared to approximately 150,000 members, predominantly from rural areas. This transformed the CPY from a small sectarian 'die-hard' and disciplined Party into an organisation that was partially democratised and opened to the masses through the PLS, while simultaneously providing the Women's Anti-Fascist Front and the League of Communist Youth with the opportunity to participate politically. By 1947 the CPY had 400,000 members (see Samary 1988). This rise of the CPY was further supported by the popularity of its leader, and the first figure of the PLS: Marshall Tito. Social changes were demanded and expected after the war. The early period was marked by a wave of popular enthusiasm and voluntary brigades that helped to rebuild the destructed country. At the first democratic elections held on 11 November 1945 and marked with a large turnout – the first time women were given the right to vote – 86 per cent of the electorate voted for the People's Front and Tito. There were certain political parties and representatives of the old Yugoslavia that ran against the People's Front, but they did not form a consistent and unified opposition. The CPY did not repress or disable the opposition, but it did also not open up space for liberal democracy. One can speculate how many votes the other groups would get if they formed a unified political party, however, the popular enthusiasm for the People's Front was unquestionably high and the People's Front would have clearly won these elections whatever the situation. 29 November became the date – the 2nd anniversary of partisan Yugoslavia – of the first major constitutional change and the new name of Federal People's Republic of Yugoslavia, which formally ended the long-distance relationship with King Peter II.

While the the political orientation of the Federal People's Republic of Yugoslavia was becoming clearer by the end of 1945, the international arena represented a major threat and a destabilising factor for the future of Yugoslavia. Could Yugoslavia remain an influential factor in the Balkans? What role would the new Yugoslavia play in the new geopolitical arena? The leadership of the new Yugoslavia was convinced that its future lay with Moscow, but it also wished to retain the political autonomy it had won through the liberation struggle. The Red Army helped the Yugoslav partisans liberate parts of the country, and, after the war, the representatives of the Federal People's Republic of Yugoslavia agreed to accept Soviet aid and experts to assist them in the socialist transition. Tito delivered a series of speeches in 1945, and in one of them we can find an essential quote that marks the clear stance of the future Yugoslav orientation: 'We have no desire to depend on anyone. We do not want to be a small change; we do not want to be involved in any policy linked to the spheres of influence' (quoted in Prashad 2007: 97). At this point it is worthwhile recollecting that already during the Yalta conference Churchill and Stalin divided the Balkans 50–50 between the British and the Soviets, while Greece remained openly 'British' territory (Fejto 1952: 25).

Thus, although self-reliance and popular support for the People's Front were undoubtedly strong in Yugoslavia, the principled attitude of Tito who publicly announced independence from the spheres of influence could prove costly in relation to Stalin and his plans for Eastern Europe, as well as the Western zone of influence around the Balkans. The conflicts between the Yugoslav communist leadership and Stalin had their own intense history, which continued after World War II, but nobody in the new Yugoslav leadership even considered a break with Stalin as an option.[1]

In the situation of tense border issues Yugoslavia could not afford to endanger their friendship with the Soviet Union. There were two border regions that were under constant pressure and one could say they were the first conflict zones of the Cold War that created definite borders between the West and East. On one hand, Yugoslavia had an unresolved border issue with Italy, especially as regards the area surrounding Trieste that was liberated by Yugoslav partisans and parts of Istria, while on the other hand an open civil war was fought in Greece between partisan left-wing resistance and bourgeois-monarchist right-wing forces from 1946 onwards.[2]

In accordance to the Yalta agreement and the idea of the British domination of the Mediterranean, any involvement in Greece was a threat to British 'national interests'. After Greek resistance liberated itself from Nazi occupation, from 1944 onwards it remained under total British domination until the end of the war, and things did not change after the war, as Woodhouse correctly argued:

> Up to 1947 the British Government appointed and dismissed Greek Prime Ministers with the barest attention to constitutional formalities. British experts dictated economic and financial policy, defence and foreign policy, security and legal policy, trade union and employment policy. (2002: 149).

In relation to the Greek civil war, Stalin never supported the Greek communists, since this position guaranteed him 'peace' over his zones of interest in Eastern Europe. Vis-à-vis the Yugoslav leadership this means that Stalin applied constant pressure to stop arming and supplying the communist troops in Greece. In other words, Stalin opposed the communist uprising in Greece.

In the border region surrounding the hotspots of Trieste and Istria, the entire region came under the joint authority of Yugoslavia and the Western Allies until the question was resolved. Trieste used to be a strong working-class city. During the war it had organised antifascist resistance, which further fuelled the fear of the Western Allies that Italy might elect communists in the first elections after the war. There was a large presence of military forces in the border region and the constant military exercises continued to exert pressure on all sides of the conflict. On the other hand, in the southernmost part of Yugoslavia, the border with Greece represented a strategic point for communist forces, i.e. the Democratic Army of Greece (the DSE) which had previously liberated large parts of Greece from under Nazi rule and were, from 1946, involved in the civil war against the British and US backed bourgeois-monarchist forces. In this battle the power constellation was moving increasingly towards the monarchists as the military equipment and financial aid was accompanied by consistent military training from the Western Allies. The latter also supported extreme right-wing groups from amongst the monarchists who exerted white terror and evacuated villages that supported the communists or the left-wing in general. However, the real beginning of the defeat that brought a wave of demoralisation and military weakening was Tito's split with Stalin. As a result of the split the strongest support for the DSE withered away and the border with Yugoslavia was closed. Following the split between Tito and Stalin, the official line of the Communist Party of Greece followed the Soviet Union and purged Titoist elements, which weakened the resistance and the DSE.[3] Furthermore, the strategic mistake of the DSE leadership in fighting the monarchist forces frontally, without proper support, resulted in several grave defeats. This meant that numerous DSE fighters, an estimated 100,000 were killed, imprisoned, or exiled (Eudes 1973).

One can conclude that it was not only Korea that felt the shadow of the Iron Curtain after World War II, but also Greece and Yugoslavia.[4] Within the context of the South-European periphery, the defeat of the Greek revolutionary forces in the civil war also marked the end of the thirteen-year revolutionary sequence in the European periphery (see Minehan 2006) that stretched from Spain (1936–39), across Yugoslavia (1941–48) to Greece (1941–49). These three cases share strong structural similarities: all took place at the European periphery, involved a strong peasant population, and were backed by strong left-wing and popular political forces/organisations; all took place within the context of both imperialist (Western, but also with a clear Soviet presence) and fascist wars; apart from Mandel's (2011) thesis on 'two wars' within World War II they also radicalised Lenin's thesis on 'revolutionary war' (1977). All of them were civil wars with strongly polarised left-wing and local fascist collaborationist/extreme nationalist forces. All in all, they were comprised of anti-imperialist, anti-fascist, and anti-capitalist elements and strove for a different social organisation of society, which they succeeded in implementing to a certain degree during the resistance itself (see previous chapter for more on the Yugoslav case), however, in Yugoslavia this was true with various degrees also for its specific road to socialism after the war.

Unquestionably, there were important differences between the conjunctures. Firstly, if we observe the temporality of Spain prior to World War II, it is clear that the Western powers followed a policy of appeasing fascist states (Italy, Germany) and remained neutral, while pursuing internal repression against left-wing forces. Secondly, the conjuncture of Yugoslavia emerged within the context of World War II, during which the superpowers were 'busy' fighting each other. This should be viewed in conjunction with the regional position of Yugoslavia, the experiences of the partisan forces that were based on strong popular support, and which already during the war skilfully manoeuvred between the Allies in order to retain political autonomy. Thirdly, despite the strong and successful antifascist campaign in Greece, its next step in 1946 took place during the Cold War, when the western imperialist forces took a clear stance against all forms of autonomous local communism – with or without Soviet support – even if this meant that antidemocratic and fascist governments would emerge as a result. One should keep in mind that after 1945 fascism still survived in pockets of Europe (Franco's Spain till 1975, Salazar's Portugal till 1974, military junta in Greece from 1967–1974). 1949 did thus not signal merely the isolation of Yugoslavia from the socialist block and the defeat of Greece, but also marked the defeat of the revolutionary left in the periphery. 1949 saw the final lines drawn on the Cold War map between the West and the East, borders that would stay untouched for the next forty years, until 1989. This does not mean that revolutionary movements disappeared from the European context, however they no longer appeared in such an intense and popular scale, and the armed resistance was displaced by riots, urban insurrections and leftist terrorism.

Returning to the role of Yugoslavia at the end of the revolutionary sequence (1936–49), the post World War II political leadership first contended the Western sphere of influence on the questions of Greece and Trieste, while the next important issue openly accentuated the conflict with the Soviet Union. Yugoslavia advocated the idea of the Balkan Socialist Federation already during World War II. During the antifascist resistance, the CPY attempted to unite the Communist Parties of Albania, Greece, and Bulgaria and the first serious attempt to orchestrate a meeting of different partisan resistances in the Balkans took place in 1943. One of the main demands was to create a central military body that would coordinate the struggles against fascist occupation.[5] This initiative was stopped by the British.

After the war the Bulgarian communist leader Dimitrov, who advocated for a big federation that would include Albania, Yugoslavia, Bulgaria and possibly other countries, reintroduced the idea. The CPY officials first held meetings with the Communist Party of Albania (Belgrade, Hoxha) and then with the Bulgarian Communist Party (Bled, Dimitrov). On both occasions they signed treaties that intended to strengthen the political and economic cooperation. The Yugoslav proposal was structured around the idea that would include six existing Yugoslav federal units, a federal unit that would unite Kosovo and Albania and that openly addressed the national question (Lee 1983: 85),[6] and Bulgaria. Stalin considered this development not merely as a policy that was being created behind his back, but also as an immediate threat to the Soviet Union's power within the socialist bloc. This was worrying for Stalin, 'as it appeared that the germ of autonomy was spreading to Bulgaria and Romania; he was also greatly concerned by the British reaction to Balkan assistance for the Communist side in the Greek civil war' (ibid., 79).

The idea of a Balkan Federation was by no means new,[7] however this time it continued in a clear socialist way. In the moments when people from the Balkans showed political autonomy, they were immediately stopped. This was a decisive moment in which Stalin disciplined the Eastern leaderships and interrupted the Balkan federative processes.[8] It was also the moment in which the spirit of Tito began to haunt the international communist movement.[9] In the specific Yugoslav context, this meant that the Yugoslav leadership should have subjugated and accepted the withering of its 'foreign policy in a bipolar world'.[10] This seemed to be a much more realistic and pragmatic step to take, for why on earth should a small country have continued to meddle with the imperialist policies of the Great Powers in the Balkans, on the border between the East and the West, at the very point where capitalism and socialism met? However, this was precisely the neuralgic, political and geographical point from which Yugoslavia spoke and intensified its autonomy, a point in time in which the future was not yet decided.

The decision to pursue the autonomous path was extremely difficult, not only because the majority of the communist leadership in Yugoslavia was historically attached to Moscow, but also due to the socio-economic friendship, in which the Yugoslav leadership fully embraced the help of the Soviet Union. The latter had promised Yugoslavia much-needed loans to reconstruct its infrastructure and invest in factories. In Yugoslavia, the first five-year plan took place between 1947 and 1951 and the Soviet Union sent its instructors to facilitate the transition process. The process was accompanied by the formation of 'mixed companies', which enabled a swift exchange of goods and joint ventures in transport and other important industrial branches. However, these 'mixed companies' brought extremely unfavourable conditions for Yugoslavia, as the contracts always benefited the Soviet Union and the companies were exempt from taxes and not under Yugoslav jurisdiction.[11] The Yugoslav economy would be gradually integrated according to the specific needs of the Soviet Union.[12]

The political conditioning by the Soviet Union was accompanied by economic conditioning. The demand for autonomy should not be argued from an a priori position, it was suggested, i.e. against a sort of a more general but democratically planned system of exchange and production.

However, the main political decisions as to how the system should work, what and whom it should prioritise, and how much it should produce had already been reached. This became the root of the political and economic conflict that pushed the Yugoslav communist leadership into an openly antagonistic stance and a deep disagreement with the Soviet Union. In the angry exchange of letters between Stalin (the Communist Party of the Soviet Union) and Tito (the CPY), the Yugoslav response on 13 April 1948 sent a clear 'no' (oxi) to Stalin and instead of the self-criticism and subjection to the expected line it opted to take a different path. In that conjuncture this meant that the Yugoslav leadership found itself in front of an abyss and decided to leap into the void, a situation confirmed two months later: on 28 June Yugoslavia was expelled from the Cominform and became internationally isolated.[13] The Yugoslav leadership was attacked for revisionism from all sides, once for being 'overly ambitious' in its construction of socialism, then for 'colluding with capitalism', and later for 'not being ambitious enough' (Samary 1988: 77).

At the beginning the split represented a huge blow to Yugoslavia, as it became isolated in a matter of weeks, which meant it was neither politically affiliated with the West nor the East. The economic situation was also not rosy, as in 1947 Yugoslavia rejected the Marshall Plan and following the split with Stalin the first Soviet loans amounting to US$135 million which were aimed at developing the industry were cancelled (see Samary 1988). An economic embargo from the East followed. On top of all this the Soviet forces began performing military exercises on the borders of all Eastern countries bordering on Yugoslavia. The mounting pressure was aimed at delegitimising the new Yugoslav state and forcing the leadership to revise its course. However, the Soviet isolation actually led to the opposite, as Rubinstein correctly concluded, 'it consolidated the Party and the popular support backing Tito' (1970: 81–2). One should refrain from romanticising this time of unity within Yugoslavia (for a good left-wing critique see Unkovski-Korica 2016), since this consolidation came at the expense of political repression that took place amongst the most loyal communist cadres. The camp Goli Otok was assigned the role of 're-educating' the Stalinist deviation. Once again, history proved to be ironic; this time it was getting rid of Stalinism by the use of Stalinist means! Approximately 400 people died during the decade it was in operation, while some 16,000 were imprisoned within the system of camps (see Previšić 2013). This is hardly comparable with Stalin's terror campaign and gulag system; however it points to the pervasive paranoid rationality within Tito's entourage and only a gradual turn towards de-Stalinisation.[14]

The split with Stalin was not merely a negative trauma that finished the revolutionary process and socialist transition, it also opened a series of productive discussions on the future of Yugoslavia and socialism. Darko Suvin noted that it was during these years that the economic and political theory of Boris Kidrič reached its peak and developed towards democratically planned socialism. Kidrič's texts explicitly attacked the bureaucratisation of the Party apparatus and the insufficient nationalisation of socialism.[15] The new self-management model was a direct result of the split and in late 1948 Edvard Kardelj embraced the doctrine of 'many roads to socialism'. Kardelj argued that each socialist country should decide for itself on the best road in the concrete situation and that a number of developments within Soviet history also indicated that there is no such thing as a single and unified history. In the words of Kardelj: 'as it reaches new countries, new peoples, millions of working masses, who have been brought up in different conditions, the development of socialism is no longer a matter of a single country' (quoted in *Borba* 1948: 1).

It is ironic that this flowering of various forms of socialism was supposed to take place as a reiteration of Stalin's trope of 'building socialism in one country', this time in Yugoslavia. In this period the Yugoslav communists discovered the United Nations, a new political platform, which served as a possible deterrent to the war that seemed imminent. In its own way, the traumatic split with Stalin triggered and continued the partisan rupture (through other means): firstly, we can speak of a major partisan rupture within the Yugoslav foreign policy that underwent a geopolitical shift from the regional Balkan level to the global arena through the non-aligned movement; secondly, internally, the rupture resulted in the more open self-management socialism which experimented with political and economic processes. These two ruptures, each in their own way, continued the partisan rupture with the existing state of affairs, inventing a new socialist path and disrupting the Cold War map. The following two chapters will address these two 'partisan' ruptures.

5

Partisan Rupture II: The Road to the Non-Aligned Movement

The split with Stalin in June 1948 resulted in serious international isolation, and the Yugoslav communist leadership was not aware of the series of consequences that were to follow. It began with the expulsion from the Communist Information Bureau (the Cominform) and the imposition of complete economic embargo to exert major political pressure to overthrow the 'Titoists' and the military manoeuvres on the northern and eastern borders of Yugoslavia.[1] It is noteworthy that the Cominform had been formed just a few months prior to the expulsion and that its legal seat – under Stalin's insistence – was in Belgrade, where the very first official meeting took place in January 1948. The meeting brought together communist leadership representatives from throughout the socialist bloc as well as representatives from the French and Italian Communist Parties. The expulsion of Yugoslavia and the relocation of the Cominform headquarters to Bucharest was a dramatic scandal within the international communist movement that was just reforming after Stalin's dissolution of the Comintern in 1943. The new Communist International thus started with a split that nobody expected, nor was it understood by the Western diplomats and political leaderships. At first the Western representatives considered this split to be a 'subtle Communist plot' (Rusinow 1977: 35). Evidently, this position did not aid the Yugoslav leadership in the slightest, for it did not help in the creation of new contacts with the West, which could lead to a new international orientation, nor did it to protect its political independence.

Moreover, the split with Stalin was unimaginable for a large majority of Yugoslav communists at that time, who now found themselves 'defying not only one of the greatest powers of all time, but also their own past and the belief which had been their only religion and occupation for most of their adult lives' (1952: 57). This resonates profoundly with what Bini Adamczak described in the book *Gestern Morgen* (2007), in which a large majority of (international) communists still whole-heartedly supported Stalin despite his brutal policies during the late 1930s. This led to a schizophrenic universe of communist militants, who assembled critical knowledge or even personal experience of Stalinist trials, repression, and geopolitical imperial claims. The strength of the belief in the necessary coming of communism and the naive expectation that the future would somehow miraculously remedy the ills of this painful transition was stunning to say the least. This strong commitment to the communist cause, based on the belief in the inevitable communist future and the somewhat blind celebration of Stalin, persisted even in Tito, who was no simple dogmatic figure. Tito was cautious enough to escape the great purges in Moscow in 1938 – most probably thanks to his not-too-strong alignments in the factional struggles that took place before – and he was familiar with Stalin's deals with the Western Allies that had been concluded in Moscow and Yalta (for a good overview of Tito, see Pirjevec 2011). Nevertheless, in light of the expulsion from the Cominform, Tito articulated what was considered to be the prevailing sentiment among the members of the Central Committee of the Communist Party of Yugoslavia (the CPY): 'Some of us continue to hope – against hope, if you like – that this nightmare will somehow pass' (quoted in Adamič 1952: 254).

However, the nightmare continued with intensified rhetoric and public denunciations when, on 29 November 1949, on the date of the sixth anniversary of the partisan AVNOJ Yugoslavia – the Cominform passed yet another resolution, which dismissed the Yugoslav leadership as 'direct agents of imperialism and abettors of the warmongers', a 'brutal Gestapo-type terrorist regime', and concluded that 'the fight against Tito's clique … is the international duty of all Communists and workers' parties' (quoted in Rusinow 1977: 44; see Procacci 1994). Apart from severing all political ties, this also meant losing all Soviet loans and the equipment needed to rebuild the infrastructure as well as the Soviet experts for a planned economy and heavy industries, all of whom left the country.[2]

As mentioned earlier, during the first years after the war the Yugoslav foreign policy was generally in line with the Soviet's, with a notable exception when it came to the defence of the sovereignty of its new borders and its ideas pertaining to the Balkans: the questions of Trieste, Greece, and the Balkan socialist federation can be seen as embryonic attempts to foster an autonomist socialist foreign policy. In this respect, Yugoslavia hinted at the existence of a different way of establishing regional policies and articulated another road to socialism. Both axes defied the Yalta agreements reached by both sides of the Iron Curtain, the former Allies. However, now the Yugoslav leadership had no space to manoeuvre, since World War II was over, and it seemed that the time for practicing autonomy in the Balkans had become constrained. The Yugoslav leadership had to focus on a single goal: survival. This meant it had to become 'partisan' once again, i.e. rely on its own forces, but with a major geopolitical difference: even though Yugoslavia was now liberated from fascists, the issues of Trieste and Greece came as a cold shower to the former Western Allies, and the Cominform split turned their biggest ally into its new archenemy.

If 1943 was a year of political and physical survival for the Yugoslav liberation struggle, in which it tactically outsmarted and almost miraculously overcame the major Nazi offensive in Bosnia (Operation Schwarz), then 1948 was a year when the new Yugoslav state was at the brink of capitulation. Apart from the external pressures, 1948 and 1949 were also marked by an alarming situation in terms of economic crisis and food shortages. This came even though we could statistically measure the consistent fall in unemployment figures in the years following the war, and by 1948 the volume of industrial production had reached 150 per cent of its pre-war 1939 levels. The latter had nothing to do with miraculous injections/investments from abroad, but were the results of voluntary labour brigades, the general enthusiasm for reconstructing the country and the forced labour which consisted of war prisoners and political enemies (Rusinow 1977: 37). However, one should not shy away from the critical evaluation that the first five-year plan was falling behind its over-ambitious goals. Agriculture saw major food shortages, which came as a result of the faltered industrial cooperation and help that never materialised in combination with the resistance to collectivisation.[3] This grim situation pushed Tito and the Yugoslav leadership to make a decisive step that would depart both from its immediate geographic location, embedded in the (geo)political tradition and the idea of the Balkans and, for the time being, not count on the support of the socialist bloc. To paraphrase Machiavelli, Tito would start paving the path that had not yet been trodden and was in that situation unimaginable. This decision marked the four decades of Yugoslav foreign policy to come and articulated an important precedence within the international communist movement.

The Yugoslav move beyond Cold War bloc-politics did not come without contradictions and tensions. The new, third way and Third World were in an embryonic form and had become a highly contested space of old and new powers. Certain recent critics of the Titoist orientation (Unkovski-Korica 2016) would consider the initial move towards the West in terms of capitulation and capitalist restoration. This conclusion can only be reached if we abstract the entire complex historical relationship as well as the causes and consequences of the isolation that I described in the previous chapter. However, one should not become over celebratory of the skilful move Tito made in his search for economic support in dire circumstances. I would agree with Rusinow's assessment that this move came at a certain price, as socialist Yugoslavia was becoming exposed to the long-term influence of the ideological, political, and economic institutions from the West, while simultaneously becoming stubbornly convinced of the 'correctness' of its own path, which would later prove to carry a set of negative consequences for internal democratisation (neutralisation of criticism and left opposition) as well as a gradual withering away of the planned economy and of a stronger centrally organised response in a time of crisis.

One can retrospectively speculate as to what extent the Yugoslav rapprochement with the West in the late 1940s came at a price of the complete withdrawal of Yugoslav help to the Greek communists, which ended in a tragic defeat, and accepting a softer position on the two zones that had been liberated by the Yugoslav partisan army (Istria–Italy). The compromise between Italy and Yugoslavia was finally settled in 1954 with the London memorandum that saw *Zone A* with Trieste fall under Italian jurisdiction, and *Zone B* with Slovenian and Croatian Istria fall under Yugoslav jurisdiction, with the additional promise of loans for the new port in Koper. Moreover, and more importantly, immediately after the war ended Yugoslavia received medical and food aid through *United Nations Relief and Rehabilitation Administration* (in the total value of approximately US$417 million in the currency at the time), however, by 1947 this programme had almost ended. It was not until late 1949 that the US sent its first small business loan to Yugoslavia, and only a year later, again on 29 November (on the seventh anniversary of the establishment of partisan AVNOJ Yugoslavia), the US president Truman sent a letter stating support for the Yugoslav Emergency Relief Act that became a cornerstone for US dealings with Yugoslavia. The major goal was to keep Soviet power out of Europe's most strategic areas and hope that the defiance shown towards the Soviet Union by other communist regimes might become infectious (Rusinow 1977: 45). With the US decision to extend their influence in a divided Europe, Yugoslavia gained US aid and with it a lifeline to food supplies, especially between 1950 and 1953 (see Lampe 1990: 28–30), as well as military assistance, which formally ended in 1957. In 1949 Yugoslavia also received its first loans from Eximbank in Washington (ibid.: 31), with a relatively favourable interest rate of 3.5 per cent. The first loans were mainly used to help set up the oil refinery infrastructure and reconstruct a few mines. In the years to come the loans became much more profit-oriented, however this precedence that the US helped Yugoslavia enabled the latter to access the International Bank for Reconstruction and Development and the International Monetary Fund (IMF), which at first granted Yugoslavia minor loans since any major investments were blocked by various American and French bondholders from the pre-war Yugoslavia (ibid.: 36). The balance sheet of trade relations between Yugoslavia and the US grew exponentially: in 1947 Yugoslavia exported 0.1% of its total exports to the US, but this number grew to 8.4% in 1949 and 13.5% by 1950, on the other hand, in 1947 American products represented 4% of the total Yugoslavian imports, however, by 1950 this number grew to 20.6%. This considerable economic assistance and exchange enabled the Yugoslav leadership to sail through the years of the agricultural crisis and gain new space for manouevre. However, Tito made sure that the aid from the West did not come with any political strings attached and promised to repay the debts of the bondholders (1959 agreement).

This rapprochement with the US took place at the same time as the Yugoslav foreign policies started using the United Nations' platform to defend its sovereignty and started appealing for autonomist politics beyond the two blocks that threatened with a large-scale (nuclear) conflict and a new world war. In this respect, the Yugoslav road to the global arena can be seen as a radical subversion of the retrospective lenses that see the period between 1945 and 1989 merely through the lenses of a bipolar world. This world was split in a number of ways: first of all, there was the split into two worlds, the first (capitalist) and the second (socialist) world, who both fought their proxy wars in the Third World. However, this geopolitical realistic account fails to address the Third World project in its own merit (see Prashad) and does not place any importance on the anti-colonial struggles and the emergence of the Non-Aligned Movement in the development of global history.

This chapter argues that one should not comply with this dominant perception that the entire sequence of the partisan anti-colonial struggles were simply vehicles: instruments aimed at sharpening the divide between the two new Great Powers (vulgar mechanical approach). Instead, the anti-colonial and non-aligned modernity brought novelty into the (first) world by giving itself authorisation precisely by rupturing from colonial dependence. Looking back at the revolutionary sequence of the anti-colonial struggles, Kardelj argued that they were to be seen as a direct response to the fascist imperialist expansion before and during World War II and should thus be seen as long-term,

> Global anti-imperialist revolutions carried out by nations who want to liberate themselves and assert their economic and political independence. Nations did not want to be the passive objects of global divisions, for they were able to set much stronger agenda on the historic problems of ending economic and political dependence and hegemony of any sort. Many national liberation and other people's revolutionary movements in colonies and other dependent countries emerged during World War II due to their own ideas of liberation and not in order to defend their colonial masters. (1975: 10).

The shattering of the old colonial-imperial powers and the introduction of political dependence came with major contradictions, political failures as well as future dependence on one of the two blocks, however one should appreciate the radical novelty of the anti-colonial movements, the historical lineage of which can be seen a long way in the past (for a fascinating example of Haiti two centuries earlier see Buck-Morss 2009).

This chapter can thus be seen as a small contribution to the well-articulated criticism by Toscano, who argues that the large majority of the current theories on emancipation overlook the geopolitical perspective, since emancipatory political action and subjectivity are allegedly completely constrained if positioned within the geopolitical perspective (Toscano 2008: 417). However, the symptomatic absence of thought that insists on situating local insurgencies and movements only confirms the conservative or cynical approach that geopolitics is all about Realpolitik. From this standpoint we can follow merely the iron laws of imperialism and the power of brutal force, which means there can be no real transformation at this level. This cynical view is not only structured as a self-fulfilling prophecy but is often complemented by the view of the angelic position that prefers to stick to micropolitics.

Thus, Yugoslavian political experiences should not be simply written off as an expression of a fortunate climate in geopolitics, but rather map out and re-appropriate the past historical experiences despite their (subsequent) limitations. Anticolonial and non-aligned modernities opened new horizons and nurtured revolutionary political subjectivity on a global scale. However, the anti-colonial movements did not simply follow Western or Eastern 'modernisation', for the anti-colonial movement returned to the Western and Eastern metropoles in the form of weak echoes, whether it was in May 1968 in France, USA, and Czechoslovakia, June 1968 in Yugoslavia, or April 1974 in Portugal.

This is why the second half of the twentieth century cannot be seen as a single major struggle between Soviet and US imperialism, but instead as the scene for the emergence of anti-colonial movements that disturbed the colonial and imperial global maps. The 'darker nations' emerged (to use Prashad's term) and became visible to the new and old imperialist states that had to start listening to their demands. The imperialist states still stuck firmly to the politics that was supposed to have been thrown into the dustbin of history at the end of World War II and condemned at the Nuremburg Trials. Unfortunately, there were no international trials that would bring to the bench those who had committed colonial crimes, or those great powers with their secret apparatuses that conducted the most brutal crimes within the territories of the 'darker nations' during the second part of the twentieth century. If one could say that the first and second world wars were waged between imperialist powers, the Cold War was directly outsourced to already 'oppressed nations'. Despite the brutal episodes of violence and war, the anti-colonial struggles produced dialectical effects: on the one hand they opened spaces of hope, empowered the oppressed and established new communities that had to deal with the remnants of Western colonisation, while on the other hand the newly emerging states soon became integrated into the mechanisms of oppression and economic exploitation by the former colonies and new imperialist powers. The struggles in the former colonies echoed strongly through the colonial metropoles, where censorship was busy preventing anti-colonial thinkers and artists from publishing their works.[4]

All of these anti- and de-colonial contributions of the second part of the twentieth century have been swept away in the age that allegedly ended history. Contemporary neo-moralists such as Henri-Levy point out the positive sides of colonialism and the corruption of the aspiring elites and their brutal dictatorships that later switched to the support of religious fundamentalism. The condemning of non-Western nations and individuals to some sort of eternal Western dependence provides clear moral and political grounds for a series of 'humanitarian interventions' in the post-Cold War era. During the last few decades historical revisionism has been rehabilitating fascism (Kirn 2019), while a long-term analysis shows deeper connections between liberalism and fascism (see Landa 2009; Losurdo 2015). The enlightened and civilisational strong hand of the West seems to be gaining currency amongst the new right-wing populist parties and movements that are basically returning to the old Eurocentric and orientalist visions.[5] If one was to speak today about the various emancipatory and anti-colonial struggles this cannot be seen as a kind of nostalgic drive or retro-utopian speculation (i.e. what should be changed in order not to become dependent again), but rather the knowledge that these experiences moved beyond the bipolar construction of the world and their traces on their own, has historic value – and their renewed mobilisation today should counter the racist-technocratic categorisation of minor, poor, or rogues states that have taken a peripheral position within the 'global-system'.[6]

While there are many anti-colonial and de-colonial (also, postcolonial) thinkers who pointed out the emancipatory moments of anti-colonial struggles, the recent discussion on the Non-Aligned Movement (the NAM) has been rather minor.[7] What I would like to argue here is that the NAM was parallel to the anti-colonial movements and that they in some places jointly disturbed Zhdanov's doctrine of two-camps.[8] Taken from the Yugoslav perspective of its isolation and moving beyond its Balkan perspective, the NAM can be seen as a continuation of the 'partisan politics' by other means. This does not mean that the NAM had such strong consequences for the people in Yugoslavia as the people's liberation struggle had had during World War II. However, no matter how different the events were, the emergence of a new Yugoslavia and the start of the NAM were both ruptures from the existing constellations of power, and resisted subjugation to the bipolar world. At first glance, belonging to the *non-aligned movement* is not the same as being a *partisan*. As I showed in Chapter 3, the Yugoslav partisan movement and the partisan figure were clearly aligned to a specific set of political, social, and even economic demands of liberation. This does not mean that the figure of the non-aligned is not aligned to its own set of demands. In the very practice of what the NAM wanted to be and was, it became immediately clear that it did not presuppose a sort of neutral and non-partisan politics, but rather the opposite, it intended to be actively directed against the existing bipolar alignment that left the country in a severe dependence on the respective centre of the bloc (Rubinstein 1970; Prashad 2007; Stubbs 2019).

In 1955, Tito made a historic visit to India, where he argued that non-alignment is not neutrality, but rather 'an active, positive and constructive policy seeking to lead to collective peace on which collective security can truly rest' (Tito 1955: 32). The Yugoslav contribution to the invention of the NAM was not limited to becoming a symbolic ornament of the Cold War, but can be approached on the one hand through the development of the global alternative struggles of theory, ideology, and politics, and on the other hand through the formation of concrete economic initiatives and political oppositions to the bipolar world, in which the United Nations played an important role. *Neither Washington nor Moscow* might have well been one of the slogans of 1968 (McGregor 2002) and could also be seen as the slogan of the NAM.

The first step in the formation of the Non-Aligned Movement was taken in Bandung (1955), one of the more important sites of colonialism and anti-colonial fights and their future imaginary. However, at this stage it was only the Asian countries that met to discuss the possible paths in future geopolitics that authorised the Third World project. The meeting was to some extent foreshadowed by the events that took place one year earlier, when a number of Asian countries joined the pro-Western military alliances.[9] This reflected the internal splits between the Asian countries in Bandung and manifested itself in the various attitudes of national leaderships towards the anti-colonial struggles, their liberation movements and global alignments. These were extremely unstable times.[10]

Despite the deep disagreements, the conference took an important step forward in strengthening the ties amongst the (new) Asian states. Tito and the Yugoslav foreign policy experts saw great potential in the future of this movement and Prashad worded their elementary gesture and response in an appropriate manner: the *Great Powers* had Yalta, then the *Third World* had Brioni (an island in the Adriatic Sea).[11] This is where the preparatory meeting for the NAM took place in 1956 and where the political leaders of the three major NAM founding countries, the NAM *troika*, came together: Tito (Yugoslavia), Nehru (India), and

Nasser (Egypt).[12] The meeting addressed the main topics and handed out invitations to twenty-two countries from three continents, the 'darker nations' from Asia, Africa, and South America, with Yugoslavia being the only European member.

The NAM consisted of politically diverse, and even ideologically opposing states, some monarchies, others republics, some leaning towards socialism, others embracing capitalism. Obviously, the NAM was not as militant as the Chinese foreign policies, which were at a later point famously challenged by Kardelj's text *Socialism and War* (1975) that addressed the specific incompatibility of a peaceful coexistence with such a militant approach. Another fascinating political alternative emerged in the mid-1960s in the aftermath of Cuba's revolution. This is known as the tricontinental movement or the Organisation of Solidarity with the People of Asia, Africa and Latin America (formed in Havana, in 1966) that brought together radical anti-capitalist, anti-imperialist, and anti-colonial movements, and not only parties or states. Could one argue that one of the major missed opportunities on the international left during the Cold War was an encounter between the NAM and the tricontinental movement? The major leaders of the respective movements, i.e. Tito and Castro, saw themselves as in direct competition on the global stage, as 'too radical' or 'not radical enough', even though they often cooperated through United Nations, or in some other way, on the strategic issues of anti-colonial movements.[13]

The first meeting of the NAM was held in Belgrade in 1961 where Tito was appointed the first secretary general. The NAM did not have a permanent seat, but implemented a rotation principle every three years, which included all member states and respective changes of the Secretary General. Apart from that, the member states regularly met at the United Nations assemblies where they amassed ever-larger support for particular issues. The member states subscribed to the following principles: mutual respect for each other's territorial integrity and sovereignty, reciprocal non-aggression and non-interference in domestic affairs, equality and mutual benefit, and a peaceful co-existence that would promote global (nuclear) disarmament. Even though these demands might make some individuals smile cynically these days, at the time, they represented important public criticism and had an impact that was later echoed in social movements. Despite the political differences between the various political leaders, the NAM became an important agent in the global order, a political movement that started maintaining ever-stronger economic ties and was very critical towards two moments: bloc politics and the uneven economic developments that accompanied the imperialism of the Great Powers. Anticolonial struggles were no longer seen as a specific phenomenon that belonged to a specific colonial power, for they became a part of a more general horizon and movement. The NAM represented one of the most important venues and as such represented a major disruption in the Cold War world map.

However, a critical question could be asked of the NAM: was it possible to put into motion these political principles and truly disrupt the Cold War division without any military backing and with such diverse political actors? As Prashad has argued, the NAM 'would remain a political platform, a sub-United Nations, but it would only be able to act in harmony on two broad issues: global nuclear disarmament, and the democratisation of the United Nations' (2007:101).

Drafting resolutions and asserting an alternative media agenda reinforced the democratic ideals in the world of Realpolitik, where morality had long lost its place. But doesn't this merely bring us back to the impossible position: how can one act against brutal force and strive for mutual coexistence and peace? Again, any reference to a 'peaceful co-existence' from the perspective of the anti-colonial struggle does not seem very partisan, but it received political merit in light of the nuclear arms race. The NAM was successful in bringing the agenda to the international forum. The NAM demands echoed in the anti-war and student movements of '68, but nevertheless the NAM remained less successful in terms of implementing real policies. Prashad claimed that the NAM made 'more room for the darker nations – but not necessarily for the world to be reconstructed in their image' (ibid., 96).[14]

Another level of appreciating the legacy of the NAM is to observe their contribution to the political thought that evoked the concept of peace. In other words, the NAM directed its efforts into thinking and practicing peace not in terms of balance between the imperialist powers or containing the nuclear disaster until the next war emerged (as if the balance between the great powers did not emerge at the expense of the brutal wars in the Third World). In this respect the NAM was particularly dedicated to the politics that embraced peace as a political concept and principle.[15] The anti-war position and movement for peace has been assigned a declaratory and moralising role, however, it has been a strong part of the revolutionary movements for a long time, ever since the October revolution.[16]

Within international relations theory, and more generally within the history of political thought, there is a major emphasis on the paradigm of war, violence, and conflict (Balibar 2012). In other words, political history and change is read through the categories of war. This paradigmatic stance was challenged by the NAM from the outset, as it stressed its own historical experiences of non-violent politics. In India this alternative reading was particularly instructive and pointed out that the seemingly 'passive' resistance embodied in the civil disobedience movement demanded as active an engagement as the people's armed struggle. In a specific situation, the non-violent pursuit of peace and justice can be even more pertinent and successful than an armed struggle. The politics of peace was conceived as a pro-active and engaging project that went against all existing military alliances and against the paradigm of war. Advocating peace constituted the core principle of the NAM. In this sense Rubinstein correctly detected the specificity of the Yugoslav aversion to its 'membership in military blocs', which became a cardinal principle of Yugoslav foreign policy and a cornerstone of the non-aligned movement.[17]

This said, the Yugoslav striving for peace, with its important share in the development of the UN peace-keeping actions, did not run into the fetishisation of non-violent politics, especially if we are talking about the structural analysis of the demise of the old colonial world system. The Yugoslav foreign policy was openly anti-colonial even at the beginning of its own isolation and during the initial period of the NAM in the 1950s and 1960s. Yugoslavia actively supported the national liberation struggle in Burma and the National Liberation Front in Algeria. It also secretly supplied the National Liberation Front with weapons and other materials through Egypt, which provoked strong reactions from the French government. On the level of the NAM, the beginning of the 1960s saw the support of member states for the national liberation struggles of the African Party for the Independence of Guinea and Cape Verde in Guinea, the People's Movement for the Liberation of Angola, and the Mozambique Liberation Front.[18] It was in this respect that Kardelj made a clear distinction between the wars of the powerful and the wars of the weak. This is not a moral category, but a criterion upon which we can deem legitimate any armed struggle that aims to overthrow old colonial or new imperial powers.[19] Unquestionably, on the topic of civil war and violent conflicts within a country this perspective remained inoperative, but only principled in terms of respecting the territorial sovereignty.

Finally, I should add that the split with Stalin resulted in a major challenge for the Yugoslav leadership that needed to change the political orientation of Yugoslavia, which also found its way beyond the overly strong dependence on Western countries. In the beginning of this chapter I pointed out that during the 1950s, the US military and material aid was of great importance to Yugoslavia. The aid was provided until 1957, when it was abolished upon the initiative of Yugoslavia.[20] Surely, in the aftermath of Tito's split with Stalin, US politics managed to ensure greater geopolitical influence throughout Europe. Nevertheless, following Stalin's death the relations with the Soviet Union would once again become more amicable, allowing Yugoslavia to once again focus its attention on the cooperation with Eastern countries.

The Yugoslav push for its political independence – which served as a possible model for other independent roads – was thus accompanied by a desired expansion of economic activities, finding new markets and opportunities for Yugoslav trade and production and the joint planning of the infrastructure and key industries necessary for the development of new countries. In the mid-1950s, Yugoslavia started to cooperate economically with the Non-Aligned Countries and even if the importance of the NAM states was not great (in the 1960s they represented approximately 15 per cent of all Yugoslav trade), one should keep in mind the importance of the specific type of exchange that took place between Yugoslavia and these countries. Since it was denied access to the Eastern European markets, it had to 'integrate' into the global market. Yugoslavia attempted to strengthen its economy, but at the same time it also invested in the public infrastructure of the developing countries, loaned its experts and signed loans at favourable commercial terms (3 per cent interest), which – if not reimbursed – would be repaid through the barter economy, or at a much delayed date.

Yugoslavia assisted the developing countries and by the mid-1960s had invested large sums of money in them. As Rubinstein stated:

These credits involved deliveries of Yugoslav industrial foods and the construction by Yugoslav firms of more than 120 different projects: hydro-electric power stations in India, Cambodia, Guinea, Togo, Ethiopia, and Syria; cement works in the Sudan and Ethiopia; textile mills in Algeria; tractor plants in Ghana and the U.A.R. ports in Syria, Tunisia and Ghana; slaughterhouses in Mali, Tunisia and Liberia; a leatherwear factory and food processing plant in Algeria. (1970: 211).

There were also other strategic companies that would introduce mixed partnership in developing countries, from *Naftaplin* (oil drilling), *Ingra* (building transmission lines) and *Prvomajska* (machinery installation) to other big construction companies that carried out large architectural projects. The economic model that Yugoslavia developed vis-à-vis the NAM was one of the alternative attempts to found a parallel economic system that would not be based on profit-oriented criteria, but would instead, be based on mutual aid and the construction of the public infrastructure (loosely connected to socialist ideas, but without direct political control). In this regard, it is possible to note the general focus on the improvement of those capacities that would assist the emerging and evolving countries in their pursuit of an independent development. Furthermore, Yugoslavia had a range of institutions that did not focus merely on the economy, but also on the system of cultural and educational exchanges. The strategic investment to the developing countries came to a halt after 1965, when market reform reduced the government's ability for further subsidies and handing out loans to undeveloped regions and countries, while the concentration of autonomous capital within Yugoslavia was given priority.

However, one should acknowledge that the early stage of the NAM was without a doubt the most exciting and experimental period in Yugoslav foreign policy; one that went beyond purely calculative national interests and against the global dominance of the two superpowers that posited their modernizations to be the only right and existing. I would agree and conclude with Paul Stubbs, who recently assessed the Yugoslav legacy in relation to the NAM in the following way:

Whilst socialist Yugoslavia's involvement in NAM can be characterized as a kind of instrumentalization of economic self-interest, part of a search for 'new and emerging markets' through which 'export-led growth', a central mantra of 'market socialism', could be pursued, this is not, at all, the whole story. Indeed, although economic questions did become more central to the Movement over time, the initial emphasis on 'self-determination', described by many as 'active co-existence' ...

combined a genuine support for freedom from colonialist and impe-rialist oppression, the right to sovereignty and non-interference for new nation states, resistance to the domination of the two main power blocs, and an emphasis on general and complete disarmament in a world in which the threat of nuclear annihilation was ever present.' (Stubbs 2019).

6

Partisan Rupture III: Yugoslav Road to Self-Management Socialism

The split with Stalin in 1948 had immense consequences for Yugoslav socialism in terms of its internal political, social, and economic organisation. Retrospectively, the Yugoslav leadership and official state memory celebrated the split as the start of a heroic and independent road to socialism, but one must not shy away from its rather harsh political beginnings. Tito's entourage found itself in a paralysis that soon turned into political paranoia that fuelled the wave of repression in 1949–50. These were the years during which mass arrests of the die-hard Stalin supporters within the Communist Party of Yugoslavia took place and during which the secret service was very active. Why did I say 'die-hard' supporters? Most of the communist leadership supported Stalin without much reservation until mid-1948. As mentioned in the previous chapter, the split with Stalin was unimaginable, a point of impossibility within the international workers' movement that was based on the unity and guidance from Moscow. So, how would one embark on a completely independent journey, if the history and the necessary coming of communism resided with Moscow (Samary 1988: 117)? And furthermore, the question immediately emerges, who would question and judge the Yugoslav independent road to socialism? How could one reprogramme the masses and the existing beliefs and change the existing plan for the early socialist development of Yugoslavia? These were not questions and issues that one could simply sleep on and it was only after a series of harsh Cominform attacks on Yugoslavia, when it became obvious that the country was left to its own devices (survival), that the blind allegiance to Moscow and Stalin became questioned and challenged. Not everyone shared the view of Tito's close entourage, and not many believed that Yugoslavia should embark on its own path. Those who expressed their doubts too loudly, together with some dissident voices, were sent to the political prison on the island of Goli Otok. It is noteworthy that there were a few prisons of this type in Yugoslavia, which primarily hosted former fascist local collaborators, while for the new political prisoners – Stalinist collaborators – Goli Otok became synonymous with 're-education'. Typically, the prisoners conducted Sisyphian tasks under inhumane circumstances of extreme heat, which was a very cynical way of addressing the 're-education' of Stalinists. However, apart from the paranoia, one can wonder to what degree this retaliation against Stalinists who were to undergo re-education was instrumentalised in terms of the internal power struggles within the Party (Djilas 1957)? Goli Otok operated as a political camp until 1957 and held some 16,000 prisoners, however, after the reconciliation with the Soviet Union, it lost its political utility.[1]

The time that followed the split with Stalin was marked by a paradoxical situation: on the one hand there was the highest degree of censorship and repression vis-à-vis the foreign policy and the not-yet-existing party line, while on the other hand, it triggered a series of political reflections about the future development of what was to become known as the Yugoslav road to socialism. Milovan Djilas, who was in charge of propaganda, recounted a story in which he, Edvard Kardelj (the foreign minister and one of the main self-management ideologues), and Boris Kidrić (minister of economy), all a close part of Tito's entourage and the politburo of the Communist Party of Yugoslavia, first held private discussions on the idea of self-management and then convinced Tito that this was the only way forward if they wished to mobilise popular support in these chaotic circumstances and experiment with a veritable form of workers' democracy, at first on a consultative basis (Rusinow 1977: 57).

The initial paradox of Yugoslav self-management lies in the fact that its return to the early Soviet times – which were times of actual social revolution that cannot be imagined without the soviets and councils –was announced from above and implemented through the law and reform! There were no soviets or councils in Yugoslavia at that time, which is why they had to start from ground zero. In the broader political-theoretical concept, 'self-management' is not defined merely as the social management of public and social affairs, but also as including (self-)government and (self-)organisation.[2] Self-government goes beyond the organisation of producers (the classic working class) and attempts to focus on politics in all aspects of social life. Marcelo Vieta, one of today's most insightful self-management theorists, defines self-management as self-creation, self-control, and ultimately self-production: in other words, self-management is about relying on one's own capacities, through which one would then be practicing political autonomy. Michael Lebowitz sees self-management as an essential element in the production process 'insofar as people produce themselves in the course of all their activities, the very process of engaging in democratic forms of production is an essential part of producing people for whom the need for cooperation is second nature' (2012: 12). Self-management is conceived as the rejection of bureaucratic administration, the Bolshevik model, and social democracy, which represents a key measurement on the success of a self-management project (Labica and Bensussan 1999: 69–75).

In the chapters to come I will attempt to unravel the ways in which the Yugoslav historical experience attests to the dialectical movement of self-management: firstly, it was a movement implemented from above which was materialised in a dominant ideology and in the social development policy of a new state that promised to improve the material conditions for everyone; secondly, it can also be read as self-management from below, which speaks of successful and long-term practices of organising workers in specific companies and social/cultural sectors, as well as in a more antagonist sense for the state, in the form of illegal self-organisations in strikes and protests that challenged the Party hegemony.

But first things first: workers' self-management was discussed within the Central Committee during 1949 and at its second Plenum in December a major agreement between the trade unions and the federal government was signed (23 December 1949). The latter prescribed a test of elective workers' councils in 215 large enterprises (see also Suvin 2016). Next year self-management was announced also formally within the *Basic Law on Management of State Economic Enterprises and Higher Economic Associations by the Workers' Collectives* adopted on 27 June 1950.[3] The law and strategic orientation of Yugoslav socialism resulted from a series of discussions within the Central Committee of the Party and its intellectual circles that can be read as the first systemic critique of Soviet socialism and its model of planned economy. Especially Bakarić, Kidrič, and Kardelj worked on developing a theoretical frame for the emerging economic development, while many other communists turned to reading the revolutionary teachings of Marx and Engels[4] and the politics of Lenin.

The history of the international workers' movement from Stalin onwards was not a harmonious one that would cement unity, but was full of theoretical and political splits, infinite discussions on deviations and faithful continuations of Marx's words and the political actions of Lenin that structured the Marxist-communist field. However, it was also true that for the first time a representative of a socialist state, Tito, inaugurated self-management as an independent path on an international level. He conceived self-management as the true method for 'withering away the state' and continuing with the transition from the point where Leninism stopped. Tito attacked 'Stalinist deviation' and professed to move beyond the mere nationalisation of the productive means and towards a 'higher form of socialism'. He concluded that the future lay in self-management: 'This is where our road to socialism lies' (1950, in *Borba* 27 June).

It is noteworthy that at that time Yugoslavia was still following the Soviet-influenced first five-year plan from 1947. However, according to the Yugoslav communists the new state planning deviated both from the teachings of Marx and Engels as well as from the early stages of the Soviet revolution (Lenin). Apart from the ironic twist that the early or real revolutionary legacy was now conserved by the Titoist leadership, another historical irony resides in the fact that Stalin's model of constructing 'socialism within one state' was now actualised in yet another road to construct 'socialism within one state'. The repetition cannot be condemned a priori, instead, one could claim that the Yugoslav experiment was one of the rare relatively successful examples of socialism that developed different political and economic forms of workers' participation and social regulation. Despite the necessary dose of criticism, one cannot reduce the series of discussions, policies, and experimentations with self-management to the goodwill of the United States which were a result of the geopolitical situation. This would be a cynical position that ignored the legacy of struggles coming from both, above and below.

In 1949 Edvard Kardelj wrote that self-management should not be viewed as a special road recognised in a decree, as it is deeply rooted in World War II popular and partisan struggles in Yugoslavia (Kardelj 1980: 232–34). This politico-economic model was to implement two major orientations from the shared communist legacy: firstly, it would respond to Marx and Engels' 'principle of direct association of producers in order to direct the economy' and secondly, it would realise Lenin's call for the 'withering away of the state' (Kardelj 1956: 456). In one of his later texts Kardelj concluded that

> Self-management is not an invention of the Yugoslav theory and practice ... but is as old as the idea of humanism and the international workers' movement, the history of its class struggle and the history of socialist practice. (Kardelj 1977: 9).

The ambivalence surrounding the common legacy of the workers' struggles on the one hand and the specificity of the Yugoslav road on the other, points out the contradiction that could be found at the heart of the existing Soviet model. Catherine Samary believed that the Yugoslav orientation attacked the Soviet 'non-withering of the state and was analysed in contradiction with the construction of socialism or at least as a threat to the socialist future' (Samary 1988: 117). The rupture with Stalin demanded a thorough re-examination of the (socialist) state and its role in the transition towards a communist society. As a solution to the troublesome merger of the Party with the State, the Yugoslav minister of economy and one of the most prolific political theorists Boris Kidrič, advocated the 'withering away of the state'. In one of his most important texts of 1950 he claimed that,

State socialism (socialism of state) represents only the first and smallest step in the socialist revolution ... State socialism [necessarily grows into] a privileged bureaucracy as a social parasite, the throttling of socialist democracy, and a general degeneration of the whole system, [and there comes about] a restoration of a specific kind, a vulgar State-capitalist monopoly.

The socialist democratic rights of the direct producers [are the obverse of] the process of abolishing monopolies; basic is – the right of the working masses to self-management at all levels of socialist State power. (Quoted in Horvat 1976: 10).

On the one hand, in the light of the 1948 split, the post-World War II Communist Party gradually neutralised and marginalised the political opposition (dissolution of the autonomy of the Women's Anti-Fascist Front and Liberation Front organisations), while on the other hand, in 1952, the Party renamed itself into the League of Communists and entertained an ideological and political move from a conspiratorial organisation – not accessible to the public – to a more public governing political body.

At the 7th Congress of the League of Communists of Yugoslavia in 1957, self-management was defined as an attack on 'bureaucratism' and 'centralisation', while pushing to create 'material conditions that were politically and judicially necessary to truly empower the workers' and helping the 'citizens of socialist Yugoslavia to become active and direct (self)managers of social affairs' (Bakarić in Samary 1988: 118).[5] By the late 1950s the self-management model started expanding from the strict field of economy – and testing units of enterprises in all social spheres.

Thus, despite the contradictions that I will describe in the following chapters, Yugoslav self-management offered a renewal of, and experimentation with, socialist and communist thought. This created a break within the international workers' movement, however, this break did not take the form of isolation, but rather resulted in an expansion, both through the Non-Aligned Movement externally and the experimentation with political forms internally. The fact that the main self-management ideologues and politicians never took their system for granted, but constantly kept revising it, raises doubts as to whether we can truly speak of a single self-management model, which pointed to a deeper rupture in which the administrative decrees of the 'avant-garde logic' (Lebowitz 2012) were substituted for a predominantly administrative logic, supposedly accessible to all workers. Keršev̌an's (1985) excellent paraphrase states that according to a number of principal ideologues, the essence of self-management lies in the fact that the workers simultaneously work as well as perform the functions that are carried out by capitalists in capitalist societies and by the state in statist societies. This process supposedly involved the integration of labour and capital under the workers' control. Historically speaking, self-management remained utopic in many aspects and failed to fulfil all of its human and social potentials. However, it was far away from homogeneity, rather as Samary rightly claims 45 years of existence saw 'four major systems of production and exchange and four different modalities of articulating the plan and market, which, from the 1950s onwards formed self-management that became combined with different relations to the global market' (1988: 21).

The self-management system went through a constant modification of economic governance, and led to a responsive economic policy that would (self)regulate the economic activities in the transition to socialism and disperse the political decision-making from the state to the society. In more Marxist terms, we could speak of the development of a social system that would see the distribution of surplus value among the republics and people in an egalitarian way, while the workers would become increasingly in charge of the value appropriation – self-valorisation (see Suvin 2016).

Despite the call to wither away the state and decentralise the plan and federative structure, the new self-management model continued to pursue the main promise of the new state of the working people: 'socialist modernisation' would continue with the construction of a massive industrial complex that was connected to independent military capacities, which would, in the final instance, defend Yugoslav independence; furthermore, it would continue reducing the illiteracy levels that had, in pre-war Yugoslavia, ranged from 40 per cent (on average) to 75 per cent in the undeveloped regions with the massive move from rural areas (over 70 per cent of the agrarian population) to the cities. Thus, when the new decentralisation policies began in the 1950s the massive modifications were not implemented all at once. The immediate changes modified the centrality of the plan that was guided by administrative orders (bureaucracy's leading role) and the decision-making process was gradually 'decentralised' and substituted with economic instruments.[6] Instead of making the central socialist state wither away, the Yugoslav self-management developed a much more complex system of social mediations and regulation that materialised in a widespread network between different political and economic instances that discussed and negotiated future plans.

These were the pillars of self-management that formed an unstable constellation of the self-management social contract. As with any contract, it was based on exchange. However, instead of the supposed symmetry and formal equality before the law, an asymmetrical and class-related moment was embedded into the contract. Instead of applying to the 'political community' (the state), which protects individuals and their property, the social contract now *applied* to the entire society, introducing the principle of justice with the emphasis on the protection of social and economic rights. Instead of the formal equality, the operation of inequality manifested itself in the very centre of the socialist social contract, transferring the means of production to the state – in short, it expropriated the capitalist expropriators. With this fundamental operation, the new community could start guaranteeing an equal development of all individuals and parts of society.

As I have already pointed out, another transfer of rights took place within the Yugoslav self-management: now the sovereign state authority was transferred to the self-management society. At this point, yet another appropriation was carried out, transferring what was now state property to society as a whole: property was no longer private or state, for it became *social*. Despite certain formal assurances, this self-management contract left some questions unanswered: if the state was supposed to wither away in the future, who was responsible for

Table 6.1 The early socialist social contract in Yugoslavia

Primary subject: the working people	→ type of exchange ←	The socialist community
Founding act: appropriation of the means of production by the political apparatus (with subsequent disposal and redistribution)	Exchange – transfer	A workers' state, the Party vanguard
		State property
		Excluded subject: the capitalist class

the conclusion of the contracts between the self-managing agents and the self-managing community – society? In Kardelj's political ideology, the moment of mediation and political regulation would always, first and foremost, belong to the League of Communists as the key political subject that embodied the 'general will' of the 'working people'. In place of the supreme legislator and the people from the bourgeois contract, the League of Communists and the working people were introduced within the context of self-management. The League of Communists became the political force that 'invisibly' managed the Society, prepared the contract, and then maintained the exclusive right of interpreting this contract and coordinating its implementation. In its initial stage, the transfer of wealth and its redistribution in Yugoslavia had tangible and positive socio-economic effects, which, of course, came at a cost. The economic part of the contract is based on repairing the basic asymmetry and economic inequality, that is, by introducing the mechanism of expropriation, which aims to achieve equality for all, but does so by performing an asymmetrical (and for the former ruling class 'unjust') gesture to those that possess large amounts of private property, be it corporations, or wealthy individuals. At the same time the working people were placed in a politically weaker position as the subjects of this contract. The silent contract between political bureaucracy and the workers transferred the political representation to the bureaucracy, which, in exchange, had to ensure full employment and material improvement of the workers' position. Subject to the social contract, the working people renounced their access to the political apparatus, thus excluding themselves from the most important institutions of the workers' state.

Table 6.2   Transition to self-management

Primary subject: the working people	→ type of exchange ←	The socialist community
Expropriation of the state apparatus, transfer to the society, political transfer to the lower levels	Representation	Political bureaucracy, workers' councils (companies), delegate system, republics, municipalities
State property	Exchange – transfer	Social property

Finally, as seen in the above schema, the major lasting and inspirational contribution of the self-management rupture is linked to the deep transformation in the form of property. Yugoslav self-management transferred property from the state to society and actually implemented 'social ownership'. Formally, the Yugoslav politico–legal practice departed from the paradoxical conception of property qua 'non-property', being at the same time in the hands of everyone and nobody. One ought to ask who 'society' is, who represents it, and how can 'society' be in charge of the use and management of the means of re/production? This does not merely mean that everyone should manage their wages and accumulation of (social) capital, but that everyone should also participate in the use and organisation of the cultural and social infrastructure (Kirn 2014). This was a determined move beyond the standpoint of 'nationalisation' and state property, where a central agency that would dispose, manage, and own the means of production was clearly ascribed to the state and Party representatives. On the macro level the social ownership regime can be compared to what Negri and Hardt (2009) have advocated under the name of the 'commons'. Yugoslav self-management introduced and experimented with this 'third way' of ownership that moved beyond the modality between the state and private property. Dolenec and Žitko (2013) tackled the importance of the notion of the commons (back) in the Yugoslav context; I agree with their suggestion that social ownership was already a form of commons, and that it was connected to a broader anti-capitalist project that strived for the abolition of private property.

Even today Rastko Močnik sees this as one of the major legacies worth defending and advocating: 'social ownership could have opened new horizons in political practices, if its political potential had not been sapped by the apparatuses of social management' (2010). The legal theorist Aleksander Bajt believes that social ownership needs to be located in a 'double inscription'; firstly into the legal and secondly into the economic aspect, which means that 'legally, the enterprise is the owner of the means of production, whereas the workers manage it in reality. The workers' collective was thus the economic owner of the means of production' (Bajt, 1975: 159). In other words, the enterprise had the 'right of disposal', while the workers' collective had the 'managing rights'. This was the formal division of power within the economic constellation. What were the major institutional advantages and disadvantages of this property regime that implemented this division of ownership rights between the workers' collective and the enterprise? In this respect, the sociologist Veljko Rus explains that

> The workers' collective would decide about matters that relate to management, while the enterprise or rather its representatives would decide on matters that related to disposal. If workers themselves would accumulate means/resources in their working organisation, then they would be also the owners of the enterprise's capital, while if these means would be invested by other subjects, e.g. banks, foreign investors, etc., then they would have the disposal rights. (Rus, 1988: 19)

Despite the formal vagueness surrounding social property, the project of modernisation and favourable economic conditions did not bring the workers and their political and economic representatives into an antagonistic relation during the early period of the workers' self-management. In many respects, the political class realised the promise of the socialist social contract. I will argue that, especially during the so-called market socialism when the proto-capitalist tendency was gaining in strength, this formal vagueness of social property was hegemonised by the new power networkers who were pushing for the understanding of the workers' participation as the shareholders who should give greater power to the market, which tilted the ownership towards private property. The major issue in the class struggle did not revolve around the form of property – whether it should be private, social or nationalised/state – but around the management, appropriation, and distribution of value. This was one of the key notions in which the paradox of self-management could be found and this will be discussed in greater detail in Chapters 8–12.

* * *

In the first part of the book – in Chapters 1 to 6 – I followed the political-philosophical analysis of the three partisan ruptures, decisively stemming from the partisan politics of the People's Liberation Struggle. In a way even the post-war socialist revolution, the Non-Aligned Movement, and the introduction of the self-management model of (self)government were a continuation of the partisan politics, and in the tense geopolitical circumstances they preserved a certain degree of political autonomy. The Yugoslav reliance on its own forces was of key importance for the understanding of the struggle and the (non)relationship with the World War II collaboration and occupation forces. This reliance continued with the socialist autonomy from the Soviet Union at the end of the 1940s and the establishment of the non-aligned position beyond the bloc division of the world at the end of the 1950s. As an unfinished political project, Yugoslavia is the name of a political scandal and a cut into the existing coordinates of pre-war Yugoslavia as well as the international post-war workers' movement and the path to socialism. The Yugoslav experiment did not entail only the local specifics. Instead, we have to understand it as a universal politics with long-term and profound effects, which would not remain restricted merely to the context of the Balkans. In order not to encourage any further romanticising and nostalgic views of these communist historical sequences, I will add a more structural outlook to this political analysis: a critique of the political economy of socialist reproduction. In the following chapters, I will analyse the main antinomies, contradictions, and class antagonisms involved in the Yugoslav self-management model during the 'market socialism' period (1965–1973). This was the most inventive period in the political sense, as by that time the self-management political power had already been decentralised and disseminated throughout the self-management society. These processes were accompanied by a severe transformation of the economic regulations that replaced the plan and the vanguard of the Party with the market and the logic of capital. However, even in the early stages, these tendencies were resisted by the organised and spontaneous masses of the workers, whose relations with the political representatives were becoming increasingly antagonistic.

A Short Introduction to the Recent Studies of Socialist Yugoslavia

In the introduction to this book I pointed out the ideological landscape of the post-Yugoslav context, characterised in particular by an obscurantist revisionism and Yugo-nostalgic memory. Despite the ideological prevalence of this mode, these were not the only two ideological positions that defined the theoretical interpretations of socialist Yugoslavia in their totality. The latest research on recent history in political science, sociological works, and contemporary historiography has focused predominantly on the so-called 'democratic transition' in the 1990s or on the formation of democratic actors and civil society in the 1980s. The analysis of the complexity of the socialist formation was opposed by literature that supported the inevitability of the demise of socialism on the one hand and the inevitability of the 'democratic' transition, which was supposed to culminate in a national state on the capitalist horizon, on the other hand. Henceforth, socialism has only been referred to in terms of a collapsed system or even a catastrophe and totalitarianism, thus inhibiting any kind of analytical work or theoretical discussion. Even the recent discussions surrounding the 'idea of communism' (Žižek, Negri, Badiou) have consigned socialism as an idea and political practice to the 'dustbin of history'.

However, instead of laying socialism to its eternal rest, we should tackle this concept and its historical experience head-on – not to demonstrate the inevitability, but rather to demonstrate the contradictory movements that exhausted the partisan ruptures and enhanced the capitalist elements. Let us therefore begin with a good definition of socialism: socialism is a social formation, characterised by transience at its very outset – i.e., on the Marxist horizon, socialism has always been a 'transitional form', a transitory phase leading to communism, yet capable of regressing to the capitalist social relations. Furthermore, in the example of Yugoslavia, one can speak about a genuine socialist experiment, as it kept developing for over forty years, during which time it went through numerous transitions and ruptures that demonstrate extremely contradictory processes, which cannot be reduced to the general signifiers of totalitarian terror, dictatorship, or plain variations of state capitalism. In the ideologically saturated context of the 1990s, we should also mention – apart from the nationalist and orientalist (self-)interpretations[1] – the analytically sound liberal explanations[2] and, naturally, the earlier ideological (self-)descriptions of socialism in the official documents, texts, and memoires of the former leaders and theorists whom we intend to engage in a critical dialogue in the continuation.

The present analysis of the Yugoslav real socialism will go beyond simply describing certain teachings from the past that should be taken into account in the present and the future struggles for democratic socialism. It is also not meant to summon the ghosts of the past that would descend from the clouds and put on new clothes. The analysis provides a new understanding of the context and genealogy of the dissolution of Yugoslavia and socialism. In the preceding chapters I presented the thesis of the rupture-like character of the Yugoslav People's Liberation Struggle that continued in various historical sequences (the self-management construction and the Non-Aligned Movement). Even this short analysis of the emancipatory dimensions of the communist politics has shown that this was not a uniform and singular event, but rather a revolutionary process with its share of contradictions. Even more ambivalent and regressive tendencies can be noticed in the subsequent socialist movement that I will reflect upon in this chapter by applying a Marxist political-economic and critical ideological analysis to its variations. One of the guidelines for the present analysis was laid down by the French philosopher Étienne Balibar, who, in the 1970s, pointed out two pitfalls with regard to the socialist transition theories. According to Balibar, most of the Marxist analyses fell into the trap of either the so-called *stage model* of transition (stages of socialist development), which supports the evolutionary paradigm of the inevitability of the transition to communism, or the *catastrophism* which is accompanied by the utopian narration of a pure beginning and a direct transition to communism (eg. Negri, Badiou). It also needs to be underlined that the current prevailing model of transition is characterised by a progressive and linear perception of time that includes the final goal (market, democracy, the national state) and considers all processes through the same perspective (the inevitable end of socialism). Unlike these self-fulfilling prophecies of transition, this book considers historical processes to be dynamic. No matter how stable these may seem retro-spectively, I will emphasise the incessant struggles in the heart of social reproduction that barely preserve the temporary systemic balance.[3] Consequently, temporality is not homogenous in this sort of history: instead it will be traversed by regressions, deviations, condensations, and transpositions.[4]

Bettelheim pointed out that Marx was mainly focusing on the tran-sition between the feudalist and capitalist production mode. Therefore, further development of the transition theory is extremely important if we are to assess the specifics and (un)successfulness of the socialist tran-sitions. One of the most important theoretical points of the Yugoslav socialist formation analysis considers the dissonance between the formal mode of appropriation and the legal–social ownership on the one hand and the actual mode of appropriation with the manifestation of capitalist elements on the other.[5] While researching the specific political economy, it is impossible to circumvent the general reproduction of social relations as a continuous implementation of the government apparatus' techniques that consider the relations between the ideology, state, repression, and law. Srečo Kirn wrote that socialist self-management was a transitional formation with numerous contradictions, where the tension between the reproduction of the relation between labour and capital and its abolition came to the forefront:

> The law of motion of the socialist self-management transitional society is a functioning relationship between the contradictory laws of commodity production on the one hand and the contradictory intro-duction of socialist self-management relations on the other hand ... every time the historical dissolution of this relationship is placed into its local and peripheral character, a prospect for its further expansion and preservation emerges. (Kirn 1982: 55–6).

A concrete historical movement that extends from the termination and partial incorporation to the regression to capitalist relations pertains to the dialectical relationship between communism and socialism. Theo-retical analysis should therefore not ignore the appearance of deviations and regressions or assess them as exceptions that prove the rule of the 'ideal model'. Instead, it should consider these deviations in their tenden-tious motions as announcements of something that does not necessarily correspond to the historical inevitability of the past or the current official outlook.

Although there are not many contemporary and Marxist studies of socialist Yugoslavia, Catherine Samary reminds us that there have been three prevailing approaches to analysing socialism (also outside of the Yugoslav context): socialism as a new class, socialism as state capitalism, and socialism as a socialist social formation (transitional form) (Kirn and Samary 2013).

The first approach appeared in Yugoslavia with the publication of Milovan Djilas's book in the early 1950s. Djilas had been a member of the innermost Party leadership during and after the war (Dilas 1982). His book gained international popularity as openly anti-communist propaganda. However, from a more analytical point of view, its foundations are rather unsound.[6] Djilas focused on the criticism of 'the new class' embodied by the new socialist bureaucracy; however, the discussion lacks any theorisation regarding the class or the specific class relations within Yugoslavia. This approach highlights the otherwise problematic position of the Party, its relationship to the state, and its infallibility, but fails to demonstrate the broader structural dynamics and specifics of the socialist social relations. I concur with Darko Suvin, who recently pointed out that the signifier 'bureaucracy' has a meaning only if we consider it in connection with class relations, as it otherwise functions as a political expletive and not as a theoretical concept.[7] Even in the context of the criticism of Stalinism and state socialism, the assumption of the monolithic ruling class of bureaucracy, which imposes univocality upon the reactionary mass, represents a deficient thesis in the theoretical and political sense. Mastnak correctly assumed that such dissident criticism is not political but moralist, because it defines all processes as 'undefined authority, for which it is not known how it is composed or how it functions – it is only known that it is "the authority" – and it is termed "bureaucracy"' (Mastnak 1982: 40). Djilas's analysis of the history of Yugoslav socialism is a journalistic analysis of a certain political elite in a precise moment in time, and was in the best case, merely a negative mirror image of the official discourse on the inevitability of history and the vanguardist role of the Party,[8] while in the worst case, it represents one of the classic studies of totalitarianisms which reduce the history of socialism to the history of political violence and ideological univocality. In this sense I agree with the aforementioned study performed by Mira Bogdanović, who points out the prominent status and mechanism that was acquired by the political conversion in the western and liberal narrative.

The second approach is Trotskyist and presumes that neither the Soviet Union nor Yugoslavia actually ever implemented socialism but were at best 'state capitalism'.[9] This thesis condemns the persistence of monetary and commodity exchange in socialism as well as the perpetuation of the relationship between labour and capital. Due to the existence of capitalist relations during the period of socialist Yugoslavia, certain advocates of this approach exalt this thesis as a transhistorical notion of the capital. Vladimir Unkovski-Korica, for example, claims that Yugoslavia was already completely integrated into the global market at the end of the 1940s, which is attested to by the documents and discussions of the innermost leadership (Unkovski-Korica 2016),[10] while another choice for Yugoslav communists was the path that the Communist Party of Albania took later on and which would see the country becoming an isolated Stalinist island for the decades to come. Moreover, Katalenac believes that private property was always present in Yugoslavia (Katalenac 2013).[11] Obviously, if one takes pure communism as the norm for analysing a revolution or a state (re)construction, then one has already in advance condemned all socialist attempts, past as well as future, as failed revolutions. There will then never be either the global revolution that has never actually happened nor will there be communism, which brings us to the eternity of capital(ism). This reveals a leftist melancholy and specific fascination with our defeats that sees the end of the immaculate idea each time a (temporary) victory is celebrated.

As we have already seen, the partisan struggle politically abolished the pre-war capitalist and unitarian dominion of the Kingdom of Yugoslavia, while simultaneously demonstrating that it would not accept a marginal role in the bloc and economic division of the new world. This does not mean that we can speak of a clean cut with the capitalist social relations at the time, but rather that the profit margins, economic efficiency, and the global market were not the only ones that played a role in the establishment of the socialist economy. Djilas's approach to the 'new class' provided 'fertile' grounds for the subsequent revisionisms and anti-totalitarian ideologemes, while the second approach erased or suppressed the analytical difference between socialism and capitalism. Through this we lose the consideration of the rupture of the social(-ist) revolution as well as the insight into the specifics of the socialist social formation and its transition. Regardless of the problematic points, the second approach contributed important discoveries and brought critical attention to the fact that socialism – at least when its cycle approaches state capitalism – is subject to class struggle and does not necessarily progress towards communism.[12] *The third* – and current – *approach* regards socialism as a transitory formation that is no longer capitalist but strives for communist goals. This specific temporality and modality, which criticises the Stalinist thesis on 'the socialist mode of production', was methodologically summarised by Louis Althusser in his book on reproduction, as: socialism = capitalism + communism. Furthermore, according to Balibar (1991), the socialist formation is characterised by 'an unstable combination of state capitalism and proletarian tendencies within communism'. We could reproach Althusser for not producing a concrete historical study of real socialisms; with the exception of short digressions, Althusser and Balibar both remained on the level of philosophy. This does not mean that their guidelines could not contribute to the articulation of the third approach, although, paradoxically, it is thereby at risk of being labelled as 'historicism' by the Althusserian position.[13] This is why I have no reservations about infusing some Althusserianism into the excellent study of Catherine Samary and especially Michael Lebowitz, who has contributed several lucid theses in his books on socialism. The guiding thread of our analysis expands Lebowitz's concept of 'contested reproduction':

> Until socialism has developed upon its own foundations, the elements it inherits from the old society infect it, and the situation here too is one of 'contested reproduction', a struggle between two opposed economic systems. In short, to ensure the reproduction of socialist relations of production under these conditions, a specific mode of regulation that subordinates the elements of the old society is essential. (Lebowitz 2012: 33).

Concretely, I will highlight the main characteristics of the early workers' self-management from the 1950s, while the central focus of this study will be on the development of 'market socialism' between 1965 and 1973, which represented a sharp cut with the socialist self-management. The 'market' period exhibits a twofold trend: firstly, the communist elements – introduction of new types of social relations and various forms of ownership, the socialisation of the means of production and life, the abolition of private property, the prevalence of labour over capital or workers' participation in the production process, the development of a highly-functional public infrastructure, fair distribution by the state – were gradually exhausted;[14] while secondly, the capitalist elements became stronger, that is, the introduction of market elements, the development of underdevelopment, the integration into the global capital and labour markets, financialisation, and the blockade of workers.

This analysis focuses on the period between 1965–73, with the aim of locating the emergence and dynamics of the class antagonisms' condensation, the consequences of which transcend the established timeframe significantly. This period is crucial for understanding the subsequent dissolution of Yugoslavia and points to the defeat of the communist politics and the exhaustion of the partisan ruptures. Marko Kržan (2013) established that the Yugoslav socialism can be roughly divided into the following periods: 1945–64 and 1965–89. During the first period, the socialist formation was relatively successful at independently solving all of the main problems; however, during the second period, failures occurred and the solidarity model of development was abandoned.[15] The two main periods of the socialist economy should be divided further, and non-chronological categories should be introduced: in the first economically successful and politically innovative period, the principles of administrative plans (1946–52) and workers' self-management were developed (1952–65); in the second, economically and politically 'less successful' period, market socialism (1965–73) and contractual socialism (1974–89) were practiced.[16] The very last period, or at least the period following Tito's death, was characterised by a harsh austerity policy and the slow approximation towards the neoliberal model that represented the final nails in the coffin of Yugoslavia. The main thesis remains that in order to understand the dissolution of Yugoslavia we have to take into account the key contradictions of self-management that appeared already in the 1960s, during the 'market socialism' phase: the economic gap between the rich (*north*) and the poor (*south*) parts of the state; structural unemployment; increasing debts to the International Monetary Fund (IMF) and the World Bank, (financialisation); and technocratic domination over workers' control in companies (the exploitation issue). For the first time since World War II, the entire developmental model of Yugoslav self-management was threatened by the articulation of socio-economic contradictions. The market reform of 1965, which was supposed to overcome the crisis, resulted in even worse consequences. My hypothesis – along with the analysis of the contradictory processes – will allow for an insight into the formation of what Antonio Gramsci called a 'historical bloc' that defeated the leftist political powers at the end of the 1980s and dissolved the socialist system. The understanding of the dissolution of Yugoslavia calls for a long-term analysis of contradictory tendencies and ideological changes that started at least two decades prior to Yugoslavia's physical disintegration. In order to demonstrate the contrast, a concise presentation of the first period will follow.

8

The Main Characteristics of Early Yugoslav Socialism

The initial post-war period was dedicated to the restoration of the devastated state and the establishment of a planned economy with the assistance of the Soviet Union. This period was marked by profound social enthusiasm: the voluntary youth work brigades contributed to the reconstruction of the major infrastructural projects (e.g. the construction of roads, including the Brotherhood and Unity motorway, and railways). From the macro-state perspective, the Yugoslav economist Branko Horvat defined this period as classic socialist planning or administrative socialism, which began in 1946 with the process of nationalising land, property, and private capital and continued in the key industrial sectors such as coal mining, transport, and commerce (Horvat 1976: 6–9). The nationalisation of food and the food processing industry followed in 1948, while the process of agricultural collectivisation was introduced with a directive from the Central Committee of the Communist Party of Yugoslavia in January 1949. Finally, in 1958, large-scale housing complexes were included in the planning policy.

During the first period, significant problems kept occurring in regard to collectivisation, despite the relatively favourable economic results. The communist leadership attempted to ensure 'primary accumulation' by collectivising farm holdings in accordance with the Soviet model.[1] This policy was based on progressive taxation and rigid planning of what to sow and how much to repurchase, which resulted in severe resistance as early as 1950 – the most infamous example of which was the Cazin Rebellion, an uprising during which 55 'kulaks' were arrested and executed. Some farmers insisted on managing their own land autonomously and wanted to keep pursuing the retail trade, thus retaining some form of private initiative (Bilandžić, 1980: 119–21). The resistance to collectivisation nearly caused the regression of agrarian production back to natural production, which would only satisfy the personal needs and would not leave the horizon of the local market. In light of this opposition, the communist leadership discontinued forced collectivisation in 1953 (ibid., 124). It somewhat restored limited private property and retail trade within parts of agriculture, while simultaneously planning for accelerated industrialisation, which would later encourage a significant percentage of the rural population to move from the villages to the cities. Apart from the significant defiance of the rural population, who had been a key material force in the social revolution and anti-fascist resistance, that period was also characterised by the 1948 Cominform dispute, which resulted in the isolation and stagnation of the Yugoslav economy. During that period, Yugoslavia therefore relied mainly on its own devices and on the development of its military and industrial capabilities. However, at this point, it is impossible to talk about any kind of integration into the global markets, even though aid from the United States did arrive to Yugoslavia after 1950.[2]

According to Kržan (2014), a rather organic connection between the nascent bureaucracy and the working masses was characteristic of this period. Namely, only social capital existed in the economy, and this was managed by the leading Party structures. Also, these structures had been well-disposed towards the working class until the early 1960s. The post 1951 period was a period of workers' self-management socialism, which replaced administrative socialism with a combination of planning and the gradual introduction of new self-management institutions and procedures, which were supposed to predominantly operate 'from below' and unburden the political apparatus.

The Workers' Self-Management Period between 1952 and 1964[3]

It would be wrong to claim that the planned economy was completely abolished with the introduction of self-management. A reform of the economic regime took place in the 1950s. It combined various elements of a market and planned economy, but it was still decisively marked by the macro-economic policy. The latter could exert its influence through the central institutions and administrative directives and thus balance the economic and credit flows. Simultaneously, the new regime transferred some of its political capacities to lower, decentralised bodies, which focused on the micro-level of social regulation. The workers' self-management began in socialist enterprises and their workers' collectives (Samary 1988: 115). In other words, the self-management policy acquired a material basis in companies and work collectives, in which the principles of workers' self-management were gradually being introduced. If self-management was in fact implemented and how it actually unfolded depended from one enterprise to another. In some workers' collectives it was taken seriously, and the workers participated in the decision-making. Conversely, in other collectives, workers were happy to delegate their formal rights onto the technocrats/directors. Formally, the self-management model and workers' rights kept expanding throughout the following decade. Work collectives would initially manage only a third of the generated value, however, in the following decade 'the collective workers' control over the generated value started increasing'.[4] Apart from the expanding workers' control, Yugoslavia saw rapid economic growth between 1951 and 1964, amounting to 12 per cent per annum on average, compared to the 5-per cent growth in Western Europe and 9-per cent growth in Eastern Europe (Horvat 1976: 4).[5]

Several reasons can be given for these positive indicators: firstly, the post-war economy started from virtually nothing, with a displaced population and a wrecked infrastructure. As a result of a realistic plan and great enthusiasm on the part of the people, the economic growth was swift. Secondly, in light of its dispute with the Soviet Union, Yugoslavia received aid from the United States of America during the 1950s.[6] This did not result in a change in the autonomy of the Yugoslav economy, as the United States provided this aid without making any demands with regard to economic recovery or political decisions. Thirdly, the Yugoslav economy kept acquiring new markets through its Non-Aligned Movement policy. Without romanticising it, we should nevertheless acknowledge that the socialist industrialisation policy yielded extraordinary results, which were evident from the great improvement in the material life and living standards of the masses. These improvements ranged from the completion of large-scale residential buildings and infrastructural projects, which represented the foundations for the progressive urbanisation[7] in accordance with the needs of the nascent working class to the general and relatively high-quality education, which radically improved the levels of literacy in comparison with the old Kingdom of Yugoslavia and allowed for the establishment of a solid system of universities. Consequently, industrialisation resulted in the creation of the working class as well as affecting its re-composition and the general transformation of the social relations and segments of the population. Darko Suvin established that industrialisation had completely changed the landscape and scope of the working class: 'In 1945, farmers (together with almost half a million artisans) accounted for 70 per cent of the Yugoslav population of approximately 10.5 million people' (Suvin 2016). By the 1970s, the rural population represented only around 40 per cent of the total population that kept growing despite the migration. This means that the relative share of the rural population compared to other professions in Yugoslavia was almost halved in a short period of 25 years (in some places, the industrialisation lasted for over a century), while the levels of employment and activity were now much higher in comparison with the years leading up to World War II.[8] This social transformation and increased political stability in the international context implies that Yugoslavia rose from its peripheral position to a semi-peripheral status of the soundest socialist state, capable of skilfully navigating between the East and the West. During the 1950s, its relatively autonomous economic policy was also successful due to the high level of state protectionism, which ensured the development of Yugoslavia's own industrial capabilities. The following table shows the significant improvement in the social and economic indicators during the first decades.

Table 8.1   Socio-economic indicators, 1950–70[9]

	1950	1960	1970
GDP per capita (according to 1966 $US prices)	216	333	520
Mortality of new-borns (per 1000)	119	88	55
Illiteracy (share of population over the age of 10 years, in %)	25	20	15
Number of people per doctor	3360	1474	1010
Radio receivers per 1000 people	21	78	166
Cars per 1000 people	0.4	2.9	35
Urban population (in %)	21	28	39

Susan Woodward established that an innovative model of 'hybrid economy' was developed during the first self-management period, in which the strategic plans were dictated by the production and investment goals. These, in turn, defined loans, prices, and foreign trade policies, while growth was anticipated through the flow of information between companies, municipalities, and the republic. According to Susan Woodward, a hybrid economy

Combines market and socialist elements emphasizing increasing autonomy for firms and territorial decentralization. In place of planned quotas, economic regulation is conducted through the financial instruments of monetary, credit and fiscal policy (according to the closed accounting system of monetary planning), and producers are expected to respond to consumer demands (both domestic and foreign). (Woodward 1995b: 28).

During the increasing economic boom, the absence of strict administrative directives and the adoption of the logic of an ad hoc control of the quantities and proportions of production were the main policies that prevented an economy of shortages from emerging (ibid., 169–71). The 'proportions planning' was ideologically defined by Boris Kidrič, who played an important role in the development of the socialist economy, which was based on a certain level of planning (loans, export rates, large-scale projects), while a part of the entrepreneurial activities was based on market 'regulation' – meaning that companies themselves could decide what to produce and how. This is another reason why the chronic shortage of goods and materials, characteristic of Eastern Europe, did not occur in Yugoslavia during the 1950s.[10] However, even if there were no significant shortages of raw products and materials for production, as the allocation had been taken over by the companies, Korica-Unkovski shrewdly underlined the fact that, at the beginning of the 1950s, there was a shortage of sufficient and qualified labour force in certain industries (Unkovski-Korica, 2014: 108–34). These profound changes also involved discipline and the 'Taylorisation' of the working masses, resulting in a permanent regulation of the new labour force flows and, gradually, also in keeping the old labour force in 'unwanted' work positions and thus preventing mobility. In light of these mechanisms, Korica-Unkovski claimed that the communist leadership had created workers' councils with the intention of disciplining the working masses, fragmenting the workers, and undermining the trade unions.[11] This almost sounds like a conspiracy theory, and even though the People's Front organisations and trade unions became subordinated to the Party in the beginning of the 1950s, Korica-Unkovski's conclusion that this represented a complete breakdown of the communist politics seems hasty. Trade unions did indeed lose their autonomy to a certain degree, as it was easier for the Party to supervise the discussions and implement its guidelines through the new socialist organisations (e.g. the Socialist Alliance of Working People). While keeping in mind the realistic external threats (the Cominform dispute), Korica-Unkovski's thesis should also be relativised with regard to three other points. Firstly, even if it was true that – due to the broader social transformation – political supervision and discipline were evident under the new circumstances, labour collectives nevertheless started to independently control at least a part of the value that they created. In some cases, they practiced genuine self-management.[12] This was not the case before, not even on the formal level. Secondly, at the beginning of the 1950s, the political antagonism between the workers and the Party did not exist yet in any readily apparent form. However, certain power struggles did exist both within the Party and between the Party and the republican apparatuses (e.g. the prison on Goli Otok).[13] Thirdly, the actual formation of the financial sector with a freer flow of foreign and domestic capital would not begin until the mid-1960s. At this point in time, we cannot talk about any type of integration into the global market. Furthermore, the relations with the global market were not always unambiguous: there is a vast difference between a state receiving non-refundable aid (coming from the US) and a state resorting to unfavourable loans that expose it to long-term economic dependence. At the beginning of the 1950s, the communist leadership took a few steps back, ideologically speaking, which could, to a certain degree, be compared to Lenin's New Economic Policy (NEP). However, in this regard it has to be pointed out that these policies allowed for a wider spread of support for the people (the abandonment of collectivisation and the introduction of the workers' councils) as well as for political survival in a hostile environment (US aid, as well as the search for new allies and the co-creation of the Non-Aligned Movement).

In the 1950s, the reforms of the socialist economy resulted in a diverse political apparatus, consisting of federal, republican, and municipal levels. For the sake of clarity, I will hereby mention the general framework and the basic institutions of the self-management system which developed increasingly complex relations through the decades and with the introduction of new reforms:[14] the level of companies, self-management communities/municipalities, republics, and the federation.

Enterprises: The Management of State-Owned Companies and the Workers' Collectives Act (1950)

Self-management was implemented as an act in the beginning of the 1950s by the socialist leadership 'from the top'. However, we should not forget that it had initially been tested on the micro-level, in certain economic units. Goran Mušić has recently written about the initial discussions on workers' self-management, and he referred to archival documents detailing the discussions between Kardelj and Đilas in the spring of 1950 (Mušić 2015). According to Mušić, the new act ensured complete autonomy of the workers in the individual companies, which allowed for

> Discussions as well as decisions about all important matters regarding the factories ... The workers' council, which would meet once a month, elected its administrative committee and professional administration, which was tasked with all ongoing matters and headed by the director of the company. In order to prevent the estrangement between the management and the workers' collective, three quarters of the administrative committee consisted of manual workers. The members were elected annually and could remain in their positions for a maximum of two years. The director was appointed by the Party for a four-year term, however, the decision had to be confirmed by the workers' council. (Ibid.).

The history of the workers' council practices is one of the most important achievements of self-management. For the first time in history, the workers became political subjects in their own companies. They had workers' councils, where they could reach the most important decisions concerning the companies' budgets, employment levels, investments in repeated accumulation, and/or salaries. Naturally, the workers' policies had to be ensured by a good flow of precise information and sufficient time for the workers to tackle the planning.

As a result of historical development, the workers' self-management had to face two main paradoxes: *first of all*, the process resulted in the fragmentation of the working class and thus in the reduction of solidarity between the workers from different republics and various industries. Mušić claims that the establishment of the 'producers' council' in 1953 was an attempt to systemically strengthen the political activities of all workers' councils. However, in reality, a legislative system came into force that was based on geographical representation (Mušić 2013). It brought together the workers within the republics and, of course, within companies. The autonomy of the workers' councils could follow the particular logic of the company interests, which leaned towards the logic of improving the planned work quotas. In turn, this could also strengthen the competition between the companies. *The second paradox* is related to the issues of accumulating resources and the companies' salary policies. To put it more simply, this question implies two contradictory approaches: should the workers' collectives focus on the principle of the workers' control, for example on the fight to reduce the working hours and improve the salaries; or should the workers' councils implement those economic standards that could maximise efficiency and market shares and consequently result in better investments and higher income? In the changed circumstances, this issue became one of the key areas of socialist reproduction.

Community Aspect: Social Self-Management (1963)

The following played an important role in the expansion of self-management: the lower-level political communities that practiced delegative democracy; the bodies of local self-management communities, districts, and municipalities; as well as many institutions whose numbers only kept increasing with time. This field of activity assumed a number of socio-political functions, and as early as the 1950s it started practicing the principle of subsidiarity: i.e., transferring the political decision-making processes to the low(est) levels. The level of political communities would presumably contribute significantly to the planning of employment policies and agreements with companies. Furthermore, they also started organising social activities that are nowadays called public services. Social self-management was introduced in the 1963 Constitution. In 1965, Edvard Kardelj stated that the main goal of self-management was for it to be established 'throughout the entire field of social reproduction, production, and exchange of products. In view of the movement of social capital [...] it should be viewed as a still unfinished process' (Kardelj 1976: 21–2). From the level of companies, the self-management model spread to the local self-management bodies. According to Rastko Močnik, this type of 'social self-management can be seen as a compromise that has kept public services away from capitalist accumulation and state administration, while the social integration mechanism is, in this sense, expressed in the monetary form and double representation'.[15]

The latter was one of the major innovations intended to ensure the approximation to the idea of direct workers' democracy. For example, it worked quite successfully within the health sector, where the decisions as regards the services were debated by the users, health workers, and political functionaries. It also worked well in the field of cultural activities, where both, cultural producers-creators as well as cultural consumers-users, had to be represented in any cultural community institution. A variety of cultural institutions (cultural centres, cultural associations, as well as representatives of municipal authorities) would send their delegates to cultural communities.[16] In the broader field of public services, this system of representation also operated vertically: the representatives of public services would be sent, as delegates, to the councils and assemblies of the territorial units (republics or autonomous provinces); on the other hand, the territorial units would have their own representatives in the administrative committees and public service commissions. Politically, this model was very well implemented at the level of public services, and judging from Rastko Močnik's evaluation it represented a serious alternative to the paternalism of the welfare state and the privatisation of public services.[17]

In terms of finances, the public services system depended on the total domestic product and income. All employees had to dedicate a part of their income directly to the socio-cultural activities. The taxes were collected by the individual republics, while certain socio-cultural activities would even develop partial market elements.[18] Self-imposed contributions were introduced into the income and resources distribution system. These were neither a part of a private initiative that would benefit certain social groups, nor a part of a charity activity that would collect symbolic capital and operate vertically. Quite the opposite: the form of the self-imposed contributions would be specified at the people's referendums held in individual municipalities, where decisions were made as regards the public infrastructure at the initiative of either the local citizens or delegates.[19] Social infrastructure was owned by everybody, and self-imposed contributions represented a supplementary source of finance and an integral part of the new social solidarity ties – a form of self-management financing. The problems arose because this model was (once again) determined on a territorial basis – which meant that the public infrastructure was best developed and maintained in the richer regions.[20] Over time, self-management spread from the sphere of enterprises to the local municipal levels and other social sectors (education, health services, culture). It thus attained what Kardelj would call 'social self-management', or in more fashionable terms, the social reproduction of self-management.

Table 8.2 below speaks of mature socialism after 1977, but it gives a good representation of the details involved in the decision-making process in the assembly of a mature organisational form of 'self-management

Table 8.2　Multiple self-managed levels – established system in the 1970s

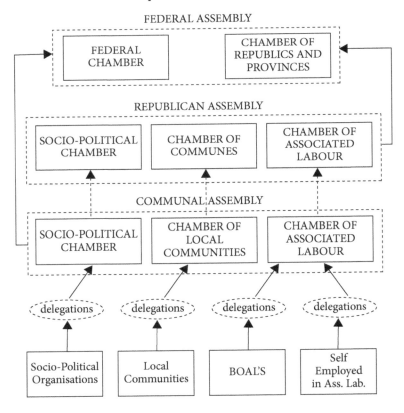

Membership of Assemblies at Commune,
Republic and Federal Level

Source: (Potts 1996: 238).

communities of interests, divided into two new institutions, i.e. into the assembly of producers and the assembly of consumers. Through the system of representation and the various institutions, the self-management process embodied all segments of society. In this manner, all individuals and social units – the producers and consumers of all activities – would presumably have their place in the diverse network of organisations. For the first time in history, their work – productive as well as reproductive – was systemically recognised and regulated. Some institutions, for example trade unions, would operate simultaneously on several levels. Following the introduction of the workers' councils, these, for a while, played a minor role and were then either subjected to the socialist political (municipal and republican) apparatus or merged with it. Their tasks focused on the harmonisation and deliberation of collective negotiations between the republic, the municipalities, and companies (industrial sectors).

The Republics in the Process of Empowerment

As a federal political entity, Yugoslavia consisted of six republics and two autonomous provinces. Every republic had a central political apparatus with a wide range of councils, assemblies, and ministries. The principles and forms of delegate, corporate, and democratic institutions were combined at the level of the republics. Representatives were elected into the assemblies. Most delegates were from the ranks of the League of Communists,[21] while the rest came directly from their own organisations. Formally, the representation of as many self-management interests as possible was ensured.

The ever-increasing power of the republics led to the stage where republics gradually became de facto states within federal Yugoslavia.[22] Following the introduction of the market reform in 1965 and the passing of the 1974 Constitution, Yugoslavia also formally – de jure – moved closer to becoming a confederate political system. Namely, the republics would organise all key social, economic, and political matters as well as steer the processes in 'factories, manufactures, agriculture, traffic and communications, pass labour legislation, as well as reach autonomous decisions regarding education and science' (Woodward 1995b: 39). At the same time, they would also collect taxes and redistribute the national income among the lower levels. Furthermore, the republican institutions would elect their representatives on the federal level, which meant that no central federal bureaucracy such as the current Eurocracy in Brussels existed – with the exception of a narrow circle of people around Tito. However, these individuals represented the political leadership rather than the federal bureaucracy. The principle of decentralisation adhered to a clear division of tasks between the republics (domestic issues) and the federation (external relations and military protection), in which the true power was increasingly becoming divided between the republics and less and less focused in the federal government.[23]

The Federal Government and Gradual Decentralisation

The highest authority in Yugoslavia, at least in the immediate post-war period, resided with the federal government and its Presidency. During the first couple of decades (1945–64), this body was responsible for the most important political and economic decisions. We could even talk about a double government system, in which one side was represented by the state political apparatus, while the Party and its political organisations represented the other side. However, these two aspects became closely intertwined, as the majority of the staff came from the Central Committee of the League of Communists, the leaderships of the republics, and from the national liberation organisations. On the other hand, the federal bureaucracy consisted of republican leaderships and other communist cadres, who had proven themselves in the various socialist youth leagues, women's organisations, trade unions, and workers' council assemblies of the Yugoslav nations.[24] The federal government was responsible for the planning and the common market. It was in charge of the financial and trade policies as well as the common defence and foreign affairs. The Yugoslav People's Army, by some referred to as the 'seventh republic', played an important role in the organisation of military tasks. In this respect, Woodward correctly observed that the Yugoslav People's Army directly and indirectly employed a significant share of the population, as the basic industries depended on the military-industrial complex and its own export plans (Woodward 1995b). The Yugoslav People's Army retained its cult status from World War II, while the state's ideological apparatus maintained the ideology of permanent readiness due to the possibility of foreign invasions (from the West as well as from the East).

During the initial implementation period of (self-management) socialism, the key task of the federal authorities was to ensure the underlying infrastructure throughout the state and to invest in strategically important projects. For example, the federal apparatus had fewer Ministries than the republics (only those in charge of common affairs). However, a wide range of federal agencies were in place and they looked after a variety of activities. One of the most influential federal institutions was the National Bank of Yugoslavia, which managed the economic activities and cash flows, set out the interest rates, and negotiated international loans in cooperation with the federal government (Horvat 1976: 311–13). Yugoslavia had a number of funds: the interventionist *Agricultural and Industrial Raw Materials Fund* that controlled the flow and supply of commodities and managed the reserves; the *Exports Fund* that set the export quotas; the *Arbitration Institution*; the *Prices and Income Council*;[25] and, last but not least, the *Investment Fund*, an important institution that ensured all republics and autonomous provinces could benefit from equal development opportunities. Alongside these funds, a number of other institutions were responsible for the business operations with the developing countries that Yugoslavia sent aid to from 1953 onwards (Bockman 2011: 241).

The 1965 Market Reform:
From Decentralised Planning
to the Logic of Capital

In short, two systems and two logics do not simply exist side-by-side. They *interact*. They interpenetrate. And they deform each other. Rather than the combination permitting the best of both worlds, the effect can be the worst of the two worlds. Precisely because there is contested reproduction between differing sets of productive relations, the interaction of the systems can generate crises, inefficiencies, and irrationality that wouldn't be found in either system in its purity. (Lebowitz 2012: 91–2).

A pure system does not exist in any social formation, and Yugoslavia was no exception. There was no unified ideal self-management model, but rather a set of contradictory orientations and policies that would, in periods of crises, crystallise into the domination of either the pro-communist or pro-capitalist tendency. After the intervention act in 1961,[1] the encounter between these two systems tilted in favour of the capitalist tendency and some authors called this 'market socialism'. In this chapter, I shall analyse the biased development of capital within Yugoslav socialism following the market reform in 1965. This tendency is associated with Yugoslavia opening itself to the global market and foreign borrowing, as well as with a specific solution for the unemployed – workers were allowed to migrate to other European countries in search of temporary work as the so-called 'Gastarbeiters'. However, Woodward is right to argue that within socialist Yugoslavia the labour market power remained underdeveloped (see Woodward, 169–73), which is why the concept of 'market socialism' cannot be used to analyse the Yugoslav model in its entirety. That said, we need to point out that the new system of regulation was enhanced by the 'logic of capital' and decentralisation, which was far from the model of equal and fair development in Yugoslavia. I will argue that this process started to decompose what Lebowitz called the 'logic of the vanguard relations of production'. As early as 1953, self-management began to renounce the monopoly of economic and political power, concentrated in the hands of the Party bureaucracy. The latter did not rely merely on the memory of the People's Liberation Struggle: during the 1950s, it was modernised, it conducted a number of infrastructural projects, and implemented a successful educational policy. The League of Communists built its legitimacy on this project of socialist modernisation, which resulted in low unemployment and considerable economic growth, and kept the League from entering any antagonistic relations with the working class. Throughout the 1950s, the political bureaucracy still possessed substantial 'social capital', which was effectively managed and kept at its disposal. Formally, the situation changed during the 1960s, when the political bureaucracy started surrendering the economic mechanisms of power to the 'market' and new political agents.

The market reform, as interpreted by trade unionist leaders, was expected to expand the power of the workers' councils, which would take over the decision-making and management of the social capital within their enterprises. The logic of the vanguard Party split into the political monopoly, which was in the hands of the state bureaucracy (the League of Communists and other political organisations), and the field of economy, formally controlled by the workers, but in reality controlled by the prevailing influence of the market forces. Following two decades of successful economic development and the establishment of an infrastructure with a relatively stable reproduction, the first serious crisis arose in the 1960s. For the first time after the Cominform dispute (1948) industrial undertakings lacked sufficient supplies and raw-materials to be able to exploit the production capacities (Bilandžić 1980: 237–39). This provided additional support to the arguments for further decentralisation. An increasing number of groups within the League of Communists of Yugoslavia argued for a greater market reform and swifter liberalisation of the economic policy, which would enable complete development of the productive forces. Due to the higher level of social progress and productive forces, the Yugoslav leadership faced a choice: either maintain the economy based on the old administratively planned and 'non-rational system', or focus on a more rational and 'free economy' (ibid., 239).

The 1965 market reform was thus neither a completely new experiment carried out by the leadership, nor a result of external forces (USA, the IMF).[2] It followed the radicalisation of the spontaneous and antinomic logic of the self-management model and was one of the unpredictable consequences of the market relations development. One could think of it as a sort of a Yugoslav New Economic Policy that wished to strengthen the local and republican self-management against the centralist state powers. Catherine Samary believes that Tito and the innermost leadership firmly supported the reform that radicalised the intervention act of 1961.[3] The new reform should therefore be perceived through a dialectical understanding of the development of self-management reproduction, which followed the global trends (financial markets, freer movement of capital) and an internal de-centralisation logic, which abandoned central planning. The following questions arose: firstly, what exactly did the new reform entail, what were its concrete consequences, and who were the new social actors who started to influence the general development of new socialism; and secondly, what and how would be produced in the future, now that the working class was formally gaining new self-management rights? The hypothesis presented in this chapter is that this period resulted in long-term negative consequences for the socialist project and Yugoslavia as a whole. The reform in question started to undermine the communist horizon and could be defined, in short, as an introduction to post-socialism and the decline of the solidarity model, which had characterised the first period between 1945 and 1965.

The most important goal of the market reform was the demand for a greater autonomy of the market as well as of the lower levels of political institutions; and the demand for greater economic freedom of production units (in this respect, the goal of democratising the workers' self-management was underlined in particular). In a more concrete sense, the reform enabled the Yugoslav economy to become more open towards the West. Let us emphasise merely the initial reform measures: the devaluation of the Dinar; reduced customs protection (fewer export subsidies); reduction of budgetary non-economic expenditure (membership fees, premiums, insurances) and tax burdens imposed upon the economy; restriction of investment spending; administrative price increases; and radical reduction of reimbursements and grants (Bilandžić 1980: 303). In the period between 1964 and 1966, these measures introduced the principle of economic efficiency and market criteria, which would eventually spread from the capital market to the labour market, and consequently even to certain non-economic activities. During this period the employment policy was handed over to the companies, so they were able to adjust the employment rates. If the economic situation was unfavourable, the companies – following the market logic – simply refrained from employing new workers.[4] The economic situation was certainly not favourable: according to Bilandžić, the economic growth amounted to a mere 2.9 per cent in the 1964–1967 period, which represented stagnation in comparison with the economic growth of 12 per cent in the preceding period.

With the introduction of the liberal economic policy, the reform attempted to deregulate the prices and reduce the trade deficit,[5] thus intervening in the previous balance between the market and the plan. The new equilibrium abandoned the macro-economic coherence and a series of redistribution mechanisms that had maintained a more equitable development of all the republics (Samary 1988: 123). Catherine Samary underlined that 'the solution to the economic problems was sought in further decentralisation, perfection of the self-management autonomy, development of a more competitive market, and integration into the global economy' (ibid., 21). The expansion of the economic subjects' self-management rights resulted in a process that contributed to the decline of the egalitarian policy. *This decline – rather than the decline of the federal and central apparatuses – was the sign that the Yugoslav communist politics was becoming exhausted.*

The advocates of the reform attacked state protectionism and the last remains of state socialism, i.e. the so-called monopoly of politics over economy. The core of the reform could be found in the following slogans: *depoliticisation, decentralisation, destatisation,* and *democratisation* (Brborić-Likić 2002). At first glance, these signifiers – the old–new political slogans – merely continued the outlined self-management development. The democratisation, destatisation, and decentralisation kept pursuing the policies of weakening the state, and called for an autonomy on the lower levels ('subsidiarity'). In practice, this was indicated by the transfer of an increasing share of the national labour income to the level of the republics and companies, which were now able to use the income more freely. The last signifier is even more interesting: *depoliticisation.* The crucial breakthrough in the dominant discourse was perhaps achieved precisely with the appeal of depoliticisation. Although it may seem the most innocent of the four appeals, it represented an articulated reaction to the previous politicisation and constant mobilisation of all social aspects of life. In fact, it merely confirmed the existing situation, as after two decades of constant mobilisation, the process of neutralising the participation with depoliticising effects was taking place.[6] The reform managed to diagnose this traumatic point and take advantage of it. Formally, the workers gained more rights, while the workers' councils could decide how much of their income should be reinvested into the accumulation and how much should be spent on salaries. However, in practice, they were gradually handing over the power to the experts within the companies.

The reformists supported liberalism and drew their ideological power from a profoundly ideological position of the seemingly unburdened expert knowledge. With regard to this question, Branko Horvat, one of the most important economists, promoted workers' self-management and argued for the implementation of the efficiency principle. The decisions in the workers' councils, he argued, should have been subject to personal responsibility, which meant that mistakes should have been subject to sanctions (Horvat 1975: 323), while the implementation of business decisions should have remained a matter of expertise rather than democracy. Expertise was thus separated from ideology and democracy (ibid.)! The argument in favour of expertise replacing workers' control can be attributed to the increased involvement and power of the scientific institutions' ideological apparatus and to the formation of technical staff that started to express its material economic interests. In other words, a social group that had already been managing certain capital in the actual production process became politically articulated and reached the final decisions as to what should be produced and how. This faction, seen as a technocracy by some and as management by others, established itself in the sphere of production, represented by the higher echelons in the industry, service sector, banks, as well as in the new ideological state apparatuses, especially science. This new environment gave birth to the so-called *liberal line* within the Leagues of Communists, which was the key propagator of the reform, decentralisation, and interests of the wealthier regions in particular, and which promoted the pro-western and export-led orientation of the Yugoslav economy. The promotion of the export and capital-intensive development model, called the 'Slovenian model' by Susan Woodward, became the most important economic interest of the liberal line (Woodward 1955a).

From a more political perspective, an important political event occurred in 1966, as the centralising line (Ranković's group) and the decentralising line (Kardelj, and later also Tito) clashed within the League of Communists of Yugoslavia (the LCY) and the innermost leadership. On the centralist side Aleksandar Ranković, the organisational secretary and head of the secret police, argued for strong 'federal institutions (especially the Party, military, and security forces), independent from the leaders of the republics' (Jović 2009: 64). On the other side, the supporters of decentralisation, who opposed this view, were gaining in strength. According to Kardelj, 'fully constituted nations' had already been established in Yugoslavia by that time, which meant that the political structure had to be changed (ibid., 62). Kardelj's group thus suggested that the common interests policy should be implemented in three areas only: 'firstly, Yugoslavia should have a common defence policy; secondly, it should have a common goal – the revolutionary transformation of the state; and thirdly, it should develop a common market area' (ibid.). This was supposedly achievable by moving away from the remains of the centralised state and towards the *federation of sovereign national states*. (ibid. 62–3). In 1966, Kardelj's vision prevailed, as Ranković and his group were removed during the 4th plenum of the Central Committee of the Communist Party of Yugoslavia and a further reorganisation of the League of Communists (the LC) and the state was proclaimed – with a significant transfer of powers from the federation to the republican and municipal bodies (Bilandžić 1980: 320–23). The international aspect of the communist struggle and federal institutions grew weaker due to the new orientation. Let us, for example, take a look at the elections in the LC: as of 1968, instead of appointing delegates at high-level forums, the elections took place within the basic organisations of the LC, which then 'elected the municipal leaderships, while the municipal conferences would elect delegates for the republican congresses and the LCY congress' (ibid., 320).

What had initially started as a call for depoliticisation, requesting that the ideology was abandoned, and management handed over to the experts, actually resulted in an extremely politicised process and a new division of political power within a new ruling class. Instead of the confirmation of the previous 'social contract' between the Party and the workers, a new ruling class coalition was established. Let me quote an indicative, symptomatic section of an official document, directly attesting to the importance of the ideological change:

The League of Communists builds on the fact that the socialist commodity production in the contemporary circumstances is the only possible form of rational social reproduction and an objective assumption of the development of self-management and direct socialist democracy. Therefore, the reform should focus on the improved implementation of the more developed and freer forms of socialist commodity production, while resisting any kind of subjectivism and statist disregard for the functioning of its economic laws. (ZKJ/9.Kongres, 1969.)

These words would not have been surprising if they were written in an economic report for foreign creditors. This passage, however, was a part of the Resolution of the LCY's 9th Congress in 1969! Along with the new constitutions (1963, 1974), the congress resolutions were the key documents that laid out the long-term goals and orientations of the self-management society over the next five or more years. In practice, the democratic centralist principle implied that the members of the LCY and other state organisations might not agree with the adopted resolutions, but had to comply with them nonetheless and adhere to the general orientation. The general orientation would be revised with the next major reform, constitution, congress, or major law. Democratic centralism assumed that the members of the LC should contribute to the implementation of that orientation in various ways. At the end of the 1960s, the LCY accepted the global market, which meant that Yugoslavia opened itself to foreign borrowing and to, as the socialist ideologues referred to it, 'socialist commodity' production. These became two of the decisive forces and key criteria for the ever-larger asymmetries between the republics and export-oriented companies, which exerted pressure on the prices of goods and wages. Susan Woodward, however, correctly presented a fairly balanced and dialectical view as to which instances in the general production became market-governed, and which remained under state control:

The leaders' concept of socialist commodity production was not a market economy, although final goods ('commodities') markets operated largely by a free price mechanism and consumer demand was meant to be the primary incentive to producers. Increasing price liberalization also occurred in the foreign sector – particularly after 1961, when … duties were progressively liberalized, and, after 1972, the exchange rate became an active instrument of policy. But the market did not apply to factors of production – labour, capital and intermediate goods, raw materials, credit in the form of working and venture capital – although monetary prices were assigned to facilitate allocation and comparative valuation and a rent was charged on fixed capital and borrowed funds. (Woodward 1995b: 169).

One important socialist political economist, Milan Korać, and a chief self-management ideologue, Edvard Kardelj, supported the viewpoint that 'elevates the commodity form or value form of products into a sort of a transhistorical postulate for all production modes or, more precisely, all product exchange modes' (Bavčar et al. 1985: 14). According to Kardelj, 'the commodity production and market are forms of free exchange of labour between self-managers' (ibid.). Darko Suvin lucidly remarked that the leading communists underestimated the step into the Western markets and blindly assumed that they are still governed by nineteenth-century market ideology (Suvin 2014). One of the rare Marxist critics of the social-ist political economy, Luka Marković, claimed that these actions actually consisted of introducing a 'laissez-faire model of socialist development ... the discussion shifted from the social to economic development ... while all the questions were dealt with from the position of *economic rationality* rather than the *proletarian revolution*' (Marković 1978: 118).

A closer look at the official documents allows us to conclude that the dominant self-management ideology was openly invaded by the liberal discourse, which was quickly supported by almost all groups as well as by the leadership of the LCY. The official documents and the market reform attest to the formal recognition of the liberal forces and to the shift in the balance of power in the socialist apparatus. The proponents of the logic of capital became the main material force, shaped politically during this process. This was one of the first signs of the phenomenon, called 'post-communism' by Buden, which started to compete with the industrial model of socialist development as well as with the position of the Party itself and the idea of communism in general.[7]

In the continuation, we will analyse the class struggles and logic of capital in the market socialism period. In order to facilitate the under-standing of the transitions before and after the market reform, the following table with a short summary of all the periods of Yugoslav socialism presents the key political forms as well as the locations and main focuses of the struggles.

Table 9.1   Political Struggles in Socialist Yugoslavia[8]

Period	Political formations	Location of the struggle	Main focuses
1941–45 Social revolution, People's Liberation Struggle (PLS)	Popular masses Communist Party People's Liberation Struggle (PLS)	Revolutionary struggle Civil war and anti-fascist struggle	People's Liberation Struggle (PLS) as the rupture with the old Yugoslavia Socialism Partisan art
1945–52 State socialism	The establishment of state bureaucracy	Autonomous foreign policy (Balkan Socialist Federation, Cominform dispute) Autarky (self-reliance) Policy of purges (Goli Otok island)	Collectivisation, nationalisation, and industrialisation International workers' movement crisis (Cominform) The logic of vanguard production relations Short stagnation Aid
1953–64 Workers' self-management	Workers' collectives and councils Bureaucracy (BC) Technocracy (TC) Non-Aligned Movement (NAM)	State bureaucracy against trade unions (for workers' councils) Anti-bloc policy: NAM Investment Fund (tensions between the republics)	Search for a balance between the market and the plan USA aid; opening toward Western and Eastern markets Mass internal migration, vast economic growth
1965–73 'Market socialism'	Ruling class faction (BC+TC) Revolutionary grassroots politics (students, workers' strikes) Expansion of critical cultural production Nationalist protests (Kosovo, Croatia)	Banks against the Investment Fund Internal retaliation against Ranković (centralists) Market North – south Republics – federation Universities Art Factories	Market reform Changes in investment management, end of the solidarity model Logic of capital Beginning of borrowing (tourism, roads, infrastructure projects) First serious economic crisis Migrant workers Nationalism and liberalism

Period	Political formations	Location of the struggle	Main focuses
1974–90 'Contractual socialism' Left and right alternative Restoration of capitalism and the emergence of national states	Weak balance between TC and national BC IMF, World Bank Federation – rich republics Mass strikes (trade unions) New social movements Nationalism and liberalism (hegemonic bloc) Implosion of the LCY and the national Leagues of Communists	International financial markets Regulation Proliferation of new self-management forms and improvement of legal communism Companies (independent capital) and republics against federation (IMF) Kosovo Changed geopolitics of the European powers after the fall of the Berlin Wall	Tito's death General crisis: austerity measures, crisis of the socialist state, inflation, unemployment Struggle for leadership in the national Leagues of Communists and the League of Communists of Yugoslavia (LCY) Democratisation of the political field Nationalism Restoration of private property and capitalist reproduction War

10

Separation I: Split within Companies, or Class Struggles from Below

Following the introduction of the market reform, the main changes manifested themselves in the transfers that cannot be explained with a simple separation from the means of production or by attempting to prove the existence of private property.[1] This attests to a specific intensification in exploitation: on the one hand, I will focus on the actual appropriation of surplus value at the level of companies (in the sphere of production), whilst on the other, I will take a closer look at the market orientation of the national product redistribution. I will therefore analyse two separations: the one *within* companies, revealing the new circumstances of the workers' competition and the antagonistic dimensions of the struggle; and the separation that occurs *between* those economic undertakings at the inter-republican level that became increasingly integrated into the global market. These separations resulted in the undermining of the social contract between the workers and the Party, establishing a new balance between the logic of exploitation and representation.

The market reform was not implemented merely in the name of greater efficiency, as the critique of the political monopoly and centralisation was initially also supported by the trade union leaderships and workers' representatives. For example, Svetozar Vukmanović – Tempo, a long time trade union leader, argued for a reform that would expand the workers' self-management and implement the idea of the working class autonomy (Samary 1988).[2] Once the basic infrastructure had been established and external dangers no longer loomed on the horizon, the circumstances were ripe for the implementation of the workers' councils' politics. According to Branko Horvat, this was the situation in which companies could finally become the basic organisations that would come together in a 'league of organisations', while these leagues would be organised in a 'federation of companies'. The market reform called for a greater democratisation of production, while the silent political foundation of the leftist, trade-unionist perspectives supported the emergence of a new class coalition between the technocracy and 'direct producers' (workers). Experts and politicised workers would supposedly represent the foundation for a new social contract that would benefit the majority in the new circumstances of self-management. This quiet wish for a new class coalition stemmed from 'economical' expectations: greater empowerment and decentralisation of companies (and regions) would supposedly diminish the state and federal involvement, which, in turn, would allegedly lead to greater workers' control, improved workers' solidarity, and smoother functioning of the economic system.

However, in reality this self-management economy did not fulfil these devout expectations. The formal rights of the workers' councils improved with the market reform, in which the introduction of greater access to financial resources was particularly important. The reform abolished the central inflow into all investment funds (federal, republican, and local), into which the companies' money had previously gone in the form of obligatory contributions. Instead, the political-territorial communities introduced the 'economic principle according to which the inhabitants of every municipality would cover the expenses involved in social services such as health, education, culture, etc.' (Bilandžić 1980: 303). Following the regional tax autonomy, the companies soon gained greater autonomy, as the abolishment of the 'high productivity tax', gave commercial companies much more funds at their disposal. This resulted in an altered distribution of income within business entities: in 1963, the remuneration within the companies amounted to approximately 31% of the product, while by 1967 this had reached 40%. In the same period, the contributions for the accumulation of investment funds decreased from 69% to 60%. Within this, the contribution for social communities was almost halved, as it decreased from 24% to 13%. Bilandžić added that the workers' salaries did indeed increase, but we should take into account the fact that due to the liberalisation of prices (the integration into the global market), the cost of living also increased and Yugoslavia registered a notable rise in inflation. In certain industries, the material position of the workers improved significantly, but what improved even more was the position of the managerial staff within banks, insurance companies, and the electricity production industry. This resulted in at least two direct consequences: the differences between the salaries in certain vocations and sectors intensified, while the tax reform resulted in improved capabilities and higher-quality services in the richer regions, as fewer resources were allocated to the federation. The motto *to each according to his labour* was soon supplemented with the slogan *to each nation (region) according to its contribution.* Bilandžić might have indeed mentioned these sociological and statistical differences in salaries, but he did not point out their origins, as his analysis ignores the class aspect. In this regard I would like to underline an excellent early study, written by Marko Kerševan in the 1970s, which transcended the belief of the official ideology at the time that Yugoslavia had a 'single class' and a 'unified working force', which would do away with the technocratic leadership of the society (Kerševan 1980: 1469).[3] Furthermore, Kerševan also criticised the 'concept of class polarisation' which froze the class conflict in the relation between the working class and the bureaucracy.[4] The latter concept suggested that socialism was still a class society, while the former position – also due to the self-legitimisation of the authorities – defended the thesis of the rare struggles and contradictions, but without the antagonism between the two classes, as only a single class existed. On the contrary, Kerševan's position was that class conflicts should not be analysed in their frozen state and that the 'objective class situation of individual groups was not given once and for all and that it was not unequivocal, but rather flexible, transitional, and internally contradictory'. (Kerševan, 1980: 50)

Kerševan emphasised the following:

> [Under socialism,] classic capitalist social classes no longer exist ... with the exclusive or explicit purpose of facilitating exploitation ...; however, social positions with class dimensions – positions that contain the *possibility* of exploitation ... – still exist. Furthermore, people in certain positions cannot be perceived as a class in advance. (Kerševan, 1985: 1467).

When it comes to class struggle, it is not enough to merely discuss the appropriation of the 'absolute surplus value' that takes place once the production process has been completed, as this value is distributed. Instead, the key moment of class exploitation should be sought in the production of the 'relative surplus value', which is manifested as the 'pressure to create surplus value'. In this regard, Kerševan's definition is predominantly based on Lenin's thought, for he claimed that 'classes are groups of people, where one group appropriates the labour of another group as a result of their different positions in the social economy system' (1985: 1468). Instead of ineffectively referring to the class struggle, Kerševan therefore proposes that the class issue should be explored within the system of other provisions (relationships of production, ideological struggles, and so forth) and that a concrete analysis should be carried out.

Marx described the specific nature of the capitalist mode of production by means of separation *(Trennung)* and the relationship between those who possess the capital and the means of production (capitalists) and those who only have their labour capacities at their disposal (workers). According to Marx, the separation of workers from the means of production is of key importance in capitalism. This can be illustrated with a simple diagram:

Figure 10.1   Capitalist relations of production

Class	Relationship to the Means of Production
Capitalists	Owners of Capital
Workers	Wage labourers

As previously demonstrated, the state and bureaucracy had the social capital at their disposal during the initial period of administrative socialism, however, the Yugoslav self-management system abolished this two-part division with the introduction of social property. Kerševan also underlined that the possibility for the 'socially-owned means of production to manifest themselves as capital' is often overlooked (Kerševan 1985: 1481). The workers' state as well as the workers-managers take the place of the capital. The logic can be cooperative or even involve shareholding.

With the socialisation of the means of production and reproduction, the role of workers' collectives became increasingly important for the production process. If we look at the general form of exploitation in the capitalist production system this originated from the private and legal ownership relations, which also represented the actual regime of the appropriation of value. However, in the self-management system, this was replaced by a regime of socially-owned property, which shifted the class dimensions to other points within the production relations. The legal separation no longer represented a dividing line. Instead, the separation took place with regard to the actual appropriation of value and the investment cycle – between the realisation on the market, the competition between the companies, and the financial capital that flowed into

Yugoslavia. At this point we should not forget that a strong class-related workers' struggle took place during the 1960s and that this often stopped the market reforms by means of illegal labour strikes. These theoretical foundations should facilitate our analysis of the market reform period.

What would Kerševan's class diagram look like if we took into account the market changes in the (re)production process? How can we answer the question as to who represented the capital during the market reform and who was on the side of labour? Formally, the workers' councils would reach decisions as regards to what and how to produce. This even established 'dual relations' in which the 'workers were wage earners as well as (nominal, formal) representatives of capital at the same time ... (while) the managers were simultaneously the actual representatives of the capital and formal representatives – commissioners of the workers' (ibid.). This is illustrated by the diagram below:

Figure 10.2   New economic domination in 'market' socialism

The Side of Capital → Workers as Managers
The Side of Labour → Workers

Capital as a social relation between labour and the organisers of the production process who have the surplus value at their disposal did not disappear with socialism, just as the value of goods or money did not. However, what did disappear, was the classic capitalist exploitation and the class of capitalists with their private ownership of the means of production. Meanwhile, the relations of domination persevered in the self-management system, regardless of the changes related to labour, capital, and the domination of one over the other. With the increased socialisation of economic and non-economic activities, the relations between labour and capital would finally tilt in favour of labour and thus improve the workers' control over production (and reproduction). We can claim that at least in the legal sense, market socialism managed to make capital autonomous and establish the foundations for better control by the workers. However, during the first years of its implementation, the reform triggered a wave of contradictory effects. The workers found themselves in a schizophrenic situation, reminiscent of Don Quixote's struggle against the windmills. According to official ideology, the essence of self-management was that the workers simultaneously worked as well as performing the functions that were carried out by capitalists in the capitalist societies, and by the state in the statist societies.[5] However, even though the workers assumed the position of capitalists, this did not mean that capital was abolished. The workers and the sale of labour power would always be rooted in the asymmetrical relationship between capital and labour.

However, if we were to be historically specific, we would need to address the tendency of this asymmetry that is exceedingly contradictory and fluid. As it happened, the introduction of the market reform increased the autonomy of the units of production, and expanded their disposal of surplus value. This resulted in the formal possibility of self-valorisation, which encompassed a fundamental contradiction: on the one hand, the workers strove for their own interests, in particular as far as maintaining or increasing their wages was concerned; on the other hand they worked against themselves and other workers who represented them in the workers' councils as the representatives of the capital and thus forced them to engage in a form of self-exploitation.[6] This meant that, as managers, the workers could decide how much of the surplus value would be invested into the accumulation cycle and how much would be allocated to wages. They also had to decide on the production quantities and how many (new) workers they should employ in the future. At this point, the form of this specific (self)exploitation becomes all the more apparent, manifesting itself as pressure against the labour market and competition against the workers in other companies. As would soon be revealed, this resulted in the extreme intensification of political demands, for example during labour strikes, as well as in the self-destructive inclinations of workers and their subconscious, as they were supposed to simultaneously (self)represent capital, labour, and politics.

Despite the more intense (self)exploitation in market socialism, it has to be underlined that the logic of representation persevered. According to Kerševan, the workers 'as the representatives of the social capital cannot directly and collectively perform the function of capitalists, but can only function indirectly through those who represent them' (Kerševan 1985: 1483). Social self-management provided for a complex system of representation, in which a wide range of social groups were supposed to be involved in the strategic decisions. The representatives of economic units were delegated to bodies of socio-political communities, and vice versa: through councils and directors the bodies of socio-economic communities were present in the economy. In political practice, two 'bad' aspirations manifested themselves with regard to 'representation'. Firstly, the strengthening of the technocratic tendencies resulted in the professionalisation of the day-to-day company management, while the planning became increasingly in tune with the market's – i.e. profit's – guidelines. The workers who represented other workers gradually became professionals or left these matters to experts, engineers, and company management staff. Secondly, the maintenance of social harmony and compliance with the social contract resulted in an opportunist personnel policy, which, among other things, manifested itself in the decline of labour discipline and diminished production of surplus value.

The authors of *Kapital in Delo v SFRJ* (Bavčar et al. 1985) wrote a sharp critique of Yugoslav socialism from the Marxist perspective, claiming that this process led to the disintegration 'as an unappeasable contradiction, embodied in the working class and the working people on the one hand and the technocracy and bureaucracy on the other hand' (ibid., 66). This idea can be believed if it is contextualised in the period of the market reform, during which a technocratic faction that resulted from the 'osmosis of company directors, bank managers, and the local authorities' gradually prevailed (Samary 1988: 169). The technocratic faction hegemonised the fields of production and ideological struggles within the reproductive apparatuses, thus creating circumstances in which it could seize 'control and management of capital with regard to labour' (Bavčar et al. 1985: 48). In the mid-1960s, the working class and the technocracy eventually became openly antagonistic, pointing at the existing class struggle in socialism.

This leads to the conclusion that the market reform by no means interfered merely with the balance between the market and the planned economy, but also prepared the terrain for a freer flow of capital and labour within the Yugoslav economy and its integration into the global system. This severely challenged the existing social contract between the workers and their political representatives (the technocracy or bureaucracy). The envisioned political goals of the market reform were only partially realised: even though the decentralisation process continued to undermine the political monopoly of the bureaucracy, the political and economic power of the technocracy remained on the rise. Instead of a greater autonomy resulting in the social control over various capitals and the transfer of power to the workers, the power was taken over by the technocrats and ultimately by the logic of capital that reoriented the socialist development.[7] This criticism of the technocratic faction helped us outline the class structure and served as a means of detecting the disintegration of the social contract. From the very outset, this contract was based on the reproduction of the social division of labour, which did not allow the workers – also due to the time shortage – to engage in any significant political activities regarding the planning of the socialist development. Instead, other economic and political representatives would think, plan, and operate in the name of the workers. For as long as the logic of representation remained contained within the context of egalitarian ideology and joint development and the political and economic legitimacy of the project was maintained, the absence of their own engagement did not bother the workers. However, the situation changed dramatically as soon as the material foundations for the self-management 'social contract' started to crumble.

The Class Struggle of Workers: The Decline of the Socialist Social Contract

We have already seen, in Chapter 6, how the social contract between the workers and their political representatives was constituted after the break with Stalin. This materialised in the infrastructure of the socialist social state, which would, ensure the following with time: full employment, basic public infrastructure, free access to public services, easier access to housing and other social benefits, and, the gradual withering away of the state and the Party. In his research, the sociologist Županov (1969) underlined that self-management involved the contract between the nascent politocracy (the political representatives of the socialist organisations) and the working class or at least a narrow section of the working class: the manual labourers. The social contract stemmed from the post-war state restoration project that was based on socialist industrialisation. By the mid-1960s this project had achieved remarkable results and laid the material foundations for the ever-growing working class – foundations that allowed the solidarity model to play an important part in international relations, thus creating strong ties.

The technocracy started gaining power during the 1960s market reform. Eventually it became a new political subject within the contract; it became a part of the economic and political representation and tendentiously constituted a new ruling class, which was hostile towards the workers. Rastko Močnik commented on this 'transfer' of power, by defining the new self-management system as a 'corporatist subjugation of the workforce in industrial production', which meant that

The political structuring of the workers into a working class was thus blocked, as this political dimension had already been taken over by the self-management mechanisms ... and the social property was represented by the companies' leading managers. In a more dynamic aspect, the individual bearers of labour power were integrated as individual consumers, while the political dimension was occupied by the apparatuses of the Party–state, which managed the social property and represented the working class *in general* (as an incorporation of corporations).[8]

In the circumstances of stagnation and crisis, the initial social contract, based on the commitment of the political bureaucracy, started disintegrating. Instead of an egalitarian development model and a formal, yet legitimate representation, a technocratic solution was imposed, proposing a 'hierarchy of coordination' instead of a hierarchy within the companies. This type of coordination distanced itself from the goal of abolishing the division of labour, as professionalisation concentrated the social power in the hands of experts. This led to the development of a fragmented market capital logic, which was in contradiction with the model of fair development and the initial operation of economic equality. This shift towards a new social contract that tendentiously returned to the liberal framework is illustrated by Figure 10.3.

Rather than any conscious policy on the part of Kardelj and other ideologues, the constant adaptation of the social contract represented the 'political unconscious' – the blind spot of self-management. The insistence on the legal establishment and formal perfection of self-management mechanisms attested to a naive faith, as hopes for the communist future were placed in the increasingly diverse and perfected legal systematisation. The more that socialist ideologues believed in the necessity of legally perfecting the self-management system (towards the end of the market period it was called 'contractual' socialism), the further away they would find themselves from addressing the actual political-economic problems. An increase in the number of contracts and laws does not necessarily ensure a greater latitude for workers nor fewer conflicts. Quite the opposite: all the legal matter – from regulations, acts, and constitutions, to the constant changes and new social contracts – has to be understood in the context of class compromise and the new political alliance between technocrats and bureaucrats (Samary 1988: 225–38).

Figure 10.3   Self-management social contract in market socialism

Ideal subject: the working people	→ Type of exchange ←	The socialist community
Productive relations	Appropriation of surplus value	Representative of the social capital: bureaucracy
Agent of self-management		Representative of individual capitals: technocrats and workers' collectives
	Distribution of national income	
Political authority	Representation	Bureaucracy as the political representative within the political apparatuses
Workers' councils, delegate system of self-management institutions		Technocracy as the economic representative in key (in)formal institutions and networks
The republics	Pluralism of self-management interests	The excluded: workers, in particular the unemployed

This meant that the new social contract was written by the bureaucracy and technocracy, while the workers had justifiably high expectations due to the worker-friendly ideology of Yugoslavia as a workers' state. Furthermore, the workers could trade in their votes in the self-management political institutions. In exchange for continued social privileges, the workers freely handed over the decisions with regard to the planning and accumulation of productive resources. Lebowitz (2012) described these types of vote manipulation and the general workers' arguments in favour of the social contract as a spontaneous workers' ideology of 'egalitarianism', which was not a part of the revolutionary politics. Once workers found full-time employment in socialism, they could lose their jobs only in extremely rare cases (sabotage, and so forth), and at least in the urban centres they all enjoyed good access to social services and infrastructure. However, the coalition of the techno-bureaucratic structures practically prevented the workers from being active within the self-management institutions. Furthermore, the workers were often insufficiently informed or did not have enough 'socially necessary labour time' at their disposal.[9] This, however, does not mean that they were only passively involved in self-management.

Labour Strikes: From Trbovlje to the Strike Wave
of the Mid-1960s (1958–69)

In Slovenia, there has been a lack of research into labour strikes which has been caused by the dissolution of socialist Yugoslavia and the defeat of the workers' politics, which had taken place already during socialism. Furthermore, the Yugoslav political authorities considered labour strikes to be illegal, thus they were not reported in the media for a long time (unless they used terms such as 'work interruption' or 'absence from work'). This important chapter in the workers' struggles has therefore not been comprehensively explored – with rare exceptions, for example in the pioneering work by Jovanov (1979) and the aforementioned sociological studies by Županov, Arzenšek, and more recently Mušić (2013).[10] The fact that strikes were perceived as illegal in socialist Yugoslavia might not attract much attention at first glance. Why would workers resist in a workers' state? Against whom would they struggle? I would like to illustrate this with a comical scene from Pavlović's film *When I Am Dead and Gone* (1967),[11] in which the company director stands up to the workers who are on strike: 'If there's something you don't like, there's a workers' council in the factory. So, solve all your issues there instead of going on strike like this!' This kind of reaction by the management was not only a part of the typical cultural critique expressed in the critical films – which tended to deliberately exaggerate and caricature in order to point out the extremes of the situation – but was symptomatic of all the highest authorities. Between 1958 and 1969 Neca Jovanov carried out a concrete analysis of labour strikes and examined the official documents pertaining to these 'conflict situations' (Jovanov 1979: 27–33; 193–203).[12] As these documents clearly show, the political authorities described the labour strikes with the collocation 'conflict situation', while the media used the term 'work interruption'.

This is understandable, as labour strikes were illegal in socialist Yugoslavia, and when they first broke out, they represented an extremely negative surprise for the socialist authorities. They first appeared in 1958 – only a year after the first all-Yugoslav *Workers' Council Congress* which was, ideally, supposed to bring together the workers and radicalise the existing trade unions.[13] Neca Jovanov (1979) travelled throughout Yugoslavia and studied various workers' environments in the 1960s and 1970s. In his book he claimed that labour strikes represented the main controversy within the self-management system, and that they indicated a severe class opposition between the workers and those who were supposed to represent them in the political system.

Between 13 and 15 January 1958, the miners in the towns of Trbovlje and Hrastnik organised a general strike, which involved more than 4000 miners, joined by other employees, trade union representatives, and Party officials. A few days later, the miners from Zagorje joined the strike in solidarity (Jovanov 1979: 130–37). Similar to many subsequent cases, the labour strike took place as a result of meagre wages. Moreover, the mine management refused to pay the miners their December salary in 1957. The media did not report on these events, as this was an illegal or a wildcat strike. It is overlooked that the representatives of the workers' collectives attempted to ensure the improvement of their working conditions – a minimum increase in wages and a cap on the prices of consumables – using all possible political means for an entire year before the strike took place. At this point, the workers stumbled upon a certain antinomy of the self-management system. First of all, they realised that the influence on the status of mining within the socio-economic division, which they could exert through the local trade union and political representations, was extremely modest (the prices of coal kept falling, and productivity kept rising). Secondly, the labour organisations would not increase their wages, regardless of the relative success and surpluses. After all other potential solutions had been exhausted, these two realisations resulted in the most radical political action: a labour strike. The strike action was relatively successful, as the workers' salaries were increased minimally in the weeks to come. They also received half of their last salary for 1957, and the League of Communists replaced a few local and trade union representatives. However, ultimately neither the workers nor the authorities discussed the broader circumstances involved in the position of the workers, which pointed towards a specific hierarchy of industries as well as revealed certain issues within the political system itself.

The number of strike actions increased during the 1960s. In particular in the mid-1960s, we can talk about a 'strike wave' throughout various branches of the economy. They were most prevalent in the more developed parts of the federation and environments with a long tradition of workers' struggle and an intensive collective work process. Jovanov ascertained (1979: 137) that the strike wave reached its peak in 1964 (271 documented strike actions) and 1965 (231 strikes). In spite of the modest media coverage and the illegal nature of the strikes, this issue became a visible form of the workers' political efforts during the 1960s. The organisers of these strikes were subjected to chicanery and described as 'hostile forces' that caused material damage. What is more, in the conclusion to its infamous 7th session, the Presidency of the League of Communists of Yugoslavia established that not only were the labour strikes not a proper way of addressing issues, but that they in fact represented 'undemocratic pressure … that abolished self-management decision-making and hindered the socio-economic development' (ibid., 29) – meaning that labour strikes were predominantly seen as an 'anti-self-management' phenomenon. The causes and certain reasons for the strike actions were nevertheless correctly diagnosed in the official documents. However, two structural contradictions of Yugoslav self-management were completely overlooked: firstly, the problematic role and position of workers in the 'institutional structure of social power' was not even mentioned; and secondly, the official authorities failed to analyse the difficult production position of workers in the 'division of material goods' (ibid. 30). At this point, an irreconcilable discrepancy between the workers and their representatives occurred, and at the same time neither of the sides had a decisive influence on certain matters any more. Instead, these matters were decisively influenced by the logic of capital and the radicalised hierarchical development of the industry, during which certain industries remained on the sidelines. In this regard, the marginal position of certain economic activities and their weaker financial conditions (the rising price of consumables, rising productivity, wage stagnation) would need to be analysed. Consequently, I am inclined to conclude that the strike actions pointed towards the class problem of socialist reproduction, albeit unconsciously at that time, and that this situation was partly used to justify the market reform.

In his recent study of the Yugoslav economy, Darko Suvin (2016) stated that strike actions were mainly limited to political organisation and resistance within the workers' own companies. They would rarely transform into large-scale protests. Suvin's conclusion, referring to Jovanov, that the poor working conditions, failure to pay salaries, and meagre wages were the main reasons for the strikes, is by all means correct. However, despite his accurate diagnosis (the fragmentation of workers), Suvin failed to mention the historical circumstances whereby the more autonomous trade union organisations remained absent, while the shortage of 'socially necessary labour time' for political engagement remained a pressing issue. If we remain merely focused on analysing the verbatim statements and demands of the workers on strike, we can conclude, without any doubt, that the strikes mostly called for reforms and that they were limited to individual companies. The workers would primarily fight for higher salaries and not so much for a more active participation in the self-management or for the revolutionisation of the processes. Suvin's ascertainment that the strikes remained atomised and fragmented holds true. We could also claim that Michael Lebowitz was right to criticise the workers for their 'narrow moral economy' of egalitarianism, which argued for the preservation of salaries and living standards. However, regardless of how justified these reproaches may be, the very frequency of labour strikes indicated the insufficiency of the self-management institutions that endangered the existing system and thus already revealed deeper contradictions.

During the reforms that 'democratised' self-management interests and expanded self-management rights, workers' uprisings would take place despite the self-management government apparatus, wishing and calling for the recognition of the workers' interests and the need to self-organise within and beyond the apparatus. Furthermore, labour strikes were important because they questioned the holy postulate of the socialist authorities: *the figure of the worker in a workers' state*. When the socialist authorities recognised that the political implications of the strikes clashed with the 'political unconscious' (Jameson 1982) of self-management, they used the underdevelopment of the self-management relations in the contemporaneous society and the damage that the workers had supposedly caused by their irresponsible interruption of work as an excuse. Conversely, the strikes would call upon the political responsibility of those who were supposed to represent the workers and ensure social solidarity. The 1960s strike wave was repeated in the 1980s, during the implementation of austerity policies. During this period, the workers became radicalised, which in turn strengthened the role of trade unions (Stanojević, 1994: 164–74). At a certain point, Tonči Kuzmanić even called the workers the regressive or nostalgic subjects of a disintegrating system (Kuzmanić 1988: 8–9), even though the labour strikes were probably one of the few leftist alternatives from the end of the 1980s that, as Mušić (2013: 9–18) suggested so succinctly, did not represent a nationalist backbone at the outset and that could only become a backbone during the process of the democratisation of socialism.[14] The labour strikes were one of the most severe manifestations of the class antagonisms in the changed circumstances of the socialist development that, on the one hand, helped to establish a front for a market reform against the central bureaucracy; while, on the other the increasingly prominent decentralisation led to the atomisation and strengthening of individual's capital, which also resulted in the increasing fragmentation of the workers' collectives.

Neutralisation of Struggles by Unemployment and the Deployment of Surplus Labour to a Neoliberal Employment ('Gastarbeiter')

Regardless of the difficult position of the industrial workers in particular, the crisis of the socialist industrialisation and market reform was accompanied by a number of political and student movements as well as alternative theoretical and artistic formations, which culminated between 1968 and 1972 (Kanzleiter 2011). This topic will be revisited in Chapter 13, while this chapter will proceed with the analysis of the composition of the working class, including those who were formally excluded or invisible according to the self-management logic. Today, as soon as we utter the word 'excluded' or 'invisible', we promptly end up entangled in a network of associations or subjected to a dissident temptation that erects grandiose intellectual and artistic beacons in opposition to totalitarian terror. Intellectuals, cultural workers, nationalist politicians, and 'thinkers' of all sorts were victims who were supposedly marginalised and excluded from the public life. However, if this were true, we would never have heard of these people, and it would have been difficult to explain the substantial production and dissemination of the national cultures in Yugoslavia at the time. The socialist authorities certainly did not ignore the dissidents, but rather subjected them to periodic censorship (confiscations and prohibitions of newspaper publications) as well as to a permanent 'illumination' by the representatives of the socialist authorities who kept persuading the dissidents to agree with their point of view. The intellectual, critical and dissident activities performed an important social role in socialism, and we could hardly claim that those involved in such activities remained on the sidelines.[15] On the contrary: in her study, Katja Praznik (2013) demonstrated that cultural intellectuals were a part of the existing hegemonic apparatus of the national culture. According to Rancière, these dissidents are not subjects of revolutionary politics, but represent a normal supplement to the way in which a police state operates. Rancière (1999) believes that those who truly radically subvert the order are invisible and inaudible in a police order – even worse, they have no access whatsoever to any cultural or political apparatuses. In Rancière's words, the politics of the excluded involves those 'parts of no-part' that the dominant logic of counting, i.e. the 'police', does not notice or take into account. Rancière's metacritique of (any) police order thus involves a certain surplus, a part of no-part, which is excluded by the normal operation/counting of the police regime. According to Rancière, true 'politics' take place in a situation of complete rupture with the existing order (e.g. with a social contract) – i.e. as something that is diametrically opposed to the search for a consensus. Only the politics of rupture can expose the position of the excluded and the uncounted – of those who are by definition not seen or heard by the police order. Rancière refers to the example of the women's struggle for the right to vote, when women demanded that the universality of the fundamental human right to vote was to be taken seriously – in other words, that every woman and not merely every man (some parts) has the right to participate in the elections and political life. To paraphrase Rancière, the (revolutionary) politics represents the active force that can break away from the 'distribution of the sensible' and thus undermine the dominant way of counting. With their politics, those who have previously not been counted, seen, or heard can open a universal dimension, as they practice the principle of equality for everyone. At the very outset, this makes them different from the mere representatives of (particular) identity politics – which must always be verified with a concrete analysis of the situation.[16]

I would therefore like to additionally historise the Rancièrian political horizon of the excluded with the 'class' moment. Instead of perceiving the invisibility and inaudibility of the excluded as an abstract effect of the 'counting logic' and the transhistorical police order, I would prefer to associate it with the analysis of the exploitation relations within Yugoslavia. In his metapolitical scheme, Rancière leaves aside the moment of exploitation, but simultaneously introduces two lesser-analysed suppositions that maintain the formality of the theory. The first assumption presupposes the existence of the natural operation of the police force that keeps excluding certain parts of society and fails to count them all. The second assumption, however, equates the invisible and inaudible with the passive (and thus as a 'natural' attachment to the police), while true politics becomes active and visible only in the moment when the excluded point out the blind spot of the police machinery and its counting. The active politics only last short term, as it is swiftly covered by the new police order with the inclusion of those who have previously been invisible. Therefore, Rancière does not focus on the logic of exploitation, but returns partly to the logic of representation, where the distinction between the active (the politics of part of no-part) and the passive (part of no-part) is not sufficiently addressed.

These assumptions are all the more difficult when they are introduced to a concrete analysis of the actual political struggles that Rancière only mentions in passing – e.g. the politics of the demos in Antiquity, Algerians during their anti-colonial struggle, and the women's struggle for universal suffrage. If we examine the political struggles within socialist Yugoslavia, the workers are the ones – at least according to Rancière – who are 'most' included in the new socialist state regime: discussions focused on the proletarian demos, the working people, in the same way as the self-management idea was materialised in the (police) self-management institutions, in which the workers and the people had their own delegates or even represented themselves. This type of handling of the police self-management order presupposes an active role for the workers. However, instead of politically activating themselves, the working class gradually succumbed to becoming passive and neutralised as a result of the ideological saturation, 'total' inclusion, and counting. As I have already underlined with regard to labour strikes, the normative revolutionary subject of the working class within the socialist metapolitics was, realistically speaking, excluded from the key institutions of the economy and only had limited access to political institutions. Even those who were supposed to be the most included (and counted) by the socialist police were not the most visible and audible in the actual political practice. In this sense, the regime of the 'distribution of the sensible' – what is audible and visible – developed differently in this concrete example: even those who enjoyed the privilege of being included in the situation were not necessarily seen or heard, which relativised the line between the passive and the active. I do not believe that it was the workers who stood at the most traumatic point of the self-management system, as they could tear down and construct workers' solidarity through labour strikes. Instead, I would like to identify those who experienced difficulties in accessing the labour market – *the unemployed* – as the people who were not counted, as the 'parts of no-part'.

It was extremely difficult for people without access to the labour market and permanent employment to access the diverse institutional network. Even worse, the lives of individuals were reduced to coming up with survival strategies, searching for flexible and seasonal employment, undeclared work, and criminal activities. Towards the end of the

1960s the Yugoslav economy no longer benefitted from full employment, and unemployment became a pressing problem, as the economic industrialisation failed to employ the new segments of the population living in the (semi)rural environment. The socialist leadership was fully aware of the unemployment issue: as early as the mid-1960s it focused on concluding international contracts regarding guest workers (Živković 2013), although it officially still promoted the myths of full employment and the idea of a permanent employee within the social sector (Woodward 1995a: 196). For the best part, unemployment was absent from the state's analyses, while the official ideologues would treat this issue with a fair degree of cynicism, as a voluntary choice, a temporary or short-term experience, which was, allegedly, an extremely rare phenomenon in Yugoslavia ('the job-seekers' communities of interest'). Woodward (1995a) underlined many issues of unemployment in light of the relations between the republics, and those between the centre and the periphery. The differences between the regions started increasing yet again: while the unemployment rates in Slovenia mainly remained between 2 and 4 per cent which meant it could almost boast about full employment, certain regions in Kosovo and Macedonia had unemployment rates that officially exceeded 20 per cent (Sundhaussen, 2012: 143). Srečo Kirn was right to state that 'the increase in unemployment rates was one of the most radical manifestations in which the position of wage recipients/earners dominated in comparison with their formal position of self-management agents' (1982: 57). In a market socialist economy, the unemployed represented what Marx calls a 'industrial reserve army'[17] – the most humiliated and affronted, who were structurally forced to either wait for new investment cycles and seasonal opportunities or enter, as precarious migrants (*Gastarbeiter*), the European labour market for a limited period. The latter presented itself as an avant-garde of the neoliberal labour market. The unemployed represented the neuralgic point at which two key logics of reproduction met: the logic of representation (without access to self-management institutions) and the logic of exploitation (the coercion and spontaneity of market forces).

The Reserve Army of Self-Management Workers: Between Flexible Employment and Migrant Workers

We could also refer to the unemployed as the dangerous class or the 'surplus population', forced to search for less formal and more flexible forms of employment and invent survival strategies. In this context, a whole range of new professions and new contracts, informal labour agreements in the private sector, as well as project work in the social sector appeared during the 1960s. In her analysis, Woodward (1995a) underlined that the new jobs (as well as unemployment) in the private sector were not recorded by the official statistics. Additionally, already in the mid-1950s, a form of precarious work had started developing in the cultural sphere that the post-Fordist thinkers ascribed to the changes of the capitalist mode of production in the 1970s. In his analysis of the changes in film production, Pavle Levi ascertained that during the 1950s, new film studios were established in several Yugoslav republics at the same time as a number of people were fired in the film industry. Simultaneously,

> Worker's councils were introduced as decision-making bodies overseeing film production, distribution, and exhibition, while the creative personnel associated with the process of filmmaking (directors, cinematographers, screenwriters) were given the status of freelance professionals. (Levi 2007: 15).[18]

The difficult access to the status of an independent artist and the irregular nature of the cultural work was reflected in the precarious situation: poorer social security, lower pensions, and unpaid vacation.

In short, flexible and precarious forms of employment were introduced in the Yugoslav labour market for specific activities (cognitive and cultural work) in the mid-1950s. In the mid-1960s, these forms of work were extended to the considerable percentage of the population that had migrated from the rural parts to the urban centres. By that time, the share of the rural population had already decreased to a mere two fifths. Vast changes in the social structure of the population took place: not only had the agricultural population decreased by 50 per cent since the end of World War II, but approximately '1.5 million fixed-term contract workers ... those who had previously been agricultural workers but now fluctuated between agriculture and industry' existed since the beginning of the 1970s. Their number kept increasing constantly (Suvin 2014: 114). Woodward (1995a: 191–92) established a detailed categorisation of the various types of labour, which she developed from the social regulation of labour: 1) unqualified labourers that kept moving from one short-term contract to another; 2) the unemployed who waited either for employers or opportunities in the informal markets on the outskirts of cities or villages (seasonal work); and 3) a large number of agricultural workers who would work seasonally in mines or other large industrial operations. These flexible forms of employment also resulted in more precarious social reproduction circumstances, poorer housing capacities, and inferior public infrastructure. During this period the first extensive illegal constructions started appearing at the edges of larger cities, but with substandard infrastructure (sheds) and poor connections with the city centres. In her study of Kaluđerica (a Belgrade suburb), Dubravka Sekulić (2012) demonstrated how the construction of social housing kept lagging behind the actual needs of the new urban population despite significant efforts and investments.

The official statistics did not take into account the new labour forms and the unemployed, hindering any later research into this issue. According to Sundhaussen, the registered unemployment in 1968 amounted to approximately 8 per cent (312,000 people), while there was no precise data for the rural areas. Moreover, by the beginning of the 1970s, unemployment in certain regions had become a long-term structural issue.[19] In the mid-1970s, Kosovo and Macedonia had an approximately 20-per cent unemployment rate – in comparison with 6.5 per cent in Croatia and full employment in Slovenia. The 1981 statistical census revealed that from the 22 million people in Yugoslavia, approximately 13 million represented the active population. Of these, only 7 million were permanently employed in the social sector. One million were officially registered as unemployed; 1 million worked temporarily abroad; while the rest were employed in the private sector or depended on flexible, seasonal, and other types of employment. We can only add that a significant percentage of the 'unregistered' workers were exposed to inferior social and economic security (Woodward 1995a: 192).

Even though the socialist authorities refused to acknowledge the unemployment problem for a long time, they did address it – from the viewpoint of the global capitalist system. The Yugoslav leadership thus attempted to 'externalise' this social issue, and as the European centre experienced a lack of (cheap) labour, a number of international contracts were signed with the governments of Germany, Austria, and even Denmark and Sweden. The reserve army of labour was thus integrated into the European capital markets, which we could refer to as the beginning of the 'European integration' process. Yugoslavia (as well as Italy, Greece, Spain, Portugal, and Turkey) would provide a constant flow of migrant workers in the period of swift industrial development in the West, which, however, slowed down in the second half of the 1970s (Chin 2009). Temporary workers were subject to special treatment, starting with thorough medical checks in their native countries and continuing with an extremely strict control of their social lives and relatively low wages for what were almost universally known as unpopular professions. The cheap labour force from the outskirts would also represent internal pressure for the workers within the Western countries, resulting in competition between the workers making it harder for them to get organised. Furthermore, besides being subjected to inadequate economic security, the migrant workers also had to live in 'terrible circumstances and put up with poor housing, but, admittedly, they received a monthly wage of approximately 750 German marks compared to the 210 German marks they would earn at home' (Suvin, 2014: 293). Not merely unqualified workers, but also highly educated and technical personnel would leave for the West.

From the perspective of the global system, the *Gastarbeiter* phenomenon can be seen as an international policy of solving the unemployment issue and temporarily (and later permanently) including this labour force into the European labour market. In most cases, these temporary workers would not remain merely visitors, however, their status remained precarious for a long time. In the case of Yugoslav temporary workers, the political leadership hoped that the workers would stay abroad for a limited time (i.e. that they would return); and that they would use the foreign currency that they had saved for future investments at home and thus strengthen the Yugoslav economy. In reality, this did not happen, as the vast majority of *Gastarbeiters* remained abroad. Furthermore, they spent their foreign currency for personal and broader family *consumption* rather than for any investments in Yugoslavia.

Based on the previously stated, we can identify two main policies of 'addressing' unemployment in market socialism: firstly, the issue was addressed with a regulated policy of contracts between Yugoslavia and the host countries, which thus gained access to cheap labour (with inferior social and economic protection and lower wages) from Yugoslavia and other peripheral countries (a neoliberal experiment); and secondly, the unregulated and spontaneous logic of market self-management manifested itself, resulting in the struggle of the job-seekers in the light of numerous informal and seasonal types of employment and the rampant grey economy. The new job-seekers were left to the spontaneity of the market and their own ingenuity: in this regard, the ideological figure of a spontaneous and versatile self-management agent was certainly brought to life! Therefore, I can adopt the basic hypothesis that by combining the logics of exploitation and representation, the unemployed represented the key blind spot of the socialist politics. In this regard, the increased dependence of the Yugoslav economy on the capitalist global system on the one hand and the Yugoslav's own inability to implement a policy of investing into social power on the other hand had become apparent. The analysis of internal class changes within market socialism must be supplemented by an analysis of the 'external' aspect of the reform, pertaining to the increased competition between the individual forms of capital and the consequences of global integration.

11

Separation II: Competition between Companies and Financialisation, or Class Struggles from Above

The transition process to market socialism undermined the egalitarian social contract, introduced economic rationality and flexible international capital business, while financial circulation expanded due to financial inflow and foreign loans. The emergence of new commercial banks was causally linked to the increased financial flows that also gave rise to direct competition between socialist companies over the distribution of resources (and their dependency on them). The financialisation of the Yugoslav economy and its integration into the global market led to increasing regional economic differences, which resulted in the most negative consequence of this process. According to Močnik, the hybrid regulation regime oscillated between 'extensive accumulation (the underdeveloped components of the Federation) and intensive accumulation (its developed components) … while the preferred growth of direct salaries was under pressure from the technocratic tendencies in the political power centres' Močnik (2010).

Močnik illustrated the difference between the developed and underdeveloped parts of the Federation by comparing two companies: Gorenje from Slovenia and Obodin from Montenegro. Both companies specialised in household appliances, and their goal was to secure a major part of the Yugoslav market for themselves. However, as is the case with most market competitors, these two companies had different foundations: apart from its considerable investment capacities,[1] Gorenje 'also had an extraordinarily well-developed network of service centres throughout Yugoslavia, which provided a firm base for its national as well as subsequent international recognition' (ibid., 142). The western parts of the state had better connections with foreign companies, and could therefore pursue more profitable contracts. These comparative advantages resulted from historical and structural circumstances: apart from the aforementioned differences in infrastructure, the richer regions were also more creditworthy, while the governments of the republics supported the big companies and banks in their own respective territories. By no means did the market reform cause the total inequality between the regions, as state interventionism nevertheless existed. Catherine Samary underlined that the planned development in the past had been at least partially unjust, as it had been 'based on extensive industrialisation with cheap raw materials and labour' (Samary 1988: 235). However, in market circumstances and times of crises, the method of 'industrialisation without specialisation' came up against its own limitations, and the differences between the poor (the south: Kosovo and Macedonia) and the richer regions (the north: Slovenia and Croatia) started to grow Močnik (2010: 142–4).[2] The reform radicalised the contradictions immanent to socialist self-management (Kirn 1982). This resulted in open conflicts in two areas: firstly, on the macroeconomic level, in the redistribution of the national income and the management of foreign currencies (which remained centralised regardless of their origin); and secondly, competition took place amongst the very companies that introduced the market criteria and – as we have already established – contributed to the ever poorer position of workers. These two areas characterised the conflicts between the republican leaderships and the central federal authorities with regard to the development and reorganisation of production units. It is in this area that the effects of the Yugoslav integration with the global capitalist system should be sought, and it is at this point that the dynamics of the local 'development of underdevelopment' started to materialise.[3]

The New Role of Banks and the Increasing External Debt

Following the reform, the National Bank of Yugoslavia retained a strong position and remained an important factor with regard to macroeconomic policy management. As decentralisation progressed, an important banking system reform was implemented, resulting in the emergence of a new economic power centre. One of the reformers' key victories was the abolition of the Investment Fund, which shifted the responsibility of managing the money supply directly to the new banks (Samary 1988: 167). Also Suvin ascertained that the new *Banks and Loans Act* had long-term consequences, as approximately 480 successful municipal banks were abolished, while a 'smaller number of investment and commercial banks, which could be established by groups of 25 companies and/or political communities' were created (Suvin 2014: 287). This process can be referred to as the concentration of (financial) capital. However, the banks had to be confirmed by the assemblies of the individual republics, which meant that they could initially lend money only in the republics in which their respective head offices had been registered. As the new banks were established by the largest companies, they also had the majority share of votes in the administrative committees and could thus make decisions with regard to loans. This financial logic of macroeconomic instruments contradicted the solidarity development model.

It is no secret that the IMF and foreign creditors entered the Yugoslav economy in a more direct fashion at the time. Consequently, a considerable supply of money or loans appeared in the financial market, and companies began to take out loans rather enthusiastically. In the event that the initial capital of a company did not measure up to the received loans, all further decisions regarding the loans were adopted by the administrative boards of the banks rather than by the employees of the companies in question (Bavčar et al. 1985: 102).[4] This issue represented one of the major financial blind spots and non-democratic shortcomings of the self-management model. The power of the new banks increased as they set liberal financial criteria (profitability) as a precondition for their loans. In return for the loans the companies had to explain and substantiate their business plans and potential demand (ibid., 197–8). The earlier bureaucracy monopoly on social capital was now replaced by a new class-related coalition that became the key political driving force that promoted the liberal development of the Yugoslav economy in the 1960s. The previous chapter demonstrated how the workers in official political institutions became blocked and increasingly removed from any strategic decisions and investments in social production and reproduction. At this point, the emancipatory potentials of the self-management project were scrutinised.

Most international loans were still allocated to the largest infrastructural projects ranging from the construction of motorways and transport improvements to the development of the tourist infrastructure,[5] and large-scale industrial installations. On the other hand, 'microeconomics' was also encouraged: in light of the liberalisation of the price mechanism and decreased customs duties on imported goods, imports were on the rise. By the end of the 1960s, inflation had increased to 14 per cent.[6] In these circumstances, a high number of new and smaller companies appeared that focused on imports rather than investing in national production. The construction of department stores (e.g. Nama) in all larger cities represented a notable manifestation of these processes. At the time the increased trade deficit with the Western economies was not as apparent, while the exchange with the Eastern and Non-Aligned Countries stagnated.[7] The negative trade balance and the repayment of loans forced the Yugoslav economy to plan for activities that would hopefully bring in more (solid) foreign currency. However, this was harder to achieve in the lesser developed economies, as payments would either arrive late or in the form of goods and raw materials. Since Yugoslavia had to repay the increasing interest on its debt every year,[8] the Yugoslav experts and economists encouraged the export-oriented economy and tourism, which would allow for the reduction of the trade deficit by securing the urgently-needed foreign currency.[9] A few major companies started making their presence felt globally in the 1960s, for example Energoprojekt (an important construction and engineering company that developed big infrastructural projects in Non-Aligned Countries), Gorenje (producing household appliances and cooperating with Western companies such as Zanussi), Lek (an important pharmaceutical company cooperating with Merck & co and Bayer), and others.

The increasingly evident manifestation of these phenomena underlines that this was a sign of the 'Americanisation' of the Yugoslav modernity or even 'Coca Cola socialism'. This moment can end up being perceived through a moralist prism that criticises consumer habits[10] and the import of the American way of life into Yugoslavia. I would challenge this retrospective postmodern fixation on consumption habits and lifestyles due to its failure to address the above structural frame, within which the Yugoslav economy became exposed to the movement of prices and changes in trends on the global market and thus became increasingly dependent on the disciplinary mechanisms of the IMF.[11] At this point, my analysis of the restructuring of socialism becomes comparable with Susan Woodward's evaluation – provided that we define financialisation as a critical point that does not consider the Yugoslav integration into the global system as a one-way ticket to capitalism 'in the sense of a global process' (Kirn 1982: 53), but rather as a system that follows its internal changes and reverse effects.

If anything, a materialist analysis should consider the hybridity of these forms and connections: neither complete fascination with the secondary phenomena (consumption) nor pure belief in the automatic external mechanisms of the global market can answer the question as to how financialisation wormed its way into the Yugoslav economy. Susan Woodward was correct in her assessment that the new economic policy increasingly depended on the 'short-term coverage (through IMF credits), to try to refinance the debt, to cut imports to the bone, and to promote all conceivable commodity exports to hard currency markets in the West' (Woodward 1995b: 51). However, this type of economic policy that originated abroad did not correspond to the general trend of decentralising the Yugoslav economy. As the political authorities were becoming increasingly fragmented and dispersed with regard to monetary affairs (loans, foreign exchange), it was almost 'impossible to have any effective monetary and exchange rate policy, let alone effective industrial and foreign trade policy' (ibid., 59). At this point, we can add that the liberal logic, asserting itself in Yugoslavia, increasingly supported the ideas focused on regional and autarkic republican economies rather than on the federal all-Yugoslav economy. The integration into the global market produced a number of centrifugal effects, leading to the radicalisation of the IMF's demands in the aftermath of the oil crisis and particularly during the 1980s. Susan Woodward believed that these demands implied the breakdown of all innovative elements of the self-management reproduction:

> Of bilateral contracts between suppliers and manufacturers; of payment arrangements through producers' cartels that rationed foreign exchange to prevent production bottlenecks; of corporatist social compacts among firms, governments, and unions to regulate wages and salaries; and of local party and government networks that had developed during the 1960-1972 period. Monetary authority should be returned to the National bank, and the independence of the bank strengthened, so that the government could implement a true macroeconomic policy to manage demand. (ibid., 59).[12]

Economics experts did not agree with the IMF programme. It might seem surprising, but the leaderships and technocracies of the individual republics opposed centralisation and an overly (neo)liberal economy.[13] At the beginning of the 1980s, Yugoslavia started implementing the IMF's recipe that involved a strong autocratic government and market discipline. As history has taught us, this would lead to war and devastation. During the 1970s, the external demands of financial capital did not match the demands of the liberal reformers: while they agreed with the liberalisation process, they by no means supported the repeated centralisation, which aimed to bring power back to the political bureaucracy. Quite paradoxically, the liberal circles, which were in favour of the market reform, opposed any foreign involvement. The rich republics and the national capital kept insisting on political decentralisation and for greater power to be handed over to the republics and companies. Therefore, the IMF's austerity policies and structural programmes failed to bear fruit politically, at least until Tito's death.[14] At the beginning of the 1970s, Yugoslav socialism reached a crossroads: on the one hand, it insisted on a market reform with negative economic consequences (diminished economic growth, inflation, increased borrowing); while on the other hand, the weaknesses of the planned development system (political investments, autarky of the individual provinces) were still being implemented. At this time, the Kosovo example revealed the most brutal antagonisms and the primary contradiction of Yugoslav (under)development.

Underdeveloped Development: The Example of Kosovo and the Breakdown of International Solidarity

Due to the variety of past development and political systems and the severe economic differences in post-war Yugoslavia, one of the key goals of the federal and communist vision was to ensure the smooth functioning of the Investment Fund and its solid redistribution policy of promoting solidarity amongst the republics. Wealth redistribution was a part of the long-term industrial policy, which financed the start-up of large-scale industrial projects in the underdeveloped regions. In his study, Mihajlović (1970) ascertained that the results of fair(er) development can only be established in the long term, and that in provinces so exceedingly different in terms of their economic development, miracles could not take place overnight. Thus, Bosnia and Herzegovina as well as Montenegro saw considerable economic progress between 1947 and 1956. However, Mihajlović underlined that already at that time, the focus should have been on new employment possibilities and improving the business environment. If we solely measured the national income and other economic indicators, we could determine that during the first stage, the underdeveloped regions (including Kosovo) advanced rapidly. However, we can only see the fuller picture if we take into account not only the above-mentioned facts, but also the indicators of social structures as the poorer regions would accumulate negative factors: from their demography, insufficient and expensive infrastructure, and poorer qualifications, through to the poor quality of their cultivated land and poorer export possibilities.[15] A more in-depth analysis reveals that the system of unequal exchange and production had also been included in the initial industrial development: it was exemplified in the system of 'differentiated prices', which favoured certain sorts of industries in the individual regions. On the one hand, the regions betting on capital-intensive industries with finished and export-oriented products would develop further; while, on the other hand, the poorer regions that produced raw materials and supplied the richer regions at subsidised prices would lag behind. We have already mentioned that this was one of the structural reasons for the emergence of labour strikes. According to Samary this system was centrally-managed, and it maintained low energy prices:

> The control of the prices of raw materials and energy, which ensured that the prices of raw materials and energy remained 30% below the average price levels, was initiated in 1954; this control. This was in line with the Investment Fund's policy of favouring this type of production in Kosovo (1988: 79).[16]

The structure of industrial capital and the level of technological and economic development indicate that certain Yugoslav regions adopted the position of the periphery, while others took advantage of their structural advantages in order to secure significant material development.

The new liberal orientation supported greater competitiveness and gave an advantage to the wealthier republics. This was made possible due to the transfer of sovereign powers to the level of the republics, which were in fact becoming autonomous states. The Investment Fund became one of the main targets of attacks of the liberal critics from the richer parts of Yugoslavia, while the federal leadership was reproached for corruption and inefficiency. It is certainly true that some of the money would vanish in the clientelistic networks of the republican and provincial bureaucrats as well as in the largest companies, which protected their positions and investments in large-scale industrial projects. This is still the case nowadays. This 'corruptive' aspect also existed in the period under consideration, even though the boundless belief in the industrial development on the one hand and the market tendency towards the autarky of the individual capitals on the other hand represented two of the more problematic aspects of the management at the time.[17] This was discussed extraordinarily rarely. Instead, the liberal circles started to criticise the fact that the rich republics had to contribute disproportionately significant shares to the central funds. From the statistical point of view, this was true: the richer republics did in fact contribute major shares to the funds – but, on the other hand, they also produced the major share of the national GDP and acquired larger quantities of foreign currencies. The question of development was thus a political rather than merely an expert economistic issue. How could one demand that the Fund be more economically rational and proportional, if this very Fund was supposed to do away with the discrepancies and ensure fairer circumstances for everyone? The Fund struggled against asymmetric relations between development and the past, which was the only possible long-term alternative in the concrete situation. As the liberals criticised the Fund's *raison d'être*, it became clear that this supposedly expert economic argument contained an increasingly apparent and extremely political goal: *the end of solidarity between the republics*. Furthermore, the liberal argument stood on feeble economic foundations. Rastko Močnik claimed that the wealthier republics benefitted considerably from the development of the underdeveloped: who else would have purchased the machines and products from the companies in the developed parts of Yugoslavia, which were far less competitive in the West? The development of the basic infrastructure and the issue of the purchasing power of the labour force in the lesser developed parts of the federation was therefore in the best interest of the wealthier republics. In the short term, the abolition of the Fund weakened the position of the underdeveloped regions; in the medium term, it even implied the partial abandonment of the already developed infrastructure of the lesser developed.

The liberal forces prevailed in the conflict surrounding the Fund, and from its ashes, the 'Development Fund' was born. Its financial role was considerably smaller: as we have already underlined, the economic sovereignty was transferred to the republics, while the lending capacities were placed in the hands of the new banks.[18] This resulted in a new development framework, in which the inter-republican planning was impaired, as the framework had been adapted to the autonomous republican economies. The insistence on decentralisation and market changes in the circumstances of the increasingly severe crisis resulted in the intensified lagging of the Yugoslav economy behind the OECD countries, while market solutions were implemented at a time when greater economic regulation was necessary. However, instead of regulation, they focused on changing the banking regulation, and this became the driving force of the new development. When the economic crisis broke out, the situation was the worst on the periphery. In spite of certain important achievements in the field of industrialisation,[19] Kosovo therefore became an example of 'poor development'.[20] Towards the end of the 1960s, Kosovo became the critical development point, where the republican, federal, and capital forces would fight either for re-centralisation, further decentralisation, or control over the social capital.

The criticism of liberal development does not mean that the (non) functional regional bureaucracy was beyond reproach: it certainly did not do enough to improve employment by organising the social power (Bavčar 1982). Another 'accomplishment' of the local bureaucracy was that it would abuse the topic of economic underdevelopment in order to translate it through the prism of national(istic) interests. In other words, as early as the beginning of the 1970s, class antagonism in the Yugoslav political scene was reoriented towards ethnic conflicts and the culturalisation of the issues (Kirn 1982: 80). In Kosovo, these watershed moments coincided with the first extensive labour strikes, demanding that work conditions be improved, as well as with the nationalistically oriented movement, arguing for a greater recognition of the Albanian nation and Kosovo as a republic. The political oppositions and economic contradictions in Kosovo resulted in a true crisis, during which the 'ongoing' Yugoslav project started manifesting itself in a new manner: the withering central state capacities resulted in the gradual disappearance of solidarity between the republics and the exhaustion of the initial emancipatory idea of a socialist Yugoslavia. A strong tendency towards the decline of socialism brought forward not only the global market in terms of commodities and foreign loans, but also disclosed an antagonistic relationship between the new ruling constellation of technocrats and bureaucrats on one side, and workers and non-workers on the other side. This antagonism and its various expressions will be addressed in the following chapter.

Socialist Reproduction and Self-Management Ideology in Yugoslavia in 1968 and Beyond

According to the prevailing historical studies, the 1960s were the years of the greatest intellectual, cultural, and political thriving in Yugoslavia (Repe 1992). According to some, this was also a period of economic prosperity linked to the commodification of everyday life (Vučetić 2012, Dimitrijević 2016). This period is most frequently identified with various groups and master-signifiers: from the Praxis School (an alternative Marxist theoretical orientation) and Black Wave cinema to strikes and student movements; from performance arts and theatre experimentation to liberal currents within the Party apparatus; and finally, a more open market and greater access to Western products. It seemed that Yugoslav self-management was living up to the image it was promoting abroad: the image of a relatively tolerant and open road to socialism. This retrospective outlook is based on the thesis that this was an embryonic form of the 'open society': the economic reforms that introduced 'market socialism' and resulted in the opening to the West also involved a certain political broad-mindedness and democratisation. Moreover, some commentators are of the opinion that this opening up of Yugoslavia was not radical enough, as Sundhausen (2012) suggested that Yugoslav socialism failed insofar as it did not implement the market reform's legal framework more consistently. This section will focus on the fundamental changes in the ideological-legal landscape of socialist reproduction during this period and underline a few dramatic turning points that heralded the break-up of Yugoslavia.

One needs to keep in mind that the opening towards the West did not come solely from the outside but was implemented from within and therefore changed the self-management apparatus and ideology. Self-management cannot be seen as a definite rupture and an invention of the independent Yugoslav road to socialism, but one should also understand how it became the 'ruling ideology' that was then tilted in various directions.[1] This understanding of ideology does not imply a purely instrumentalist approach, in which the masses were manipulated and followed the ideas of Tito and his closest entourage. The ideology should be seen as a part of the material infrastructure: as Althusser argued, it has a 'material existence'[2] and is based on the operation of institutions and their rituals. The belief in self-management resulted from all of the social relations involved in the self-management system. It was closely connected with the ideological apparatuses of the state and represented the key social connection between the collective and the individual. By means of material practices of the reproduction apparatuses, ideology leaves its mark – one of the most visible of these being, of course, the ideological subject that relies on the legal subject.[3]

This can be well followed through the major changes within the dominant ideological formation of 'self-management' that occurred during the 1960s. Even if self-management was the most important ideological formation that grew through legal documents, political institutions, and economic practices, we can trace its heterogenous aspects: from elements of anti-Stalinism and anti-fascism, decentralisation and the critique of bureaucracy, to Marx's focus on the association of producers, industrial productivism, liberalism, and other ideological influences. The 'ruling ideology' means that self-management became ubiquitous, which Marx defined as 'a particular ether which determines the specific gravity of every being which has materialised within it' (Marx 1985: 37). The dominance of this ideology was further reflected in the specific pragmatism of the ruling class, who applied the term 'self-management' to all social changes and political-economic reforms. During the first period of self-management, which lasted until 1965, egalitarianism and a balanced development of all republics were the decisive principles of the self-management ideology as represented by the political bureaucracy. However, according to the perspective of 'decentralisation', a strong and liberal ideological framework was formed and represented by the technocracy with its expert knowledge and technical expertise. Thus, very dissimilar and even opposing ideological positions as well as political, expert, and scientific discourses would be translated into self-management, even at the official level. We should nevertheless not forget that one should not equate the 'ruling ideology' and the 'ideology of the ruling class'. The latter would acquire various emphases in different periods: from revolutionary socialism and partisan internationalism to democratic centralism and even Stalinism, liberalism, and, last but not least, nationalism. Even though there is a connection between the 'ruling ideology' and the 'ruling class', it is not necessarily a direct one: the ideology of the ruling class is not 'totalitarian' and cannot be isolated from society and propped up as an external manipulator of the entire society. Even though Stalinism was the prevalent ideological position of the Party leadership during the historical period at the end of the 1940s, returning in the wave of repressions at the beginning of the 1970s, this does not imply that Stalinism remained the (only) ideology of the ruling class, as this ideology was opposed in various political and economic deliberations and struggles for domination within the political apparatus. In the previous chapters (Chapters 9–11), I pointed out the historical formations of class society within the 'market self-management', starting with bureaucracy as the only political representative (social capital) and proceeding to the amalgamation of bureaucracy and technocracy (independent capital). At this point, technocracy became the ruling class.

As a rule, the ruling class asserts itself by dominating the productive relations and appropriating value. At the same time, the ideological hegemony of the ruling class enjoys 'relative autonomy' from its structural place in the mode of production, which means that the causal relationship does not go merely in one direction (objectivism). The ideological hegemony, on the other hand, asserts itself in view of internal and external 'challenges' and struggles, during which particular divergences from and recuperations of anti-hegemonic positions take place. Therefore, the relations between the productive process and the ruling class can only be dissected through the analysis of the hybrid forms and temporary class alliances that ensure the reproduction of the existing social relations. The ruling class is thus not the only driving force that can exert control over all of the ideological apparatuses. Instead, according to Althusser, the class struggle is at its most dynamic precisely in the field of ideology. Ideological struggles take place on a daily basis: they are a part of the constant patchwork of provisional results of the struggles that keep ensuring its legitimacy.

In the previous chapters we have demonstrated that even the major social contract and the central tenet of egalitarian social development (socialist industrialisation) was eventually challenged and replaced by a more competitive developmental model. Then again, even if such drastic changes to the Yugoslav self-management were indeed at play, a strong belief seemed to exist that an improved legal framework for self-management and pluralist interests could mitigate the conflicting forces and tensions and bring about actual communism. Could one argue that the legal and contractual tradition remained one of the major blind spots of the Yugoslav self-management ideologues who saw socialist law as the key social mechanism and moral supplement that would mould and direct the changes in production relations?

The law and the contractual legal tradition were undoubtedly extremely elaborate. In terms of their content, the majority of the developments contained openly 'communist' elements: from social ownership to the fascinating legal term of 'associated labour', which brought together the producers and the consumers; from the expropriation and ultimately socialisation of the means of production, to workers' self-management, which eventually spread to all aspects of social reproduction. I am more fascinated by the naive belief of the socialist authorities that legal contents by themselves would result in communism, rather than by the 'communist contents' per se. It seems that the socialist ideologues ascribed legal acts from the political and economic relations with the actual and formal power of abstraction – as if they spontaneously adopted the belief that the mere legal form was something neutral, without any conflicts or pitfalls. The fundamental recipe for development could thus be summarised with the formula 'industrial modernisation + the withering away of the state by means of law' – with the latter succumbing to severe difficulties at the moment when the economic crisis broke out and the market reform took place. The withering away of the state, which can be understood as the dismantling of the bureaucratic monopoly and centralisation, does not mean that the state did not exist in Yugoslav socialism. In fact, we could claim that multiple states – republics – emerged within Yugoslavia and practiced a large degree of political autonomy, while technocratic domination meant the strengthening of independent capitals and weakening of state's ability to manage social capital.

Even though the market reform period 'boasted' of the creation of numerous excellent legal documents that expanded the political decision-making of the workers and everyone who contributed to the self-management society to the level of the entire system of social reproduction, this did not mean that these legal documents were also observed in practice.[4] Thus, Igor Bavčar was, in spite of the recognised importance of social property, right to claim that ownership relations were legal-formal relations, meanwhile the moment of managing the actual production circumstances remained something completely different (in Mauke 1982: 8). The greatest obstacle to the development of social property, supervised by the workers, was the blockade within the social management apparatuses.[5] In other words, the legal documents and policies of the Party organisations by no means guaranteed the sanctioning of the informal class balance of power, established within the social property regime. As it was, the market changes were promoted by the official policies themselves! Even though, during the first two decades, the industrialisation formula and the legal systematisation of self-management yielded decent socio-economic results as well as ensuring a political consolidation that did not antagonise the working people, the theoretical 'consistency' of this formula was severely shaken by the very first serious economic crisis that followed the market reform as well as by the political answers to the exploitation 'from below' – i.e., the exploitation that resulted from the increasing number of those who had no access to work (surplus population) and had to either lead a miserable existence or leave the state (as migrant workers).

There is an openly antagonistic and class-based character that can be followed through what Lebowitz has called the socialist 'contested reproduction' – that is, through the social processes and relations that took place in the realm of the state apparatus, law, and ideology. In the previous chapters, I argued that it is not enough to measure the 'degree of exploitation' of workers in socialist Yugoslavia during the 1960s.[6] The class struggle is not simply measured as a statistical index or defined through a sphere of consumption that became increasingly apparent in the late 1960s (Vučetić 2012). Class struggle and its fundamental principle – exploitation – are to be found in social relations and material conditions that need to be considered from the 'standpoint of reproduction'. Balibar correctly pointed out the following:

As opposed to the production of things, the production of social relations is not subject to the determinations of the preceding and the succeeding, of the 'first' and the 'second'. Marx writes that 'every process of social production is at the same time a process of reproduction. The conditions of production are also those of reproduction'; and at the same time they are the conditions which reproduction reproduces: in this sense the 'first' process of production (in a determinate form) is always-already a process of reproduction. (1970: 271).

However, the 'standpoint of reproduction' needs to be understood with the clear awareness that in spite of the market reforms, this took place within the socialist framework, capable of regulating the flows of capital and labour through an array of political institutions – i.e. it was capable of restraining the proto-capitalist logic and imposing a different temporality. Moreover, the standpoint of reproduction became dialectical in so far as it took into account not only the ideological figures and the dominant ideology, but also the resistances that materialised during the struggles of the working people and other political subjects.

Due to spatial constraints, I will focus solely on the most symptomatic indicators of the changing ideological figures of self-management and the political subjectivities that expressed dissatisfaction with the proto-capitalist tendencies and the official ideology. Ideological figures exhibit symptoms of social divisions, meaning that these 'master-signifiers' do not represent the ultimate ideological principle, but rather a way of developing and manifesting the strengths of the 'position of enunciation'. In the socialist state, the key investment was indisputably embodied in the figure of the *worker* and the *working people*. This can be followed through the analysis of the media, legal documents, political texts, and, last but not least, the role ascribed to this political subject with the arrival of communism. However, did the working people remain the main political figure even after the introduction of the market reform? Was the self-management ideology still controlled by the vanguard subject of the proletariat that supposedly carried out the revolutionary project together with the Party? Even a fleeting glance at the official documents from the congresses of the League of Communists of Yugoslavia, the Yugoslav Constitutions, and the texts written by the main ideologue Edvard Kardelj is sufficient[7] to ascertain that even the 'official' line of socialist leadership would not always talk about the working class, let alone a homogenous and sole political subject: the Party (headed by Tito). Moreover, in the political discourse as well as in everyday situations, we can identify the heterogeneity and plurality of political figures that resulted from the long-term ideological struggles and protests within and on the outside of the League of Communists.

My thesis is that the new ideological figures developed their legitimacy and positions of enunciation with the arrival of the market reform and the mass protests at the end of the 1960s. At the time, numerous political referents gained public recognition that could roughly be divided into three new figures: *firstly, the figure of man* in the sense of re-interpreting the young Marx (the Praxis School) and the subsequent Party re-appropriations; *secondly, the figure of the market*, later also self-management communities of interest and pluralism (liberalism); and *thirdly*, the emergence of the *figure of the nation* and thus national-ism, which fatally undermined the partisan ruptures and the initial social contract. These figures clearly indicate that we are no longer dealing merely with a strict class moment and a connection with the level of pro-duction, but rather that the focus shifted towards ethnic dimensions and the level of general reproduction. The 1974 Constitution of the Socialist Federal Republic of Yugoslavia is by all means the most important political document that dates back to the end of the market reform. In this Constitution, matters became complicated as soon as it came to the key subject of sovereignty and political activities. What was the supreme body in which the socialist forces and efforts were invested? The 1974 Constitution stated that in Yugoslavia, all 'working people, nations, and nationalities' (Ustav SFRJ, 1974: 4) held 'sovereign rights' and that 'all authority belongs to the working class together with all the working people living in the cities and villages' (ibid., 483). Somewhat later, the signifying chain of holders of sovereignty was also joined by 'citizens' or 'residents'.[8] To sum this up: the working class, the working people, city municipalities and village communes, citizens and residents, nations, and nationalities were all holders of sovereign rights and authority. These definitions are within the scope of the aforementioned hypoth-esis, meaning that three different principles were at work when it came to sovereign subjects: firstly, the working class/the working people, who belonged to the sphere of production and the classic Marxist theory; secondly, citizens-residents as a liberal category, who were now included in the broader social reproduction, stemming from the expanded self-management, and who announced the habitus and the everyday life and activities; and thirdly, the nations and nationalities, which heralded the re-emergence of the ethnic principle and the decline of the initial principle of 'brotherhood and unity'. In short, the 1974 Constitution of the Socialist Federal Republic of Yugoslavia can also be interpreted as a historical compromise between the key ideological positions and political groups that developed during the decade of market reforms. The Constitution thus appeased the extremes of the technocracy and bureaucracy on the one hand and the post-1968 leftist and rightist oppo-sition on the other.

From Worker to Man and the Leftist Opposition as
the Key Driving Force of 'True' Self-Management

In the previous sections, workers were presented either as a mass of uncon-
nected producers, excluded from the self-management institutions,[9] or
through the sporadic (self)organisation during labour strikes and other
forms of resistance. With the introduction of the self-management
political apparatus and the development of the workers' state, the referents of the working class and the working people became increasingly
empty terms – mere placeholders in whose name official policies were
implemented. The constant use and implementation of the apparatuses
resulted in the ideological over-saturation with the figure of the worker,
which became the air that everyone breathed and would therefore often
trigger a superior or even a severely ironic attitude amongst the 'cultural
critics'. During the period in which the social contract was crumbling,
this ideological over-saturation was one of the reasons for the additional
ideological crisis of the figure and politics of the working class.

However, this ritualisation of the working class was not the only fundamental political and theoretical problem to have arisen. The critical
question, best articulated by the representatives of the leftist opposition within the self-management system, was the following: how could
the new communist critique intervene in a political system that, on the
declarative level, represented the anti-system (self-management as the
withering away of the state) and ideologically argued for the same goals
of universal emancipation, socialist revolution, and empowerment of the
working class? In the mid-1960s, the League of Communists' 'position
of enunciation' was challenged by three major political agents: firstly, by
the critical and alternative currents within the sphere of the politicised
culture (especially within the so-called Black Wave film, see Kirn 2012b);
secondly, by the dissident Marxist Praxis school who organised annual
gatherings of Western and Eastern Marxists on the Croatian island of
Korčula (Marković and Cohen 1975) – the 1968 meeting carrying the
title 'Marx and Revolution'; and thirdly, the greatest political response
was embodied in the labour strikes and the student movement. These
three agents remained heterogeneous and loosely connected – i.e., the
revolutionary situation in 1968 did not produce any new lasting political
bodies that would challenge the Party as a political bloc. I would nevertheless argue that these groups and movements occupied a space
that, albeit tentatively, produced a triangulation between art, politics,

and theory. This triangulation with what were clearly mass elements and a revolutionary programme (of the student movement) bore some resemblance to the 'partisan ruptures' while there were at least two major differences in comparison to the previous partisan ruptures. Most importantly, the new partisan triangulation that emerged at the end of the 1960s occurred in very different historical circumstances, for it took place during the global wave of criticism aimed at the existing authoritarian order, colonial legacy, and imperialism, but also as a specific critique of the Yugoslav 'market socialism'. Secondly, this new partisan triangulation did not have any lasting effects as it did not lead to an encounter between the progressive forces, the masses, and the new (or old) political bodies. Instead, we are dealing with sporadically strong but isolated political events and the dissemination of artworks and theoretical texts that created a progressive framework for the left-wing opposition.

Despite their 'weak messianic power' (Majewska 2016), the events of June 1968 presented a political rupture within Yugoslavia that was, on the one hand, seen as an expression of solidarity and an extension of the global events, whilst on the other hand it represented a specific response to the very particular constellation of the Yugoslav market self-management that had explicitly attempted to tackle the failing socialist development in light of the worsening economic crisis, ever higher numbers of migrant workers, and rising unemployment. This is why the student demands never focused merely on the autonomy of knowledge and increased rights for the student population. The students did not subscribe to any nationalist or anti-communist slogans and would not be seen as protagonists of the market mentality. On the contrary, if we analyse the majority of their slogans and demands, we can note an expression of a genuine and broadly left-wing opposition – a communist critique of socialism and the global order. The examples of the most popular slogans/demands included 'We want more communism, not this kind of authoritarian socialism' while the appeal 'Down with the red bourgeoisie!' was particularly suggestive. One of the most expressive symbolic documents of the period can be found in Želimir Žilnik's film *June Turmoil*, which was filmed during the student uprisings on 4 and 5 June 1968. Due to the agility and willingness of his film crew, Žilnik, at the time a young and critical filmmaker, was able to document the events at the newly-renamed Karl Marx Red University and its epicentre, the Faculty of Philosophy, which announced a seven-day strike and the occupation of various faculties. The students in Belgrade also adopted a resolution programme that aimed to attain certain genuine self-management rights and goals (see Alcoy/Olujić 2018). Four major demands were made that explicitly addressed the increasingly apparent 'social inequality' that could be resolved by distribution alone: the 'increasing unemployment' and the existence of temporary and flexible employment, which should be abolished, as well as the 'strong bureaucratic forces' and the need for the democratisation of the political space. Finally, the students demanded that their situation should be improved. The discussions became increasingly radicalised, and for the first time since Yugoslavia was formed, the leadership headed by Tito was openly – if somewhat ambivalently – challenged. Dragomir Olujić – Oluja was one of the organisers of these events. He discussed the major stakes involved in renaming the University of Belgrade into the Karl Marx Red University, taking into account the context of Tito:

> If we are to address the issue of Tito as an undisputable authority, we need to define our positions in relation to him … you might have noticed that on our posters Tito was depicted wearing a partisan uniform … during which Tito's role was indeed undisputable. Secondly, at the beginning of 1968 there was an initiative to rename the University of Belgrade after Tito; thus, one of the reasons we have renamed it the 'Karl Marx Red University' was to put an end to this initiative! (Alcoy/Olujić 2018).

Student protests gradually spread to other major university cities – Sarajevo, Zagreb, and Ljubljana – where assemblies and protests were organised in front of the university buildings. The socialist leadership was aware that the situation was grave as it was facing an escalation that could result in the general discontent of society, which could potentially not be solved by police repression and the local authorities. Plamenić (1969) argued that this was a dramatic event that could be best described as 'insurgence'. As soon as the student general assembly in Belgrade called for a seven-day strike and started to protest in the streets, showing solidarity with workers, the leadership decided to intervene. On 9 June, Tito addressed the students across the country. He recognised the downfall of the socialist authorities who failed to address the students as political subjects and admitted that their criticism of the material conditions and employment problems was well founded. He also stated that the rising inequalities and 'all those questions of investments and the pursuits of investments have clouded our thoughts ... which made us forget about the people. However, we cannot make objects without people'.[10] Tito's speech also steered clear of interpreting the student protests as a foreign intervention conspiracy and instead thanked the students and the working people for their constructive criticism and asked for their future assistance in building a better society. Tito concluded his speech by suggesting that if he was unable to 'resolve these issues, then I should not hold this position any longer'. One becomes almost nostalgic if one compares this speech to the discourses of the current leaders such as Macron, Trump, or May, even though the political function of Tito's speech needs to be understood clearly: in order to appease the sharper revolutionary criticism and neutralise its political potential, he recognised the general plea of the students. This recognition did not remain purely on the symbolic level, for it led to the adoption of two new laws a few days later. The Central Committee of the League of Communists in Belgrade first adopted an act that doubled the minimum wage and came into force the following month; then it implemented the Trainees Act which forced companies and state institutions to employ a certain percentage of young high school and university graduates.

Both the students and the workers received Tito's speech and the announced laws enthusiastically and saw them as successful results of their protests. In the following years, students were granted greater autonomy and became more active within the University structures, while an array of student cultural centres, student publishers, and even a student radio station (Radio Študent) were established in Ljubljana. This was a historical sign that it was possible to democratise socialism and that confrontations with the socialist leadership could bear fruit other than repression. However, in the longer-term, the potential revolutionary encounter between the student protests and labour strikes was prevented and the mass student protests were neutralised (Black & Red correspondents, 1968). Student movements still continued to sporadically emerge across Yugoslavia, but they were now seen more as temporary affairs carried out by smaller groups of engaged students. Student assemblies and occupations kept occurring until 1972[11] when the core group was arrested and put on trial in Belgrade, while some of the most critical professors connected to the Praxis Marxist group were banned from teaching at University level (Marković and Cohen, 1975). The openly repressive side of the socialist authorities – from the softer forms of pressure and censorship to arrests and expulsions – manifested itself after a delay, at a time when the 1968 revolt had already faded away.

The 1968 revolt was immensely 'educational' for all left-wing revolutionary forces within and outside of the Party: what was to be done when the proclamation and its contents were occupied by an alleged revolutionary agent (the League of Communists) headed by the partisan veteran Tito, who defeated Hitler and Stalin, but was now seen to increasingly often struggle for the control of the state apparatus by ritualising the authorities and emptying the radicalism of self-management figures? The defeat of 1968 and its aftermath was not so much a result of the rise of neoliberalism (as retrospectively stated by Boltanski and Chiapello, 2007), as it was a result of the inability of the left-wing progressive and mostly anti-authoritarian forces to produce a permanent political body that could confront the state power. When Althusser wrote his essay on Ideological State Apparatuses, he was not interested in how ideology and the apparatuses functioned and transformed individuals into subjects, instead, he wanted to understand what had led the events of May 1968 to fail. He derived a strong lesson on the relationship between the dominant class and state as allegedly neutral agents in the mediation of the class struggle:

> Class struggle, where one class is powerful and violent only because it is the dominant class, in other words, exercises its force and violence upon another class (which is also a force) that it must, in a never-ending struggle, hold in check if it is to maintain the upper hand over it. The relatively stable resultant (reproduced in its stability by the state) of this *confrontation* of forces (*balance* of forces is an accountant's notion, because it is static) is that *what counts is the dynamic excess of force* maintained by the dominant class in the class struggle. It is *this excess of conflictual force, real or potential, which constitutes energy A*, which is subsequently transformed into power by the state-machine: *transformed into right, laws and norms.* (Althusser 2006: 109).

If the new left was serious in its criticism, it should have pursued the struggle more ambitiously and persistently. In the event that the contemporaneous socialist authorities indeed merely preached rather than implemented truly socialist policies, the new left should have taken Tito's statement that he would give up the power seriously and risked an existential engagement. At this point, it was clear that Tito and his 'partisan' generation had clung to power for too long, thus blocking the regeneration of the socialist movement, while the certain quandary within the 'anti-authoritarian' position – its preference not to take over power – also came to light. It seems that the connection with the working class – the union between the left-wing movement and the striking workers – remained unrealised, while the red bureaucracy could only barely appease the situation by adopting declarations and ensuring minor improvements to the material circumstances.

The alternative cultural critique – which, however, cannot be retroactively equated with anti-communism,[12] even though a decisive distancing from the working class can indeed be noted – contributed to the political discourse paradox of the new left. This distancing is not a matter of aesthetics or a struggle against social realism, however it can be perceived as a reaction to the ideological over-saturation. At the time, the most symptomatic points of the new alternative 'interpellations' manifested themselves most visibly in the so-called 'Black Wave' films, which pointed out the failures and digressions of the socialist transition by presenting the existing self-management system in the characteristic 'dark' colours. Ironically or realistically, these films revealed the gap between the ideals and the reality of self-management,[13] while simultaneously introducing new types of anti-heroes into the world of film – protagonists for whom there was no room in new socialism or who expressed hopelessness in light of the declared optimistic will and the new man. Apart from introducing the new anti-hero figure, most of these films also presented the figure of the worker and the places of work (factories) in a negative manner: the workers were portrayed either as the victims of the local Party dignitaries or as gullible masses that could be easily manipulated with a bit of cheap entertainment.[14] In their own way, these film depictions took part in the deterioration of the figure of the worker, dominant at the time – which could, on the symbolic level, be referred to as a subversion. However, this failed to ensure any progressive political effects: at best, these works contributed to the depoliticisation of the workers and their potential allies in society. Only exceptionally would critical works of art – more specifically, Black Wave films – attempt to re-appropriate the figure of the working class.

It is hard to draw a line under the political and theoretical position of the political (students) and artistic left, but generally we could say that they were closer to the more anarchic theorisations of freedom and emancipation, to positions outside of Party politics, and to other sorts of political organisation (movements, protests, labour strikes). The figure of the (yet again) new and true man probably represents the most reflected-upon theoretical-political consideration of the 'new left'. Man became the key designation of the incomplete emancipation of self-management and the referent that paved the way beyond the ideological hegemony embodied in the League of Communists. The humanist-Marxist school and the Praxis magazine group – consisting of a number of philosophy lecturers (Gajo Petrović, Predrag Vranicki, Mihajlo Marković, Milan Kangrga, Zagorka Golubović, Svetozar Stojanović) and related researchers in the field of sociology (e.g. Rudi Supek) as well as economics (e.g. Branko Horvat) – were the most deserving for this ideological breakthrough. For our current purposes, the most important theses of the Praxis representatives can be identified by reading the early writings of Marx, while, speaking more broadly, they can be seen as the Yugoslav version of the Frankfurt School or certain tendencies in Western Marxism (Stojaković 2012: 50–55). The Praxis school became globally famous for its summer school, which it organised on the island of Korčula between 1963 and 1973, and which was attended by the most important Marxist representatives from the West (e.g. Bloch, Mandel, Fromm, Lefebvre, Habermas, Fink) as well as from the East (e.g. Kołakowski, Heller, Kosik, Marek). The basic theoretical-political orientation of the Praxis school was best summed up by one of its founders, Mihajlo Marković:

> Man is essentially a being of praxis, i.e., a being capable of free activity by which he transforms the world, realises his specific potential faculties, and satisfies the needs of other human individuals (Marković 1975: xxviii).

The members of the Praxis school argued that an individual's activity and development should represent the foundations upon which one can begin to build the collective's activity (Tadić and Horvat et al. 1975: 406). This did not involve merely a deviation from the position of the working people, but also a transition from the collective to the individual, which went against the ideological constellation of the League of Communists. Instead of the working class, Praxis underlined and focused on the conception of man as described in the early writings of Marx, which had only begun to be translated and published at the time. Let us refer to a single characteristic excerpt from Marx's *The German Ideology*, which functioned as a political-exploratory announcement of the Praxis school's efforts and argued in favour of realising man's capabilities:

> [...] while in communist society, where nobody has one exclusive sphere of activity but each can become accomplished in any branch he wishes, society regulates the general production and thus makes it possible for me to do one thing today and another tomorrow, to hunt in the morning, fish in the afternoon, rear cattle in the evening, criticise after dinner, just as I have a mind, without ever becoming hunter, fisherman, shepherd or critic. This fixation of social activity, this consolidation of what we ourselves produce into a material power above us, growing out of our control, thwarting our expectations, bringing to naught our calculations, is one of the chief factors in historical development up till now. The social power, i.e., the multiplied productive force, which arises through the co-operation of different individuals as it is caused by the division of labour, appears to these individuals, since their co-operation is not voluntary but has come about naturally, not as their own united power, but as an alien force existing outside them, of the origin and goal of which they are ignorant, which they thus are no longer able to control, which on the contrary passes through a peculiar series of phases and stages independent of the will and the action of man. (*MECW*, vol. 5: 47–8).

The new man in the new communist society would supposedly finally control his productive capabilities and put a stop to the estrangement process. This understanding of man is fundamentally linked to the reinterpretation of 'praxis' as a creative human activity of self-realisation, based on the universality and the utopic dimension of man as praxis rather than merely the subject of property and the law.[15]

Ozren Pupovac assesses that Praxis humanism rests on the central notion of man as not 'confined to the finite conditions of nature or society; but rather, it is a matter of affirming the infinitude of human capacities for thinking and acting' (Pupovac 2011). The Praxis school projected radical subjectivity onto the figure of man, where human freedom supposedly consisted of the signifying chain of equivalents for thinking – will – action – self-fulfilment. The radical humanism of the school rejected the biological definition of the human essence and the naive anthropologisation of man, but remained at least partially loyal to the tradition of the anthropological-eschatological orientation of the early

Marx. At this point I agree with Slavoj Žižek's critique, in which he determines that the problematic core of Praxis' 'Heideggerian Marxism' lies in the maintenance of the 'naive belief' in the existing self-management. As Žižek's wrote: the Praxis school positivised 'the essence of modern man, which was supposed to be the internal essence of self-management' (Žižek 2000: 113). In their early period the members of the Praxis school remained politically dedicated to the idea of communism and did not argue for the abolition of self-management. Also, they were staunch critics of nationalism and wished that conditions would be ensured in a self-management system for individuals to realise their full potentials. However, while their political orientation was in the early phase not questionable,[16] their theories proved problematic at the point where man's realisation had to be ensured in the broader struggle for the abolition of the division of labour within socialism. This point has a bearing on any construction of a socialist alternative that calls for long-term intellectual and political efforts. This monumental effort could not be initiated merely by the theoretical appeal of the Praxis school to realise human capabilities. Instead, it should have been accompanied by politics aimed at changing the material circumstances – in short, by a political organisation within or outside of the Party. If the critique regarding the division of labour is intellectual, then its political abolition must not remain only on the theoretical level.

As the work at hand also stems from an Althusserian perspective, the Praxis school's critical insistence on a theoretical humanism that solely politically envisions the process of estrangement can be seen to be rather self-evident. The appeals to the figure of the abstract man push certain aspects of the Praxis philosophy back to the liberal horizon of the legal subject of the Universal Declaration of Human Rights. The man of Praxis does not only wish to conclude a contract and be equal in the eyes of the law, for he also wants to develop his potential. Just like the young Marx, the Praxis school was interested in human emancipation, ingrained in the radical line of the heritage of the Enlightenment.[17] The major shortcoming of the Praxis school was its complete lack of analysis of class antagonisms in socialist Yugoslavia. Since Praxis thinkers believed in something similar to genuine self-management, they promoted the full development of man, which meant that they substituted political economy for political emancipation. In the main texts written by the Praxis thinkers we can note a deviation from the social and economic rights towards political freedoms and communication rights.[18] Let us not forget: the Praxis thesis of emancipation always starts with the individual and only proceeds to collective emancipation in its second stage. As if after becoming conscious of the processes of estrangement, here – in the self-management world – people would realise what the mechanisms were and conceive their true (self-management) essence.

Regardless of the idealistic-humanistic core of the Praxis school members, their theoretical interventions were not left without any material effects. Moreover, some of their critical discussions encouraged broader political discussions and enriched the artistic production as well as the student movements towards the end of the 1960s. With its theoretical work, the Praxis school opened a new theoretical space. In those revolutionary years, the school became the intellectual counter-apparatus that kept introducing new ideas amongst the student population. We could even claim that it started undermining the intellectual-ideological primate of the Party. As I have previously mentioned, the socialist authorities' responses to criticism were initially politically calculated and the critiques were partly integrated into the obstruction of 'market socialism'. However, a few years down the line, the Party leadership would retaliate against the representatives of the 'new left'. Following a wave of arrests of student leaders and the prohibition of the works by certain visible representatives of the Praxis school at the University of Belgrade, the summer school on the island of Korčula was also abolished. Despite the tragic end of the Praxis school in 1973–74, the new orientation of the LCY adopted certain elements of the humanist discourse, at least on the ideological level. By emphasising the right to self-management as the most sacred of all *human* rights, while expanding the spectrum of the working people to the level of citizens (residents), paradigmatic shifts occurred with the introduction of the 1974 Constitution of the SFRY. However, the right to self-management was defined rather loosely:

> The right of the working people and citizens to self-management shall be untouchable and inalienable. This ensures that everyone can reach decisions with regard to their personal and common interests within the organisations of associated labour, local communities ... as well as all other forms of self-management and mutual association (Ustav SFRJ,1974: 529).

The focus was therefore placed on the working *people's* right to political engagement and, in particular, on their right to reach decisions with regard to their *personal* and common interests. The political aspects of the self-management apparatus, where the working *people* and *citizens* could realise their self-management goals, were also listed.

A few years later, when the Party was eager to relativise its revolutionary past, the figure of man became an even clearer item on the agenda of the official socialist politics. The works of Edvard Kardelj rarely mention the union of the working class and the proletarian dictatorship (Kardelj 1977), however, terms such as self-management interests, consensus and agreement between the self-management workers, and even the search for happiness gradually made their way to the forefront (ibid., 174–6). Let me quote from a speech Kardelj delivered in 1976:

> The happiness of man does not depend on the state, the system, or political party, but on man himself – not the man per se, but in the context of equal relations with others. In these relations, man needs to freely and in a self-managed way (control) master his particular and general social relations – and through appropriate democratic organisational forms also the state, system, and political party as the instruments of his self-management practice. The vanguard of socialism ... has a single goal: to create conditions – in relation to a given historical moment – in which man will be free in his personal expression and creation (production), and that he will – under the social ownership of the means of production – work and create freely in order to pursue his happiness. This is self-management. (Kardelj in Stanković 1977).

Kardelj did not refer to an 'abstract man', but suggested a new figure of an 'actual human' and underlined the 'personal happiness' of the individual rather than that of the entire society as the goal of self-management. With this move towards the self-management atomism of interests, the shift away from class-related issues was signalled by the party ideologue himself. Later in his life, Kardelj even stated that true self-management would not be implemented by Tito or the Party, but by the 'individuals' themselves: 'We all suffer from the same illusion ... that we can find a miraculous system, institution, parliament, a single or multiple parties, all of which can – through ministries or similar mechanisms – solve the problem of human happiness' (ibid., 175. In *Borba* 1977). Self-manager thus becomes the holder of all social functions, to paraphrase Marx, a bureaucrat in the morning, a technocrat in the afternoon, a collective agitator in the evening, a cultural worker during the night, and a good parent throughout. It is impossible not to recognise the ironic 'return of the repressed' man from the Praxis philosophy in Kardelj's humanism, at a time when the political horizon began openly adopting the Euro-communist tendency.[19]

Liberalism and the Figure of the Market

The market reform period was light years away from totalitarian univocality. We could describe it as a very open political, economic, and ideological phenomenon of liberalism[20] that developed as an internal criticism of socialist progress – partly as a result of the appearance of the first pragmatic applications of nationalist arguments related to the status of the republics and their economic sovereignty. The following section will focus on liberalism.

In Yugoslavia, liberalism emerged from the unproblematic acceptance of the logic of self-management development, decentralisation, and the market. It gained its political expression in the middle of the 1960s when the federal regulation renounced the solidarity between the republics. Jasna Dragović-Sosso was right when she claimed that 'different conceptions of "Yugoslavisms" in the course of the 1960s as essentially unifying notions were effectively abandoned ... in favour of the affirmation of Yugoslavia's national diversity and the call for economic decentralisation' (Dragović-Sosso 2002: 29). The fact that the political bureaucracy was losing its social power did not mean that this power was assumed by the workers. As I have already demonstrated, the new holders of social power were to be found predominantly within the triangle between the directors of companies, new banks, and local political functionaries, who were politically active in the republican sphere, and supported regional development that consequently enhanced national awareness.[21] This explains the importance that was given to the discussion on the 'fairness' of the national product and foreign currency distribution, which led to the first paralysis of the federation and the crisis of national relations between the republican and federal institutions.[22]

The end of the 1960s was the most symptomatic period for liberalism in Slovenia. It was characterised by one of the most resounding scandals that shook the relations between the nations and announced the retaliation against the liberal orientations within the Party apparatus. The dispute related to the highway scandal was provoked by the schedule envisioned for the allocation of the enormous IMF loans to the republics and local communities where the highways were to be constructed.[23] The distribution of the substantial loans was subject to a silent agreement based on the national criterion: if a republic did not get a loan in the first round, it would receive one in the subsequent round. In 1969, the Slovenian delegation expected to get a part of the loan to finance various sections of the highway; however, the money was allocated to other parts of Yugoslavia. A part of the Slovenian delegation was not present at this meeting; thus, the decision was not properly presented to the public and a communication breakdown occurred between the federal and republican leadership. Over the following days, a media frenzy focused on the exceptional 'priorities' of the centre and the underprivileged position of Slovenia. This was followed by official meetings on local levels, which were 'directly' affected by the loans. In the local and regional committees of the League of Communists of Slovenia, one could hear – for the first time since World War II – openly nationalist statements about 'the southerners', the exploitation of the Slovenian economy by the centre, the unfair distribution of the national product, the excessive and inefficient implementation of the federal budget, and even some calls for the independence of Slovenia. Despite the extraordinary public and media spectacle and the general support for the liberal demands in the context of the motorway scandal, these events did not trigger any mass manifestations in Slovenia. Instead, they provoked a competition within the League of Communists of Slovenia, in which the prevailing liberal line attempted to further the demands for a greater autonomy of the republics. At that time, the liberal line – in ideological agreement with the Croatian comrades – demanded a confederacy that would *de facto* set up the material circumstances for the secession of the republics.

The dominance of the liberal lines within the League of Communists was characteristically summarised by Bakarić, one of the leading economic theorists and communists, who stated the following after the Congress of Self-Managed Workers in 1971: 'We could say that we communists were in the minority within our own organisation regarding a series of issues' (1983: 518). This meant that Tito and Kardelj's inner circle had to acknowledge the ideological power and push for a more liberal governance, as well as temporarily concede to the demands for a political reorganisation and greater autonomy of the republics. Certain points of the liberal response reveal a post-Fordist tendency that was supposed to replace the industrial development[24] while arguing for entre-preneurship, efficiency, and flexibility, along with the newly-introduced term 'innovations'. The economist Ermin Kržišnik claimed that the Slovenian economy should focus on banking, the service industry, research, efficient use of its geostrategic and transit location, exclusive small-scale industry, engineering, and computer science. The liberal paradigm focused on increasing accountability to particular entrepre-neurial interests. However, Tito and his closest associates in the federal political apparatus were not prepared to give in to the demands that would radicalise the market reform and strengthen the liberal line even further. This resulted in a counter-offensive by the old leadership, which 'disciplined' the liberal leaderships and personnel in the repub-lican leagues of communists. The liberal resolution of the crises was hereby suspended, and the forces of technocracy were at least temporar-ily defeated. Tito skilfully used the arguments that originated from the students' and workers' protests, criticising the 'red bureaucracy' and the increasing differences between the republics. Despite this purge, which demonstrated the power of the innermost leadership of the Central Committee of the Communist Party of Yugoslavia, Tito's circle did not strengthen the federal institutions with the new orientation. Although the market reform did not continue with the same pace, the commercial banks and republics remained the main holders of social power within the new development. In the governing discourse, the adjective 'market' was replaced by 'contractual' socialism of self-management interests,[25] while the economic policy remained dedicated to the proven concept of industrialisation with market elements, which continued to obstruct the workers' self-management.

Nationalism and the Subject of the National State: From the 'Right Deviation' towards New Politics?

Nowadays, the research on nationalism in Yugoslavia stands on excep-tionally shaky foundations. Certain approaches put nationalism second, considering it a mere expression of the economic trends. This absolves the Party cadres of all political responsibilities for the consequent collapse of the political organisation. However, other approaches reduce all developments to the national prism, thereby all too eagerly confirm-ing today's dominant ideology that sees Yugoslavia as an 'artificial entity' and carefully fosters the myth of eternal ethnic hatred.[26] During the first period of socialist Yugoslavia, the national question was of secondary importance. Nevertheless, this was not simple proof of the power of the official anti-fascist ideology or a result of the manipulation of the masses, as some anti-totalitarians might add. No, during the first period, the success of the socialist project became the political criterion of the fact that nationalism was of no importance to the political agenda. Based on a more equitable economic development, the socialist project – in its early phase – respected the relative autonomy of the republics and the accelerated investments in the basic social infrastructure, which was accessible to as many citizens as possible. The socio-economic problems emerged in the mid-1960s, along with the first wave of nationalist outbursts, which should not be overlooked. Critical analyses of nationalism during the socialist period were rather scarce. I would like to underline the pioneering works by Jasna Dragović-Sosso, Andrew Wachtel, Hrvoje Klasić, and Audrey Budding and others, which have broadened our horizons and helped us to at least define the field of intervention. These works contributed significantly to a more detailed analysis of the ideological forms of the new nationalist movements, the role of intellectual and cultural hegemony,[27] and the cultural-ideological apparatuses of the late and mature socialism.

During the first self-management period, integrational ideas prevailed, at least on the level of discourse. According to Dejan Jović, the efforts were focused particularly on advancing the concept of 'brotherhood and unity' which stemmed from World War II (Jović 2008: 62–81). The official ideology emphasised the anti-fascist legacy of the People's Liberation Struggle, which had become a strong part of the collective memory and was present in practically all artistic genres and activities. However, with each passing year, the presentations of the heroic character[28] of the People's Liberation Struggle became increasingly mythological, which triggered increased faith in the infallibility in some people, while the new generations started losing their belief in the partisan legacy. What do we share with this past experience? The socialist ideologues were naive in their optimism that the nationalist 'remains' of the past would disappear in the light of the socialist society. The underestimating of the nationalist phenomena was inherent to the ideology of enlightened socialism. During the political and economic changes that took place in the 1960s, the socialist leadership never truly dealt with the nationalistic tendencies. These tendencies were seen by the leadership as a regression towards the rural mentality and pre-war Yugoslavia,[29] which, among other things, pointed at the inability of the socialist authorities to re-evaluate potential local fascism. Instead of re-articulating their own partisan experience, they resorted to repression, while the space for discussion remained limited/ineffective.

Not everyone remained silent on the topic of the rise of nationalism: one of the more progressive outlooks was presented by Horvat, who understood the rise of nationalism as a reaction to the general feeling of economic insecurity. The mass exodus of the rural population to urban centres resulted in material scarcity and the severance of social bonds for many newcomers, while the economic deprivation of certain regions brought forth considerable unemployment (Horvat 1976: 38). In a way, the aforementioned new-leftist critiques, which accused the authorities of betraying the revolutionary ideals, contributed to the articulation of the frustration and disappointment with the authoritarian and rigid character of the League of Communists of Yugoslavia and its leadership. The structural problems of unequal development and economic back-wardness were becoming progressively nationalistic: the old opposition between the evil centre (Belgrade), the largest nation (Serbia), and all the others – as well as the egotism of the rich (northern) nations and the periphery (the underdeveloped) – came to life. Instead of the inte-grational idea of Yugoslavia, the argumentation of the new economic policies was increasingly expressed through the prism of building autarkic communities and developing the economic sovereignty of indi-vidual republics. We could search for the main reasons behind the rise of nationalism in the socio-economic changes. However, such a framework remains not specific enough, as it only points to spontaneous ideological reactions.

Recent critical research has indicated that the nationalist ideology never truly disappeared, not even during the initial period of socialist Yugoslavia.[30] Moreover, the anti-Albanian (and anti-Roma) sentiment had been present since the end of World War II in everyday ideology as well as in the official political organisation of the new Yugoslavia. Let us bring attention to the unsuccessful negotiations between the Albanian and Yugoslav communists as well as to the autonomous region of Kosovo, formed *within* the Socialist Republic of Serbia as a result of a compromise. As a result of the historic political antagonism and the extremely unfavourable economic position, a part of the local bureau-cracy in Kosovo resorted to nationalism during the 1960s. At the end of that decade, certain political groups demanded for Kosovo to be granted a more equal status within Yugoslavia, which would have implied the proclamation of the seventh republic (Magaš 1993). The protests were suppressed, and the federalist concept of 'brotherhood and unity' was replaced by Kardelj's confederal and more autonomist concept of self-management that had already shown the first positive results (Jović 2008: 62–81). The matter of nationalist outbursts and identity politics were therefore not merely secondary expressions, but rather an increasingly articulated political conflict and a part of the cultural hegemony.

We should highlight one event that failed to garner a lot of attention, as it was deemed a purely 'linguistic' and scientific matter. In 1954, linguists adopted a hypothesis that Serbo-Croatian was a single language with two variants.[31] In 1967, this hypothesis was contested by *Matica hrvatska*,[32] which argued for the separation and restoration of Croatian and Serbian as two autonomous languages. The scientific discussion was followed by the demand for the official recognition of this separation, while in Serbia certain intellectuals, cultural workers, and linguists started to defend the thesis of one nation and one language. This discussion was a controversial and symptomatic indication of 'science' becoming political. In political reality, these linguistic demands backed 'the beliefs of the right-wing' and called for republican sovereignty. As Hrvoje Klasić (2012) pointed out in his analysis of *Matica hrvatska* (which became one of the key cultural-political centres of the national renaissance and a catalyst for a mass movement already at the beginning of the 1970s), important political shifts took place only a few years later. Certain historians and interpreters believe that the Maspok movement (in the original *masovni pokret*, literally translated as *mass movement*) was the main representative of the 'right-wing deviation'. However, it would be more appropriate to consider it as the beginning of organised nationalist politics, promptly adhered to by different social groups such as intellectuals, liberals from the League of Communists, and students. This movement was also publicly supported by the League of Communists of Croatia, who used certain Maspok arguments in their struggle against the forces of centralisation. However, when the liberal demands were articulated within the national(-ist) horizon, they failed to retain any progressive demands. On the contrary: they became more conservative. Maspok can be seen as a response to the failed revolution of 1968, as a conservative response, or even as testing grounds for the anti-hegemonic forces, which – due to the growing popularity of the nationalist ideology – contributed to the mounting tensions and conflicts in the ethnically mixed regions (e.g.

in Krajina), in which the majority of the population was Serbian. The original demands for linguistic separation were joined by the economic demands for foreign exchange sovereignty and the political demands for Croatian independence. The nationalist movement now associated the linguistic dissimilarity of the Croatian language with a political reference: Croatia was supposed to become a state of Croatians without Serbs, which became a part of the imagery of the ethnically pure territory that would become a reality in the 1990s.

The nationalist outbursts should therefore not be considered merely as an expression of the economic crisis or as a reappearance of suppressed contents. At the beginning of the 1970s, the socialist leadership faced mass – on occasions even anti-communist – public criticism for the first time since World War II. These policies should therefore not be referred to as a deviation, but rather as an emergence of the politics of a radically opposite political imagery. The ideological formation of the nationalist movements consisted of anti-communist and traditionalist components, references to national culture, and even the rehabilitation of local fascism. By 1971 the situation was out of control, as Tito openly underlined in his speech: 'Would you like to return to 1941? This would be a true disaster' (in Rusinow 1977: 299). In the following months, the nationalist movement was repressed, some of the leaders were arrested and sentenced to prison, and the entire political apparatus of the League of Communists of Croatia was subjected to a thorough purge (Repe 1992: 250). In this case, the reaction of the Central Committee of the Communist Party of Yugoslavia and Tito's leadership circle was no different than it was in the case of repressing the left-wing deviation, however, it failed to resolve the national issue. In the short-term, the purges managed to re-establish political control. However, this brought an end to the relative freedom of political and media expression and resulted in a more consistent control over the cultural apparatuses and artistic production. From the long-term perspective we can claim that the repression revealed the impotence of the old partisan generation that was no longer able to rule without resorting to force and relying on Tito's personality.

In 1974 a confederal orientation, which emphasised ethnic identity as a political stipulation, was openly included in the Yugoslav constitution, which indicated that the leadership moved a little closer to the ideological compromise of a new Yugoslav entity.[33] However, this pragmatism of the authorities, pointed to an internal disintegration: it is one thing to compromise with the left-wing, but coming to terms with the nationalist imagery is something completely different. This leads us to the conclusion that the ideological amalgam of liberalism and nationalism is of key importance in the understanding of the historical bloc that was victorious at the end of the 1980s. What initially seemed to be a puritan linguistic practice of separating languages and reviving the (elitist) national culture would soon transform into an alternative model of the political constitution that did not have much in common with the class and federal entity of socialist Yugoslavia and the working people. The old model of 'one nation in one state' resurfaced. This model – as the name clearly indicates – promotes the nation as the utopic subjectivity that is fuelled by ethnic substance and that finds its most appropriate political form in the *national state*.

The Re-Stalinisation of the League of Communists?

Tito and his leadership were pragmatic in exploiting one 'deviation' today and another tomorrow, as they saw fit, and they mercilessly conducted a thorough purge at the beginning of the 1970s. The political repression might have purged the left and right deviations, but it failed to solve the economic contradictions. It merely led to a shortage of personnel in political organisations, making room for opportunistic cadres and resulting in the resignation of progressive forces (Goldstein 2005). The League of Communists of Yugoslavia and its national leagues of communists were those who lost the most as a result of this 'clean-up operation', while a part of the old partisan generation headed by Tito remained at the very top of political power. The historian Ivo Goldstein considers this to be one of Tito's greatest political mistakes, which took a heavy toll after his death.[34] The socialist leadership did not take advantage of the situation to renew the bond between the masses and the Party. Instead, it tried with all its might to maintain its power. Ernst Petrič, a Slovenian young generation liberal, has come up with an interesting summary of the rise and (temporary) fall of the liberal tendency:

> From the historical point of view, Slovenian liberalism was an attempt to democratise 'socialism' in what were still premature historical circumstances. This was not possible due to the rigid monolithic social and ideological model that had to be ground down before it would collapse ... And as it collapsed, it was clearly impossible to salvage it anywhere in Eastern Europe. This is why the path led towards the right

and the restoration of the rather rudimentary forms of capitalism, instead of leading towards democratic socialism. If the liberals had succeeded in Yugoslavia and Dubček in the Czechoslovak Socialist Republic, etc., something might have remained of socialism, after all. In this sense, socialism had its historical opportunity precisely in its liberal version, including ours. Those who crushed it buried socialism in its positive sense. (Quoted in Repe 1992: 236).

It is impossible to disagree with the part of the text claiming that the historical responsibility for the destruction of socialism should fall on those within the socialist leadership who stifled the possibilities for a different development of self-management by repressing the liberal line, the workers, and the student opposition (Kirn 2015; Goldstein 2005; Repe 1992). The leadership indeed failed to recognise the 'left deviation' as the only chance to revitalise socialist power, a quest for a radically different socialism, and a future to fight for. The declarative position of this quote, which already attests to the inevitability of the end of (real) socialism and Yugoslavia, represents a greater problem. Liberalism could have played an even more heroic role in this story, salvaging what could possibly be salvaged from a sinking ship. With this act of salvation, liberal socialism would have paved a quicker path towards the end of socialism, which was not far from the truth. The only thing that Petrič forgot to add was that, in the meantime, liberal socialism had mutated into social liberalism that characterised the Slovenian transition of the 1990s and later began to ravage the socialised means of (re)production. At the same time, it is impossible to label this imagery a 'right deviation', as it would have stayed within the Yugoslav and communist horizon. Instead it introduced – from the very beginning, at least ideologically – an anti-hegemonic bloc of national liberalism on the horizon of the bloody disintegration of Yugoslavia.

The period between 1969 and 1972 unquestionably brought about the most intense ideological struggles that introduced new ideological figures – man, market, and nation – which, to a considerable degree, shed a light on the general crisis and stagnation of the League of Communists and led to a more pragmatic reproduction of the socialist authority. Politically, we can speak of a period in which both the revolutionary and counter-revolutionary movements emerged, and of how following the political repression this contributed crucially to the exhaustion of the League of Communists.

13

The Contradictory Movement of Socialist Civil Society in Slovenia during the 1980s: The Beginning of the End of Yugoslavia

In the previous chapters I outlined the 'market socialism' period and indicated the intense economic contradictions and ideological struggles it involved, as well as outlining the political antagonisms of the self-management project. This is not to say that the tragic destiny of Yugoslavia had already been decided by the early 1970s. There was no indication that self-management would end in bloody ethnic wars: we could argue that the disintegration was a result of long-lasting internal and external processes on the one hand and radicalised confrontations at the end of the 1980s on the other. If the 1960s clearly illustrated the economic contradictions that surfaced after the introduction of the magical market formula, then I will argue that the 1980s clearly revealed all the heterogeneous and antagonistic political positions that appeared in the profoundly altered regional (the enlargement of Europe) and geopolitical (the end of the Cold War, the demise of the Non-Aligned Movement) circumstances. I suggest that we consider the main antagonisms not merely through the self-management apparatus that expressed the economic conflicts between the core and the periphery, but also through the gradual growth of the counter-hegemonic bloc, led by the socialist civil society, that contributed to the break-up of the state.

First, we have to ask ourselves whether there was such a thing as a socialist civil society? Do the debates within the context of this 'liberal' framework imply a return to the formal division between the (socialist) state and civil society and its interests and conflicts in the times of socialism? The early theoretical framework of self-management was built upon Marx's early criticism,[1] which explicitly targeted the bourgeois division into the formal realm of the state and its citizens on the one hand and the realm of civil society on the other. This division obfuscates the class relations, and should as such be abolished. Initially, Kardelj and other self-management ideologues hoped to overcome the centralist state and bureaucratic monopoly with the market and 'socialist commodity production' in the 1960s, however, following the wave of political discontent in 1968, the 1970s brought the 1974 Constitution and the Associated Labour Act (1976), which was at the time seen as the new magic formula. This law was the brainchild of Edvard Kardelj and could be described as the crowning achievement of 'legal communism'. In 1970, Kardelj became the leader of the constitutional commission, which was to become his main legacy as well as the last major Yugoslav reform that was discussed and implemented across all social levels of self-management. The 'Basic Organisation of Associated Labour' became the central political entity, which spread into the political and social infrastructure. Producers were thus joined by the organisations of users of the social infrastructure. The idea behind this was that a genuine cornerstone for self-management democracy would develop from these elementary units of self-management interests and society would outgrow the state, thus abolishing the vanguardist role of the Party. Despite the best intentions of legal communism, the 'self-management' of society became a mode of social reproduction, the major effects of which included fragmentation through decentralisation. In his critique of both the self-management apparatus as well as the retrospective interpretations of the 'civil society', Močnik stated the following:

> Civil society was a slogan of anti-communist movements in the world of European Real Socialism and … it was also the most important 'alternative' ideology at the beginning of the reconstruction of capitalism in those countries. In terms of ideology, this 'alternative' – at least the most vocal factions in the countries of the former Soviet bloc – was liberal-democratic: it contended for the consequent realisation of the ideology in the name of which capitalism was being reconstructed … and helped introduce capitalism to former socialist countries: it maintained the illusion that a democratic and working-people-friendly 'capitalism with a human face' is possible. (Močnik 2014).

Despite this valid criticism of civil society, the giant social apparatus of self-management enabled plural forces to emerge and started major confrontations that first expanded the democratic horizons rather than merely restored capitalism. This chapter provides a condensed overview of the power struggles against and within the established self-management apparatus, while geographically I will limit myself mostly to the analysis of the most vibrant scene that took place in the Socialist Republic of Slovenia. Moreover, while certain critical and Marxist literature focuses on the concepts and processes of post-socialist transition (Buden 2009; Gajić and Popović 2011; Močnik 2010a; Veselinović et al. 2011), other literature sees the demise of Yugoslavia through its 'destruction' initiated by 'external forces' (Magaš 1993). The latter are most commonly identified with the harsh austerity policies enforced by the IMF after Tito's death, which targeted Yugoslavia's political and economic system (Woodward 1995b). Some researchers have recently highlighted geopolitical shifts and the increasing economic dependence that facilitated the greater influence of other European powers which interfered by supporting and recognising the independence of the northern Yugoslav republics: Slovenia and Croatia (Živković 2015, Gonzales 2018). In 2005, Sabrina Ramet accomplished an important synthesis, when she managed to assemble the major studies that focused on the external and internal factors of the disintegration of Yugoslavia.

I would like to add to the critical and already well-researched role of the IMF, the geopolitics, and the crisis of federal and communist organisations, an analysis that focuses on the development of internal political forces and antagonisms. There were at least two key antagonisms that need to be examined: firstly, the one between the centre and the periphery, which was expressed through the official confrontations between the republics and the federative government as well as by the power struggles within the Party and its organisations; and, secondly, the confrontation with the civil society and the labour strikes, or the struggles from below that openly challenged the legitimacy of the self-management apparatus and created imaginaries that looked towards the past as well as the future. We will see that within the socialist civil society, the diversity of struggles and social groups often expressed highly contradictory and even opposing demands. The hypothesis will be developed dialectically, pointing out that these agents can be seen as the late vanguard of the democratisation of the socialist system, while they were also the vital part of the new imaginary beyond Yugoslavia and the promoter of national liberalism that eventually spread within the self-managed apparatuses of the Yugoslav republics.

The Emergence of the Democratic Civil Society during the 1980s

Numerous Slovenian political commentators and analysts consider the civil society that emerged during the 1980s as the genuine initiator of Slovenian democracy, without which there would have been no 'democratic transition' in the 1990s (Fink-Hafner 2000; for my criticism of transitology, see Kirn 2017). Some even celebrate this period as the birth of the 'Slovenian democratic revolution' (Balažic 2004). Juxtaposed to this retrospective liberal narrative, we can find certain conspiratorial-nostalgic narratives that argue that the events of the 1980s should be interpreted as a part of a Western conspiracy (and CIA involvement) that sponsored the dissolution of Yugoslavia and which also took place through the civil society (Trček 2016).

Boris Buden, one of the main critics of the transitional processes in the post-socialist context of the 1980s and 1990s, defended the democratic legacy of the civil society, while being completely aware that the subsequent process turned into a disaster, which Buden describes vividly as 'the collapse of the state, horribly destructive civil wars, ethnic cleansing, atrocities, human losses, economic breakdown, political chaos, etc.' (Buden 2007). On a more philosophical level, the position of Buden and myself challenges two dominant narratives regarding the developments in 1989: firstly and most obviously, the apologetic stance of Fukuyama (1992), who views the end of socialism as the 'end of history' and a triumph of Western liberal democracy; and, secondly and perhaps more interestingly, the allegedly contrasting view put forth by Alain Badiou, one of the most vocal representatives of the 'idea of communism'. Badiou (1998) claimed that *nothing took place in 1989* but the restoration of capitalism and liberal democracy, which, rather than constituting a triumph, turned 1989 into an 'obscure disaster'. Although these two philosophers come from different political camps, neither of them sees 1989 as a revolution. Fukuyama believes that 1989 revolved around the liberal democratic triumph, which brought history to its end. On the other hand, Badiou considered this event as a representation of the liberal restoration of the state of affairs. It is interesting that these politically opposed arguments share two central aspects of 'transition' and the role that the civil society played in it. Primarily, on the general level, their respective theoretical viewpoints are not interested in tackling the processes of transition but conclude in their respective claims of 'the end of history' and that 'nothing had changed' after 1989.

Secondly, they both failed to properly assess the past social formation, i.e. *socialism* – this contradictory social formation from which the transition took place. If we are to follow any of these political reasonings, we must forget about the existence and dynamics of the various socialist and democratic revolts and organisations that took place in late socialism. Also, these views would have us forget that there was a precise and qualitative change between federal and socialist Yugoslavia – no matter how much of the partisan rupture had withered away by the 1980s – and what happened in the 1990s with the resurgence of nationalism, primitive accumulation of capital through wars, and the gradual 'integration' into the European economic landscape. The socialist civil society was thus neither an ideal harmonic society that conducted a democratic transition, nor was it a simple effect of neoliberal restructuring. Instead, I will argue that the civil society expressed the contradictions involved in the self-management of society and in the long-term power struggles and ideological conflicts.

During the 1980s, two major agencies competed with the Party: the socialist civil society and the workers' opposition, which openly addressed the political and economic crisis and started forming an alternative. However, this alternative history should not overlook the fact that the trigger and actual 'detonator' for the rise of the civil society was to be found in alternative art and most notably in punk music. The 1980s was excellently summed up by the theorist Maja Breznik, who argued that 'punk was actually a detonator of the democratic revolution in the 1980s, since the political transformation only superseded the social transformation in which punk played such a vital role' (1995: 79).

How did these political, artistic, and theoretical practices take place and what did they encounter during the early 1980s? Who were the main political agents? How did the reactionary tendency subject the democratic transformation and, as Breznik rightly pointed out, turn it into a 'nation-building' idea and 'restore capitalism on neo-liberal beliefs'? (ibid.). As already mentioned, the early 1980s witnessed major destabilisation enforced through economic discipline: the IMF austerity packages (Magaš 1993, Woodward 1995b) did not result merely in the shortage of commodities, but also in drastic increases in unemployment rates as workers started losing their jobs or were forced to declare bankruptcy (Géraud-Legros 2006). Beset by constant internal struggles, the ideological legitimacy of the socialist leadership crumbled, while the social contract continued to be undermined. On the one hand, the rich

Yugoslav north had full employment and enjoyed a very strong social infrastructure and considerable growth, while, on the other hand, the southern regions saw unemployment rates increase to over 20 per cent and had a very poor infrastructure and economic output. The political responses came from the regions subjected to these extremes.

The civil society – or what some refer to as the political alternative (Močnik) – was first born in the early 1980s in the Socialist Republic of Slovenia. There was a strong clash between the progressive theoretical, artistic, and political practices and groups in the urban centre(s) during this period. Similarly to the 1960s, the triangulation between art, theory, and politics produced lasting effects that would soon be described under the general signifier of 'alternative'. In general terms, the latter pushed for a deeper democratisation process and the introduction of political rights and freedoms. Breznik (1995) argued that punk detonated what at first glance appeared to be a solid façade of self-management. From the very outset, the ideologues of the League of Communists considered punk 'dangerous', 'anarchist', and even 'fascist'. The strong reactions and the surveillance carried out by the both secret police and police could be seen as a trigger that transformed the tiny art scene into a popular movement amongst the youth and the urban scene (Tomc 1985). The initial 'artistic' phase was followed by organised and politicised groups that were active in various fields, from the cultural scene to the student circles (Radio Študent, theoretical and political journals) as well as within established Party organisations, most notably the League of Socialist Youth of Slovenia. The media sphere and the freedom of expression were of utmost significance, and as Močnik suggested, this process took place throughout Yugoslavia:

In the 1980s, the Yugoslav alternative launched significant battles regarding the right of expression (Article 133 of the Federal Penal Code, which criminalised 'verbal delict') and other human rights (especially in connection with the Belgrade trial against the organisers of the Free University in 1984-5). Henceforth, the term 'civil society' started to be associated with struggling for human rights and the rule of law. It was self-evident for many participants that we were striving for human rights within the framework of the socialist state. (Močnik 2014)

The various political agents primarily wanted to expand their leeway and include new rights into the discussions on self-management.

If their initial actions, which seemed to be of a limited scope, were relegated to the intellectual and media sphere, then by the mid-1980s additional protests, actions, performances, proclamations, and strike actions accompanied its course. It should be stressed that these groups addressed issues such as LGBT rights, ecology, feminism (Dobnikar 1985, Jalušič 2002) as well as the peace movement (Mastnak 1992, 2005) and labour strikes (Stanojević 1994). They articulated extremely diverse demands – from the recognition of new political, social, and economic rights, the equality of minority groups, freedom of speech, and rejection of the death penalty, to the demilitarisation campaign that challenged the sacred position of the Yugoslav People's Army (and introduced the conscientious objection to military service) and the workers' demands for better working conditions and higher wages. Lively discussions took place in weekly publications such as *Mladina* ('Youth') and the more specialised theoretical journals (*Nova Revija*, *Problemi*, *CKZ*, and the *Tribuna* student newspaper), artistic magazines (*Literatura*), and on Radio Študent. The renaissance of the events and publications in the early 1980s represented the breeding ground for the famous Ljubljana encounter between critical Marxism and psychoanalysis. Moreover, art groups such as the NSK, Borghesia, Gržinić/Šmid, and others catapulted themselves into the Yugoslav politico-artistic space, later to be recognised by the West as an Eastern variation of retro-avant-garde art (Arns 2006). However, a more liberal approach could be retrospectively identified in some civil initiatives and their dealing with the recognition of identity, or specific single-issue mobilisation (see Močnik 2014), whose main focus was not on undermining the general politico-economic orientation of the socialist self-management of Yugoslavia. In their theoretical and media proclamations, critical theorists would not spare their criticism and would openly target the sacred authorities and power structures, as well as the ideological indecisiveness of self-management.

If these new political groups were initially not represented by any official political organisations, this changed with the counterhegemonic and leftist takeover of the League of Socialist Youth of Slovenia (the ZSMS), which was, as a subsidiary socialist organisation, a part of the state's political apparatus (for a critical assessment that views ZSMS as a sort of neoliberal agent, see Radojević-Kreinzer and Podvršič 2018). The ZSMS would regularly provide the majority of the personnel for the League of Communists as well as hold some critical views. However, in mid-1980s Slovenia, it started to openly challenge the course of the federation and the republican leadership (see also Balažic 2004). The leading members of the ZSMS played a role in alternative media and public discussions, organising and financing cultural events and exerting political pressure. One could argue that ZSMS's role was essential – it was a transmitter that worked between the political groupings from below on the one hand and the representatives of the republican and communist leadership on the other. This was a strategic position with actual political power (infrastructure) that could work both ways, either intensifying or softening the 'alternative' discourse and demands. If the existing infrastructure permitted the political and cultural associations to access spaces and finances, then the civil sphere influenced and pushed the ideology and institutions of self-management towards democratic reforms. The first part of the 1980s did not witness any major political events that would result in what Mouffe and Laclau (1985) refer to as the 'chain of equivalences', which would bring together different demands, challenge the socialist system, and overthrow it. In retrospect, the parallel existence of alternative spaces, journals, discourses, and actions resulted in the formation of a progressive civil society that created its own 'critical public', which was not yet in an openly antagonising relation with the official political apparatus.

The increasingly acute confrontation within the federation (for more details see Jović 2008) addressing the resolution of the economic crisis and the future course, the increasing external pressures on the fiscal and monetary policies, as well as the ritualisation of Tito's legacy (the Day of Youth, monuments dedicated to Tito) attested to the mounting crisis. In view of this, it is hardly surprising that a major subversion originated from within the field of art, which was particularly sensitive to the issues of symbolic representation and future imaginaries. A number of artist groups decided to intervene in the sacred ideological kernels of contemporaneous socialism. The New Collectivism poster that won the public call for the most sacred of all holidays (former Tito's birthday, the Day of Youth) in 1987 became highly controversial. After the award was announced and given to New Collectivism, one of the critics brought to the attention of the commission that the group merely re-designed an old Nazi youth poster to which they added the small twist of changing the symbols. This could lead to the interpretation of New Collectivism and the NSK (Neue Slowenische Kunst) as a group of agents provocateurs fighting the 'totalitarian rule'. However, one cannot speak merely of the shocking effect, but of a politically effective consistent strategy of 'overidentification' (Dolar 2015).

This act exploded in public as well as within the communist organisations, which held special meetings dedicated to this case. It did not only make the group instantly famous, but also questioned the ability of those who governed and cultivated the legacy of Tito and the Day of Youth to judge aesthetic issues. Obviously, the decision as regards the poster was revoked, and New Collectivism experienced a wave of reproaches deeming them 'fascists' and enemies of the state. This event did not merely put a temporary stop to the group's activities, for it also pushed other similar groups under the increasingly politicised scrutiny of the role of art as well as encouraging a specific reinvention of the utopian and avant-garde premise. I would argue that these groups and their encounters with the theoretical and political scene have made lasting contributions to the democratisation of contemporaneous socialism, despite their ambivalence in terms of the political programme. This general democratic civil society lasted until 1987 and was not limited solely to Slovenia. Artistic and political movements also appeared in other Yugoslav regions, but with different intensities and at different times.[2] Certain victories within this period indicated that a different *democratic socialism* was possible, and to a certain degree it was practiced relatively successfully. It can be argued that the political alternative consisted of groups that were ideologically heterogeneous and included radical socialist, democratic, and liberal tendencies.

If it was indeed punk that led to the democratic civil society, as Maja Breznik believes, then the late 1980s saw a dramatic change within this constellation:

When the nationalist and separatist political forces that democratically took over the power halted, at least temporarily, the transformation (by diverging it into nation-building) and the restoration of capitalism on the neoliberal premises, the alternative artistic production focused on the more ambitious 'artism', perfectionism, and even elitism. (1995: 79).

However, apart from what Breznik calls the 'artism' and 'elitism' that influenced the new national culture (she was probably referring to the NSK that could be seen as a cultural retro-avant-garde of the ZSMS), one should not overlook a whole array of national pop bands that were embraced by the masses during that period. Moreover, the radical democratic processes of the 1980s were first appeased internally, as I will show in the following section; only later were the democratic agents also disciplined externally, when the need to re-educate them in the democratic culture was demanded by the West and the (neoliberal) shock therapy was implemented during the late 1990s and 2000s.

From the Democratic to the Nationalist Political Alternative

Eastern Europe after 1989 resembles a landscape of historical ruins that is inhabited only by children, immature people unable to organize their lives democratically without guidance from another. They do not see themselves subjects of a democracy that they actually won through struggle and created by themselves. It has been expropriated from them through the idea and practice of the post-communist transition, only to return now from the outside as a foreign object that they must reappropriate in a long, hard and painful process. (Buden 2007).

Turning to the intense period between 1987 and 1991, one should keep an open eye for the increasingly rampant economic crisis, the fierce struggles within the state apparatuses for the domination over the communist organisations, and the emergence of openly nationalistic tendencies within the republican leaderships (Jović 2009). It is unclear whether the move towards the nationalist positions first emerged within the socialist apparatus or within the civil society, but it is clear that the initial demands for a deeper democratisation of socialism were increasingly becoming substituted by the more nationalistic views that started subscribing to the capitalist imaginary (e.g. the calls for private property, see Géraud-Legros 2006). However, if the demands for a more liberal and free-market form of self-management were not surprising given the nature of the economic crisis, neoliberal restructuring, and the geopolitical changes of the late 1980s, including the shift to openly nationalist positions, they should still not be explained solely from the perspective of the communist elites that pragmatically converted and embraced nationalism. The demands for independent nation-states were first made within the new political alternative outside of the official political apparatuses, and they can be traced back to certain intellectuals and civil society movements. This section will thus focus on the crucial events and agents that resulted in the formation of the new alternative that 'nationalised' the former coalition between the socialist reformers and the liberals. At least three major political events that occurred between 1987 and 1990 had a lasting impact on the withering away of Yugoslavia, the implementation of the 'one nation in one state' model, and the decline of the democratic civil society that would construct its imaginary in the Yugoslav perspective. These were: the nationalist academic revolts in Slovenia and Serbia; the JBTZ Trial; and the culturalisation of the workers' struggles in Kosovo.

Let us begin at the turn of 1986–87, which is arguably the central departure point for the rise and the ideological legitimacy of nationalism. At this point it is important to highlight the initial driving force of nationalism, which was later on wrongly ascribed to the workers and peasants from the rural regions who waged the wars during the 1990s. This has become a liberal theme based on class racism that wanted to exculpate one's own class's positions during the 'democratic' transition: how can we explain the carnage that followed the allegedly democratic heaven of the 1980s? However, the actual struggles in 1986–87 brutally and honestly show that the first nationalist programmes were drawn up by the leading intellectuals from the various republics. In Serbia, a sixteen-member committee was set up at the Serbian Academy of Sciences and Arts with the task of analysing the general situation, and its Memorandum leaked into the public in 1986. A year later, sixteen dissident (and mostly anti-communist) Slovenian intellectuals published No. 57 of *Nova Revija*, a special issue of the magazine published as a response to the Serbian Memorandum. Both the Memorandum and the 57th issue of *Nova Revija* focused on the 'national question' (Serbian and Slovenian, respectively) and on the way in which the status of each nation within Yugoslavia was dominated by centralism (the malevolent Belgrade, the vile legacy of Tito).

The Memorandum overtly challenged the autonomy of the provinces of Vojvodina and particularly Kosovo, made a case for Greater Serbia, and established a topos of who was the victim and who the aggressor:

In the spring of 1981, open and total war was declared on the Serbian people, which had been carefully prepared for in advance in the various stages of administrative, political and constitutional reform. This open war has been going on for almost five years. It is being waged with a skilful and carefully orchestrated use of a variety of methods and tactics, with the active and not just tacit support of various political centres in Yugoslavia, which they are taking no pains to conceal and which is more ruinous than the encouragement given by our neighbours. (SANU, 1986).

The Memorandum correctly assumes that Kosovo, and to a certain degree Serbia, were most severely affected by the economic crisis and austerity measures. Problems as well as social and ethnic tensions between the Albanian and Serbian population were clearly evident. According to the Memorandum, these tensions worsened with the increased autonomy that was granted to these provinces in the 1974 Constitution. Evidently, there was no mention of the strong military presence or the fact that the majority of the police forces in Kosovo consisted of ethnic Serbs. Furthermore, the suggestion that the riots and protests can be described as over five years of 'open and total war' can definitely be seen as a blatant exaggeration that was to become an important part of the nationalist war discourse. The Memorandum also took a long detour through a few centuries of uprisings of the Serbian nation in Kosovo and described yet another alarming situation concerning Serbs in Croatia. It is extremely telling that the Memorandum barely concerned itself with the Yugoslav and socialist future at all, instead focusing solely on the future of the Serbian nation and culture that had been left to 'decay'. Serbia supposedly needed to 'take the initiative' after four decades of stagnating within socialist Yugoslavia, and the Memorandum stated that 'the first requirement for our transformation and renaissance is a democratic mobilisation of all the intellectual and moral forces of the nation' (SANU, 1986). Despite the fact that the official Party organisations condemned the Memorandum, many prominent figures of the period – including Slobodan Milošević – later adopted these arguments during the power struggles between the various factions, while the main authors of the Memorandum became the most active political representatives of the transition.

A year after the controversial discussion took place in Serbia, the 57th issue of *Nova Revija* was published. Alongside the nationalist perspective that it shared with its Serbian nationalist colleagues, it also included the first systematic programme for the independence of Slovenia. As the editorial board concluded, 'this is an initiative for a different reflection on Slovenians and a new understanding of Slovenian statehood that will be constituted in the institutions of a potentially sovereign nation and in its everyday life according to the demands of the new historical epoch'

(1987: 2). The issue consists of a number of different sections, ranging from philosophical Heideggerianism (Urbančič's 'The Yugoslav "Nationalist Crisis" and the Slovenes in the Perspective of the End of Nation, Tine Hribar's "Slovenian Statehood"') to more historical pieces. The most pivotal section was represented by the plea for the reconciliation between partisans and fascists within the Slovenian nation (Spomenka Hribar), which, to say the least, remains controversial even today (Kirn 2019). This was followed by contributions addressing the political and legal system in Slovenia; treatises on suicide and Slovenian emigration; articles on the Slovenian educational system, literature, and religion; and an important section dedicated to the civil society. Most of the political, legal, and philosophical texts evoked the inalienable right to national self-determination and reinforced the mission to fulfil the dream of a sovereign Slovenian state. Some of these articles were more obviously critical of the existing socialism and the League of Communists, while other texts emphasised the uniqueness of Slovenia to establish a critical stance towards the 'myths of Yugoslavia' and the 'shared Slavic' history and separate them from the true Slovenian path (Pučnik 1987: 143). If this could be ideologically seen as avant-garde, politically, many of the contributions published in the 57th issue of Nova Revija called upon the League of Communists to take the 'road towards independence'. Following the publication of issue No. 57, the ZSMS organised a public discussion in which the editorial board of Nova Revija had to defend its programme and the published articles. The entire editorial board was pressured to resign. Nevertheless, the magazine was not censored: it kept receiving funds and was allowed to continue publishing. In the following years, it published an even more specific programme that called for Slovenian independence and the introduction of private property.

These academic documents shared a deep national aspiration for the determination of the Serbian and Slovenian nations, even if they were formulated by a minority of the nationalist and liberal intelligentsia in the socialist republics of Serbia and Slovenia. However, if the Slovenian version potentially wished to bring forth the disintegration of Yugoslavia and the affirmation of an independent and sovereign nation-state, the Serbian Memorandum implied a more expansionist agenda – they aspired for the territories in which the Serbian nation had lived historically – which, however, did not go against the 'integrity' of Yugoslavia. Thus, the theoretical foundations for national independence were established.

Another major political event can be seen as the realisation of the Slovenian dream and the ideological-theoretical calls for independence. In 1988, during the so-called JBTZ trial in Slovenia, the nationalist ideology started reaching the masses at the same time as the national programme started manifesting itself in the new surge of mass protests with tangible effects that would soon start to resonate strongly within the protests as well as within the Slovenian Party leadership. The affair started when four journalists and political activists – Janez Janša, Ivan Borštner, David Tasić, and Franci Zavrl (also referred to as JBTZ after their surname's initials) – were arrested by the military police and brought before a military tribunal. Immediately after their arrests, on 31 May 1988, the Committee for the Defence of Human Rights was founded, and it soon extended its membership to 32 left- and right-wing political activists and intellectuals. In a matter of weeks, the Committee managed to collect 100,000 signatures in support of the four defendants (Žerdin 1997). The sporadic gestures of solidarity gradually developed and ultimately resulted in ten thousand people gathering in front of the prison where Janša, Borštner, Tasić, and Zavrl were awaiting their trial. Since the four defendants were accused of betraying military secrets, they were tried at a military court that aimed to impose stricter control in Slovenia – which had, by that time, seen many new alternative political, cultural, and theoretical practices. As was the established practice of military tribunals, the trial was conducted in Serbo-Croatian, which was the *lingua franca* of the federation. However, the defendants claimed that it was their right to reply in Slovenian and thus refused to respond. The goal of imposing stricter control over Slovenia and disciplining its communist leadership and the civil society backfired and started to alienate the Slovenian people from Belgrade and the federal powers. On 22 June, one of the largest protests (with a turnout of more than 40,000 people) took place in the centre of Ljubljana. For the first time, those who protested in the streets and supported the political alternative were greeted with sympathy or even openly supported by the communist leadership. The four were sentenced to prison terms ranging from six months to four years for 'betraying military secrets' concerning the possible actions of the Yugoslav People's Army in the event of the disintegration of Yugoslavia. They became Slovenian national heroes as soon as they were imprisoned. Janez Janša became one of the most famous Slovenian right-wing politicians, and would later serve as Prime Minister, the leader of the opposition, and the 'eternal' President of the

Slovenian Democratic Party. Franci Zavrl – at the time the editor of the *Mladina* weekly – would go on to become one of the richest people in Slovenia.

On a more general level, this was the historical moment of concatenation that hegemonised and homogenised the political alternative: it succeeded in uniting the diverse political agencies and positions within Slovenia against the malevolent authority from the centre of Yugoslavia. The birth of the nationalist moment was tolerated by the Slovenian socialist leadership to a considerable extent. Moreover, it was even used to gain the upper hand in the struggles within the federation and they took advantage of the old cliché regarding the dirty and alienated centre (Belgrade) that dominated over the smaller republics. This was the period that would later become known as the 'Slovenian spring', characterised by close cooperation between the different levels and instances within and on the outside of the self-management apparatus that would organise the transition to independence and the capitalist economy. The main groups of the Slovenian spring and nationalised civil society would transform into the new political parties in a couple of years. It was at this moment that the conservative and nationalist groups gathered around the Catholic Church became active agents within the civil society. As early as 1987, while assessing the ideological work and actions of the Church and its civil representatives, the political theorist Tomaž Mastnak spoke of the danger of 'totalitarianism from below' (Mastnak 1987).

The next major event for subsequent nationalistic uprisings took place in early 1989, when the socioeconomic situation in Kosovo exploded. The conflict had been 'culturalised' as a case of ethnic hatred between Albanians and Serbs, while in reality the region had witnessed the most dramatic decline in social standards and infrastructure. In an area with the greatest mineral wealth in Yugoslavia (and with the huge Trepče mining complex that employed over 20,000 miners in the early 1980s), labour strikes had become a recurring phenomenon (Kirn 1982). However, the people here did not demand independence or ethnically-cleansed factories, but simply wanted better wages and improved material conditions. In light of the increasingly critical escalation, and with Slobodan Milošević already announcing that the autonomy of Kosovo would be curtailed, more than 1350 miners went on a hunger strike deep inside the mine. For over a week, the strike continued in terrible conditions, resulting in one of the most dramatic and arguably the longest underground strikes in history. The strike ended with the hospitalisation of more than 180 miners and the removal of the pro-Milošević Albanian leaders of Kosovo from their positions. This was seen as a temporary victory for the working class. However, the strike was brought to its end by a police intervention carried out by the anti-terrorist squad, which arrested the remaining 50 miners barricaded 850 metres below ground. Milošević managed to declare a 'state of emergency' through the Presidency of Yugoslavia. This remained in force for a considerable duration and allowed the Serbian police forces to intervene.

These events propelled Milošević to the top of the League of Communists of Serbia and gave him the upper hand in the power struggles within the federation. At the same time, he was also able to initiate the so-called 'anti-bureaucratic revolution' against the resisting leadership within the autonomous province of Vojvodina. Not only was he successful in revoking the constitutional right of the regional autonomy of Kosovo, he even managed to have the 'last word', as he organised – together with the Orthodox Church – a grand rally at which he held a momentous speech in front of a million people in Gazemistan upon the commemoration of the 600th Anniversary of the Battle of Kosovo (1389–1989). Celebrating 600 years since the Serbian aristocracy had lost their power to the Ottoman Empire, disguising it as a religious and nationalistic festivity of a Greater Serbia, and hinting at the possibility of future armed struggles cast a shadow over many parts of Yugoslavia.

Both the Slovenian and Croatian socialist leaderships, as well as a variety of civil initiatives throughout Yugoslavia expressed solidarity with the Trepče miners. The Slovenian Writers' Association and the ZSMS were particularly vocal in focusing their attacks on the Serbian aggression. In other words, the political and cultural representatives swiftly culturalised and nationalised the central class antagonism and used it for their own power struggles against the Serbian leadership and the central federal authority that was pushing for reforms. At the press conference on 2 March, instead of class issues, Jožef Školč, the President of ZSMS, even went so far as to argue that Albanians in Kosovo were like the Jews during World War II (*Gorenjski Glas* newspaper, 3 March 1989). The ZSMS representatives even published images of the Stars of David as an expression of solidarity with Kosovo, which was obviously a highly manipulative move: not only was it insulting to the victims of the Holocaust, but it was also used as a part of the demonisation campaign against the Serbian leadership and the Serbian people. The events that followed became a catalyst of the federation's internal struggles with regard to the constitutional reforms as well as within the communist political elite. Instead of rethinking the entire project of socialism and Yugoslavia with regard to its 'weakest link' – i.e., the failure in Kosovo, where class exploitation of the workers and the logic of underdevelopment were expressed to the extreme – the leaderships all across Yugoslavia made a dreadful mistake: they saw the miners' strikes as a vehicle for their respective nationalist agendas. This was a point of no return for the leaderships and cemented their future positions; pushing towards the destruction of Yugoslavia.

The Slovenian civil society and socialist leadership saw the rise of the Albanian and Serbian nationalism as the central indicator of the 'civilisational' distance between the European Slovenians and the barbarian Balkans (Močnik, 1999). The JBTZ trial and the events in Kosovo were used to portray the enemy in Belgrade, in what became a symbolic reconciliation between the old socialist elite and the new agents and political parties that would compete as part of the elections in Slovenia in April 1990. The democratic election brought to power the anti-communist coalition DEMOS, while the former political force the League of Communists (now embodied in the Party of Democratic Renewal), still remained an important agent, and received a considerable share of the votes at the first election. The first democratic elections, conducted in what was at the time still socialist Yugoslavia, represented the institutional culmination of the 'Slovenian Spring', which can be perceived as the date of the symbolic death of the civil society. As the ideological struggle at the end of the 1980s became both anti-Yugoslav and anti-communist,[3] the hegemonic bloc of nationalists, liberals, and former communists united in a new political constellation that called for Slovenian independence. These new parties and the old-new political Party all aspired to liberal democracy and private property and saw their future only in European integration.

At the time, all conflicts were viewed through the nationalist perspective, however they should not be interpreted in such simple black-and-white terms – as if they were simply conflicts between what were supposedly purely progressive and rich northern republics with their civil democratic spheres (Slovenia and Croatia) on the one hand and the backward and nationalist centralist forces epitomised by the figure of the formerly Western-oriented banker Slobodan Milošević (Serbia) on the other hand. The questions as regards the future constitutional form of Yugoslavia – whether it was to be a federation or confederation, the urgency of the harsh reforms – stifled the future of the common state. Probably one of the most indicative events took place on 22 January 1990, during the 14th Congress of the LCY in Belgrade, when the Slovenian delegation left the meeting in protest (for details on the League of Communists and this event, see Centrih 2015). The decision to stop all communication and discussions within the LCY and take the road to independence was, to a certain degree, understandable after an entire decade of tough battles, stifling political processes, the vacuum that followed Tito's death, and the geopolitical changes. However, in economic terms, this road can be interpreted as a road of calculated self-interest, aiming to protect the well-being and the accumulated wealth and infrastructure of the richer countries that had benefitted from the rest of the federation.

The referendum for the independence of Slovenia took place in December 1990, while the Croatian referendum was organised six months later, in May 1991. In both cases, the vast majority voted in favour of independence (around 80 per cent of the entire electorate). The political leaderships of these countries thus formally declared their independence on 25 June 1991. The new states were first recognised by the Vatican and Germany with what Woodward termed the 'German policy of preventive recognition' (1995b: 200), siding with the Croatian and Slovenian leaderships vis-à-vis the Serbian leadership, the Yugoslav federal government, and the Yugoslav People's Army. The breakdown of the Cold War order and the demise of the socialist bloc was inscribed into the new European horizon of the German national reunification that triumphed in Fukuyama's famous announcement of 'the end of history'. However, in the case of Yugoslavia something went terribly wrong. Structurally, the Croatian and Slovenian political leaderships assumed a typical 'comprador' elite position within the emerging European order. They were tasked with the following: a dispossession of social ownership and the swift introduction of private property in all social areas; turning towards NATO and the European Community; and lastly, the implementation of independence, which was recognised by the reunified Germany that was at the 'head' of the European Community (the EC), announcing the political dissolution of Yugoslavia. Following the break-up of Yugoslavia, the old federation was substituted by the 'one nation in one state' model and the proliferation of small ethnic states. Due to the economic, political, and ideological confusion at this time, this situation produced an even more intense crisis, especially in ethnically heterogeneous areas: what was one to do with the segments of the population that wanted to stay in socialist Yugoslavia, or those who now wanted to exert their own right to self-determination (e.g. the Serbian population in Krajina, Croatia; or the Serbs and Croats in Bosnia and Herzegovina that would secede a year later, in 1992)? Ethnically, Slovenia had been a very homogenous space, but this was not the case in most of the other republics and regions. The same model could thus not work in other situations, if one did not deploy force and/or the army.

The goal of this book has not been to analyse the 'final' dissolution of Yugoslavia and the onset of the ethnic wars in the 1990s. However, I wish to here at least outline some of the central reasons and causes behind the internal demise of the socialist and Yugoslav project. Further-more, apart from underlining the clear responsibility of the transitional national-liberal leaderships, democratically elected in what were still socialist republics in 1990–91, I nevertheless claim that the immediate European 'international community' recognised the new states pre-maturely and contributed to the escalation of the violent break-up. Woodward rightly ascertained that the Slovenian and Croatian declara-tions of independence at the time faced

> Substantial opposition within Yugoslavia … Europeans, for example, handed a victory to the confederalists. The federalists lost to the EC, not to a domestic vote or an elite political fact. The EC also defeated, by elimination, the third party to the constitutional conflict, the Yugoslav federal government. (1995b: 201).

Furthermore, one of the last genuine political forces in socialist Yugoslavia at the time was, paradoxically, the Yugoslav People's Army, which was not yet dominated by nationalist officers and generals. In the post-war period it enjoyed the status of the seventh republic, for it possessed its own industrial complex and enjoyed considerable autonomy. Once the EC started treating the Yugoslav People's Army in terms of the illegitimate aggressor, it turned 'into an independent actor in the political contest … from trying to hold Yugoslavia together and protect army assets to devising and defending a state-building project of its own' (Woodward 1995b: 201). Since the Yugoslav People's Army was not consulted during the negotiations with the EC and was pressured by civilian powers, Milošević started throwing out the old pro-Yugoslav and Titoist personnel, replacing them with pro-Serbian and pro-Montenegrin officers in early 1992, which basically led to the subjugation of the Yugoslav People's Army under Serbian interests and also to the long-term war.

These were the specifics of the road towards the capitalist market, which was, in Woodward's words, the 'road to tragedy' caused by the republican political elites, foreign creditors, and Western governments. The foreign creditors and Western governments demanded Yugoslavia commit 'political suicide':

> They require governments to reduce their own powers. They also do so at the same time that the demands on government, particularly the necessity to protect civil order and to provide stability in the midst of rapid change, are ever greater. Without a stable civil and legal order, the social conditions that are created can be explosive: large-scale unemployment among young people and unskilled urban dwellers; demobilized soldiers and security police looking for private employment; thriving conditions for black market activities and crime; and flourishing local and global traffic in small arms and ammunition. A sense of community under these circumstances is highly prized, but not because of the historical persistence and power of ethnic identities and cultural attachments, as the ethnic conflict school insists, but because the bases of existing communities have collapsed and governments are radically narrowing what they will or can provide in terms of previously guaranteed rights to subsistence, land, public employment, and even citizenship. (ibid., 17)

With the fall of both socialism and Yugoslavia, their banners of the partisan struggle, the Non-Aligned Movement, and self-management, yet another socialist road sank in the quagmire of wars. The nationalist bells tolled and the flags of the once-defeated local fascists and World War II collaborators were flown by the newly-elected presidents and their supporters, who would massacre each other's armies and the civilian population during the 1990s. Although this tragedy should preclude any nostalgic yearning for a paradise lost, this does nevertheless not mean that these lessons cannot guide us in the current situation.

Conclusion: After the 1991 Yugoslav Deluge, the Rise of the New Europe

Partisan Yugoslavia was an expanding and ever moving island of liberation, a utopia that floated across the stormy war-torn sea. Once liberated, Yugoslavia became an inspiration to the oppressed and a synonym for a political, geopolitical, theoretical, and even economic *scandal*. A scandal, a veritable *partisan rupture* that broke off with the mainstream ideological frame, be it capitalist realism or the Stalinist socialism that existed at the time. Yugoslavia created a decisive break within the international workers' movement that was, on the state level, dominated by Stalinism. It also stood for a rupture that could not be integrated into the scenario of the global political elites and their bipolar world nor into the subsequent nationalist-liberal revisionism that followed the fall of Yugoslavia. The *partisan struggle, self-management,* and the *Non-Aligned Movement* were all fruits of laborious struggles and the work of communist (and other) leaderships and the masses from a single generation. This book has argued that the most prominent and long-term break took place during World War II, when the antifascists and partisans succeeded in transforming the negative politics (the fight against foreign occupation) into a veritable social revolution that was supported by the masses. Yugoslavia was a part of the revolutionary sequence on the periphery of (Southern) Europe, which resulted in defeats in Spain (1936–39) and Greece (1941–49), and the victory of the liberation struggle in Yugoslavia (1941–45). In its own way the Yugoslav partisan rupture contributed to the revolutionary tradition of the oppressed, and some of its various consequences, visions, echoes, as well as unintended effects, have been covered in this book.

Chapter 1 provided the theoretical frame necessary for a deeper understanding of the 'partisan figure' and 'partisan rupture'. This chapter critically distances itself from the figure proposed by Carl Schmitt and offers a few notes on the theoretical differentiation between the telluric (ethnical) and universal partisan struggle. Furthermore, I elaborate on the Althusserian–Badiousian notion of rupture: firstly, rupture is not understood as a one-off event that is carried out by an already established agent that would merely overthrow the *ancien régime*. The partisan rupture yields strong consequences and is seen as a starting point of the revolutionary process that transformed the subjective forces as well as the objective conditions. Furthermore, the time, space, and subjectivity of rupture are inefficient and authorised by themselves, i.e., by the interiority of the struggle. In other words, the rupture is not teleological (subject to historical necessity), but contingent and unpredictable. Finally, the rupture results in strong consequences in thoughts and actions that oppose the dominant system of oppression and exploitation.

Chapter 2 provided a broader historical background to the first Yugoslav partisan rupture and analysed the central economic tensions and political antagonisms in the pre-war Kingdom of Yugoslavia. The bleak picture of the semi-fascist dictatorship in the Kingdom illustrates the major whys and wheretofores of how the Yugoslav Communist party and the masses of oppressed people revolted through uprisings, protests, and wildcat strikes. Furthermore, I pointed out how essential the experiences of the international brigades in Spain were in the light of the looming fascist war. The antifascist struggle and the various political agents of dissent and international solidarity infused new dimensions to the strategy of the People's Liberation Struggle. Even though the communists emerged victorious in the war ridden landscape due to their skilful organisation of the masses and the waging struggle, the partisan struggle cannot be reduced to a retrospective Party history.

In contrast to the official ideology of socialist Yugoslavia, Chapter 3 advocated the view that the People's Liberation Struggle (PLS) in itself became a central agent and event that initiated the new Yugoslavia. One should not take anything away from the Communist Party of Yugoslavia (CPY), its organisational and ideological work, its long-term clandestine modus of functioning, and the fact that it held an avant-garde position within the PLS. However, its leadership – with its conspiratorial and sectarian modality due to the constant interwar repression – as well as the social-political composition of the Party, changed radically during the war. The CPY became a mass organisation that ran parallel to the open and mass democratic forms of the people's liberation councils that were predominantly left to their own agility and capacity to organise the struggle and life in general.

The Yugoslav partisan movement was the only movement that included people from different religions, of both genders, and from all nationalities. Partisans created an imagery of a new future that differed radically from the other two existing political principles: the partisan movement differed from the fascist occupation and their prospect of the new fascist Europe that was based on racial hierarchies and ethnical hatred; whilst it also differed from the old forces that identified with the government of Yugoslavia in exile and were, in the military sense, represented by the Chetniks. The latter waged war on the partisans and terrorised the local population. In terms of a future horizon the Chetniks wanted to merely continue, under open Serbian national dominance, the pre-war Yugoslavia. In opposition to the two principles based on ethnical hatred, the PLS did not struggle in the name of an exclusive nation that would be predicated on an eternal national substance. The PLS was clearly based on antifascist solidarity, on the equality of all nations and nationalities and social emancipation. Furthermore, the PLS became a revolutionary mass movement that was predominantly comprised of the rural population, and which was supported not only by the CPY, but also received vital contributions from the Women's Antifascist Front and the Youth Communist Organisation. The PLS's central innovation was to combine national and social liberation in a specific form of a deter-ritorialised (anti)state. To this end the PLS developed its own mobile infrastructure, comprising political and cultural (counter)institutions on both the liberated and the occupied territories. It reached its peak during the second meeting of the Antifascist Council of the People's Liberation of Yugoslavia in November 1943, when the delegates from the Yugoslav resistance declared a partisan revolutionary government that cut all ties with the old Kingdom of Yugoslavia. The latter was formally recognised by the Allies, however, the Yugoslav partisan movement relied on its own forces and capacities and thus risked its future. A set of tremendous political consequences unfolded as a result of the partisans liberating Yugoslavia on their own, and this was reflected in *the establishment of the federative and socialist Yugoslavia*.

The post-war reconstruction was linked to a number of strategic challenges for the new Yugoslavia, such as the severity of the split of Yugoslavia from Stalin and the Cominform in 1948 assessed in Chapter 4. Yugoslavia became isolated in a period in which the future of Trieste and the Primorska region were being decided and the civil war in Greece was taking place. Despite some short-term defeats and a strategic setback for the CPY in the Balkans – the closure of the border, withdrawing the aid to the Greek resistance following Stalin's trade of Greece to the Western powers, and the failure to form a Balkan socialist federation –

the Yugoslav leadership stepped on the path to a new model of socialism and moved beyond the Balkan horizon.

Chapters 5 and 6 took a closer look into the pioneering times of the workers' self-management (SM) and the Non-Aligned Movement (NAM). These two post-war partisan ruptures did not employ the guerrilla tactics and revolutionary organisation deployed during World War II, however I claim that they continued with partisan politics by other means which yielded local and global effects. The 'internal' rupture departed from the critique of Stalinist bureaucratisation and the dominant model of nationalising the means of production and developed into the model of workers' self-management and social ownership. Undoubtedly the most successful and experimental period of self-management took place between the 1950s and the mid-1960s. On the other hand, the 'external' rupture resulted in the Yugoslav communists turning towards the rest of the world and participating in the establishment of the Non-Aligned Movement. The NAM was officially launched in 1963, with Tito becoming its first (rotating) president and Belgrade its first headquarters. The NAM became a political platform for a variety of countries that were engaged in antinuclear and anti-colonial efforts that would decentralise the bipolar world. In short, the three partisan ruptures (the PLS, SM, and the NAM) constituted a kernel of revolutionary politics that yielded consequences on the local, regional, and even global level. The first six chapters of this book examine what the partisan ruptures meant for the emancipation of the oppressed in Yugoslavia, which can be read as the interlacing of emancipatory ideas, practices, and struggles. Finally, this part of the book can be read as an attempt to reanimate the partisan figures by un-blocking the current situation of neoliberal authoritarianism and the dominant ethno-nationalist doxa.

Chapter 7 critically evaluated the most recent academic literature on 'Yugoslav studies' that, in the light of the breakup of Yugoslavia, have mostly focused on the democratic processes of the 1980s, the transition to a free-market, and the ethnic wars in the 1990s, all of which are bundled under the banner of post-socialism. The major thrust of chapters 8–12 invites readers to focus on the self-management period (1965–1972), which can be considered as the beginning of the transition towards 'post-socialism'. In juxtaposition to the first 6 chapters, that could superficially be read as a sort of nostalgic dwelling on and romanticising of the past's heroic moments, the second part of the book offers a rigorous critique of the 'next' stage of the socialist transition that regressed towards capitalism. Chapter 8 provided a historical overview of the central features and agents of Yugoslav self-management, while Chapter 9 focused on the period that was coined 'market socialism' and sketched the negative results of the market reform advocated by the communist leadership(s). These chapters depart from the definition of socialism as a 'contradictory social formation' that combines capitalist and communist elements; instead analysing how the historical transition to 'market socialism', disguised under the banner of decentralisation, brought a strong capitalist tendency that dismantled the interrepublican solidarity and reversed the effects of the partisan ruptures.

With the aid of a Marxist analysis and Lebowitz's concept of 'contested reproduction' Chapters 10 and 11 focused on the central antagonism and paradox of the self-management project. How could the socialist transition reconcile the introduction of market and the global capitalist economy with its promise of strengthening the working people and building interrepublican solidarity? The market reform revealed one of the central blind spots of self-management, which on the discursive and economic level targeted anything that smelled like centralised authority: the 'socialist market' was celebrated as a force that would resolve class tensions and fight bureaucratisation. The contradictory movement that strengthened the logic of capital took place on two levels: *firstly*, on the macro level, as could be seen in the relocation of social capital that affected the development of the entire federation and the fair distribution of the national product that functioned as a social transfer from the richer to the poorer regions. The market reform dismantled the central institution of the Fund for Investment and transferred the power to re-locate funds and provide loans to a set of new commercial banks that strengthened the position of the republics vis-à-vis the federation. The underdevelopment of certain regions further favoured the richer parts of Yugoslavia that competed on the market. *Secondly*, the conflict took place within the system of socialist enterprise(s), wherein the economic decentralisation and freedoms legally guaranteed more freedom for workers' self-management. In reality all strategic decisions were concentrated in the hands of the directors and engineers – known as the technocracy – who were in favour of the market reform and its implementation. The core struggle for the management of social and independent capital therefore took place within the enterprise (e.g. contesting wages and investment), where workers were partially blocked out by the technocracy. Even though the market reform granted workers additional rights to decide over the accumulation process within the enterprise and thus valorise their wages, it did not contribute to the expansion of the time necessary for reflection and political activity of the working people. Furthermore, the (self)valorisation process, and the path to rising wages, resulted in doors closing for new workers. Workers became structurally alienated from other non-workers, and were prevented from truly entering the self-management institutions: due to their lack of time, energy, and interest, on the one hand they continued to be *represented* by the political bureaucracy in their formal representative bodies, while, on the other they were represented by the technocracy in their workplaces. Once the new ruling class coalition of the technocrats and bureaucrats formulated the liberal programme that opened up Yugoslavia to the global labour and capital market, things only became worse. The implementation of the market reform had negative politico-economic effects: the exploitation within enterprises strengthened, unemployment started rising, and the differences between regions intensified the (infra)structural disadvantages of the underdeveloped regions. Even though the decentralised state apparatus still managed to contribute to the improvement and growth of the social infrastructure (through social housing, hospitals, nursery schools, and schools), it performed rather poorly in terms of strengthening the labour power and the power of those who were about to enter the labour market. The figure of the migrant worker was a symptomatic sign of the transition towards capitalism (post-socialism) as well as the first testing ground for the flexible (neoliberal) workforce and market on the European scale. The separation of workers from the political and economic instruments influenced their decision to organise hundreds of labour strikes during the 1960s.

Chapter 12 brought to the forefront the self-management politics from below and the most tumultuous moments between 1968 and 1972. This was a period that witnessed the first explosion of revolutionary democratic, cultural, and political activities: from wildcat strikes and student movements to various cultural (Black wave) and theoretical activities (the Praxis school). This amalgam of theory, politics, and culture emerged from the failed promise of the Yugoslav leadership, while advocating the implementation of genuine self-management. Because of this, the struggles were initially read as a leftist or communist critique of the existing socialism. However, this was not the only answer to the political crisis. In the early 1970s Yugoslavia experienced a series of nationalist outbursts: from the disputes that emerged over the distribution of financial loans to regions (the 'highway affair' in Slovenia) and incidents and nationalist protests in Kosovo, to the major unrest in Croatia that saw the rise of the movement called 'Maspok'. The latter included students and parts of the republican communist bureaucracy, who, for the first time since the war, articulated nationalist, anti-Yugoslav, and anti-communist feelings. Alongside the political analysis this chapter also provides a critique of the ideology that shows how the figure of the working class shifted towards a more loosely defined figure of the 'self-manager' and the related concepts of man, nation, and market. Instead of reviving the partisan ruptures and promises of self-management in cohesion with the communist youth and left-wing critics, the Titoist leadership opted for a wave of repression that dealt equally with the left and right-wing 'deviations' within the political and cultural realm. Some protagonists of the 1968 unrests were arrested, some were stopped from working (in university and in film), while others left the country. The repressive end of this period illustrated the exhaustion of the partisan ruptures and the failure of the political leadership to organise and promote social forces that could shift the capitalist tendencies towards a more communist sequence.

In the final chapter I took a closer look at the emergence of democratic forces in Slovenia, the wealthiest republic in Yugoslavia and the republic that is usually considered a good example of the transition towards liberal democracy. The civil society that emerged in the 1980s brought with it dramatic reversals and internal contradictions. The initial period could be provisionally termed as efforts to 'democratise' socialism. The political composition of the movement was extremely broad, ranging from the League of Socialist Youth (part of the official political apparatus) to students, ecological activists, cultural groups, feminists, and LGBT rights groups. This colourful political movement was hegemonised during the second part of the 1980s, when the civil society took a more nationalistic turn during the military trial against four journalists (the famous JBTZ affair) in and after 1987. During this period of austerity policies and the political vacuum that followed Tito's death, the 'avant-garde' intellectuals from Serbia (Academy of Sciences and Arts) and Slovenia (Nova Revija) openly called for national independence. Socialism, Yugoslavia, and the withering away of the classes and the state were now largely forgotten and social issues were now read exclusively through nationalistic lenses. Kosovo, an autonomous province and structurally the 'weakest link' of the federation became a site of confrontation for the nationalistic political elites (most notably from Slovenia and Serbia) that were deciding on the future of Yugoslavia and the reforms that were to take place within the federation. With the ever-increasing austerity reforms demanded by the IMF and the ever-poorer economic situation, the calls for dramatic changes and new leadership intensified.

The Yugoslav self-management model did not fail because it was not liberal enough, but because it was not *communist* enough.[1] It failed to spread the revolutionary politics to all fields of society and it also failed to reanimate the link between the masses, the working classes, and the LCY. The constant criticism of the State pushed the self-management model on a path of 'deregulation' that brought liberalism to the forefront of the ideological confrontation. The path to *actual* self-management was hijacked by the bureaucratic-technocratic coalition. Class antagonism became visible and acute despite the impressive legal documentation and formalisation of the ever-growing socioeconomic and political rights of the self-managed workers and communities. This was not merely a defeat of the left-wing forces and for socialism in Yugoslavia and the former East, for it also influenced the demise of the Keynesian welfare state model in the West.

The Rise of New Europe?

The fall of the Berlin Wall brought some political and economic freedoms for citizens of the socialist bloc, but also other extremely negative processes: class exploitation intensified, national minorities became marginalised and oppressed, nationalist and conservative religious views were revived. The former East might have contributed a major conservative counterrevolution in the 1990s, but only by becoming an export target for West Germany. It is noteworthy that the famous meeting between Helmut Kohl and Ronald Reagan at the Bitburg cemetery where some SS soldiers are buried, dramatically shifted the official borders of World War II memory from antifascism to national reconciliation. The famous *Historikstreit* –Nolte's rehabilitation of Nazism that was academically defeated – strongly echoed in Eastern Europe. Finally, the newly reunified Germany became the central state upon which the new political elites of the Eastern countries modelled themselves. The call for the reunification of Germany was in fact the very first Trumpist slogan of the new Europe: *make Germany great again, and with it Europe!* Europe had its own Trumpism well before Trump came to power in the US. The German shock therapy model of reunifying with its Eastern part showed the East how it should behave and how the transition should be executed. There was no discussion, no new constitution, no class compromise, but a meticulously planned takeover that was packed with modernisation and foreign direct investments.

Once neoliberal triumphalism reached Yugoslavia, we witnessed its most brutal results: ethnic wars and rogue capitalism in the small (in) dependent states. What represented a victory for the new Europe and neoliberalism on the one hand, represented a total defeat of the emancipatory struggles for democratic socialism and the revolutionary legacy on the other. The Yugoslavia of 1991 confirmed the total exhaustion of the three partisan ruptures: the socialist federation, self-management, and the non-aligned movement. Yugoslavia was no longer seen as the model for universal emancipation, a different road to socialism, and the non-aligned movement: a genuine *third way*. The latter was taken over by the Social Democrats who embraced neoliberalism, while Yugoslavia began to be associated with much darker metaphors and judgements: ethnic wars driven by the irrationality of formerly brotherly nations now fighting each other, the ultimate corruption of the comprador mafia political class, and the general absence of a 'democratic culture': in short, it became the site of Balkanisation. This was the time for people from Yugoslavia to forget about their achievements and start from below zero.

The partisan ruptures did not follow the historical necessity that were instituted and driven by the Party. The successful social revolution with transformative effects was a result of the encounter between the struggling masses, the cultural revolution, and the organisational capacities of the Communist Party, the Women's Antifascist Front and the League of Youth Communists. If there was no historical necessity for the rise of a new Yugoslavia, the same can be said for the fall of socialist Yugoslavia. In retrospect one can see the reasons for the breakup in the complex swings between the internal implosion of the self-management model, the nationalistic recomposition of the political elites, the external harshening of austerity, the crisis of industrialisation, and the wider neoliberal advancement. The exhaustion of the partisan ruptures also mirrored the inability of the communist leadership to conduct the historical task of renovating socialism and merely embracing the global historical trend with a nationalistic face. Yugoslavia withered away into multiple small nationalistic states and neoliberal capitalism – everything that the partisan ruptures stood against.

The prevailing liberal argument on the demise of Yugoslavia can be seen in the reiteration of the inefficiency of the socialist economy and its appalling levels of debt. From a comparative and global perspective of increasing financialisation one might, at first glance, not note anything unique that would make socialist countries more prone to debt in relation to the global capitalist economy. However, financialisation shows that the disciplinary instruments are implemented once again on the (semi)peripheral countries through austerity, privatisation, and other forms of shock therapy (Živković 2013). In the specific example of Yugoslavia, I would like to stress that, firstly, the Yugoslavian debt was nowhere close to the level of debt of its successor states a few years later or nowadays (see Obradović 2018); secondly, that Yugoslavia was receiving major loans from the mid-1970s onwards, which was a result of both the high trade deficits with the West and the changing climate of the global economy; and thirdly, that with the help of the IMF, who finally decided to sign off a fraction of the debt in 1989, Yugoslavia was able to repay some of its interest on its debt.

However, the price Yugoslavia paid for returning the escalating debt and its interest to IMF was excessive. The price cannot be measured in purely economic terms, for it brought with it a series of social and political consequences: the austerity policies resulted in mass redundancies in factories, stagnating wages, and deteriorating social infrastructure, meanwhile the IMF's political demands for the centralisation of self-management, a system that from its very beginnings strove towards becoming less centralised and more democratically organised, brought the republican leadership to a standstill at the federal level. With the rising inflation levels (in 1989, inflation hit 1000 per cent) and the increasing political crisis within and between republican leaderships, Yugoslavia was brought to its knees. The most logical representative of the recovery that would orchestrate paradoxical centralisation policies *and* an 'anti-bureaucratic revolution' in Yugoslavia, as demanded by the IMF and the neoliberal ideology, was nobody other than Slobodan Milošević, the head of one of the largest banks in Yugoslavia.

This book has not focused on the transition towards authoritarian capitalism in Yugoslavia and how its essential part could be found in the ethnic wars that took place with the complicity of the 'international community'. However, certain parallels can be drawn between the

Yugoslav breakup and the current major crisis in the new Europe. This is why the demise of Yugoslavia and its 'avant-garde' call to make new small nation-states great again should have been taken much more seriously. The death of Yugoslavia and the birth of (new) Europe do not only coincide historically but have some *unheimliche* spectral resemblances in the way political and economic processes unfolded. Let us recall that it was during the wars in the Balkans, when Yugoslavia was singing *destroy, destroy,* that Europe announced its triumph, with *Insieme, unite, unite Europe* which was the winner of the Eurovision Song Contest in Zagreb and proclaimed the European integration process, which was inaugurated in 1993 by the Maastricht treaty.

The spectators and audiences could enjoy a Manichean division of the new capitalist reality: on the one hand, the fall of the Berlin Wall, the end of socialism, and the Maastricht treaty, on the other hand the Siege of Sarajevo, massacres in Srebrenica, and the Dayton treaty. On the one hand we had the logic of cosmopolitanism and liberal multiculturalism under the regime of capital homogenisation in Europe, on the other hand we had right-wing populism, parochialism, re-traditionalisation, the marginalisation of minorities, and the dispossession of the working classes. When we are pushed against the wall with a dominant 'alternative' the choice has already been made for us: either we choose Europe as the lighthouse of freedom and democracy, or the Balkans as the space of backwardness and eternal ethnical animosity (Močnik 1999). This alternative repeats the long-established liberal–conservative ideological trope – Europe or the Balkans – that excludes the possibility for any political autonomy and future that could be imagined within the Balkans and for the people in the Balkans. Furthermore, it forces people from Yugoslavia to forget their historical experiences, the radicality of the partisan ruptures and their experiments in workers' self-management and other emancipatory movements within socialist Yugoslavia. The negative image of the Balkans thus carries a racist and (self)orientalising ideologeme that functions as a 'phantasmatic screen' onto which we can constantly project anything negative. Instead of attempting to understand the rise of authoritarian politics internal to the transition towards neoliberal democracy and capitalism, everything can be reduced to the eternal identitarian, religious, and ethnical animosities. It is not surprising that this – alternative is not an alternative at all, for it, from the very start, openly favours the necessary transition to the paternalistic Western/European/free market. This narrative also functioned as an exculpation mechanism obfuscating the complicity at the beginning of the war and Europe's tremendous failure to deal with the wars in its backyard.

Choosing new Europe as a phantasmatic screen of everything positive has a long history with a material basis. Let us not forget that the European Southern periphery with Spain, Portugal, and Greece, which represented the previous enlargement of the European Community was created on the horizon of the welfare state and the democratic renewal following the period of fascist rule. From this emancipatory perspective, led by the democratic and socialist movements in the 1970s, the (temporary) defeat of fascism in Europe in the 1970s painted an optimistic vision of the European future. This was whole-heartedly embraced by the elites and the inhabitants of most former socialist countries, who wanted to become a part of Europe at any cost. Dreams of a new community were linked to the democratic promise, the hope retrospectively seen as a naive belief, that the free movement of capital and labour, as well as the protection of human rights and democratic standards, would be safeguarded by the new European Union. One could say that the very first major challenge – the wars in the Balkans – indicated that the European Community failed to address the consequences of its premature recognition of Slovenia and Croatia. There was no unanimous European policy as regards the post-Yugoslav context and the US had to intervene, while fully acknowledging the authoritarian ethnical politics. The international community led by Clinton, resolved the war by confirming the ethnical model of one nation – one state. Instead of Europe ironically smirking at Trump's slogan 'Make America great again!' we should acknowledge our own process of making nation x great again: from the reunified Germany becoming great within new Europe, to its plural echoes in the making of Slovenia, Croatia, Serbia, and now Britain great nations again.

Bringing together the destruction of Yugoslavia and the current crisis of the EU periphery does not provide us with a recipe as to how we could break the current deadlock, or make a prediction of what is going to happen with the rise of the extreme-right in Europe and the crumbling of the European neoliberal project. What this short conclusion can point towards is the political fact that all major revolutions of the twentieth century started on the periphery, and that an alternative world is possible even in times when there is allegedly no alternative and no history, be it revolutionary or counter-revolutionary. Speaking about the partisan and socialist Yugoslav past can be seen as a critical meditation on the mistakes of socialism as well as an affirmation of the old victories of the oppressed. Finally, it is only the patient and increasingly determined work of the working classes, their intellectual and political capacities, insurgent revolts and radical labour and party organisations that will bring about a new socialist strategy for a different future.

Notes

Introduction

1. Lešaja analysed 19 years (1990–2009) of the cleansing of books that were deemed ideologically problematic in Croatia and reached an estimate that approximately fourteen per cent of all library books have been either burnt or destroyed in some other way. This number does not include the usual share of the book-stock that needs to be removed due to the lack of space (austerity).

2. Mirt Komel viewed the Yugoslav wars through the topic of primitive accumulation (2011), however a good selection of texts focusing on the post-Yugoslav context and a few other Eastern European countries can also be found in the edited volume *Kroz Tranziciju* (Gajić and Popović, 2011) and one on primitive accumulation edited by Hajdini (2013).

3. For a good analysis of the ideological transition see Buden (2009); for a critique of post-fascism, see Močnik (1995) and Kuzmanić (1999), especially in relation to xenophobia towards migrants and people from former Yugoslav republics in Slovenia.

4. For a good historical overview of the transition process in Yugoslavia see Močnik (2008), also see edited volume by Veselinović (2011).

5. Balibar and Wallerstein's (1991) collective effort launched a critical approach that accounted for the relative autonomy of instances and political subjectivations that relate to race, gender, and class. See also the introduction to the edited volume of Burchardt and Kirn (2017).

6. A number of serious historical and cultural studies agree that the Yugoslav experience cannot be reduced to the totalitarian paradigm, see Centrih and Kosi (2007); Centrih (2011); Kuljić (2010); and Jovanović (2012), nor can it be simply applied in the more general context of the Eastern bloc, see Ghodsee (2011); Sable and Stark (1982). For a juxtaposing view see Schöpflin (1993).

7. From museums of totalitarian art (Amsterdam, Sofia) and the Museum of Totalitarianism (Kiev) to the House of Terror Museum (Budapest) and museums of recent national histories that formed a unified front on the historical convergence or continuity of the two totalitarianism(s) within the former Eastern bloc (Radonić 2009, Ghodsee 2014, Koposov 2017). For a detailed and critical analysis of the musealisation of the East in the example of the House of Terror Museum in Budapest see Boris Buden (2009) who rightfully claimed that people in the East soon had to forget that they were the ones who conducted the democratic changes at the end of the 1980s;

deprived of a political past they had to recognise their lack of democratic culture and perform a kind of self-orientalising gesture. For a broader view on the long-term political criminalisation of communism through EU institutions and political discourse see Neumayer (2018).

8. Mitja Velikonja wrote *Titostalgia*, a book that predominantly covered the nostalgic practices surrounding Tito (2009).

9. Louis Althusser elaborates on the philosophical critique of the teleological thought along the ideological line origin–subject–goal in the Marxist theory and certain forms of Hegelianism (1976).

10. Jović pointed out that the transitologists are not interested in the transition process of where societies have moved from, and then to. Instead they apply extremely technical and normative models in order to evaluate the current stand of a particular society (2010: 65).

11. Due to spatial limitations this book cannot offer an integral and exhaustive study of all historical periods and all major topics within workers' self-management. For the period following the market reform I would recommend reading Darko Suvin's book (2016) that contributes important elements for further analysis, while the thematic collection edited by Velagić (2009) sheds some much-needed light on the issue of women and social reproduction that are here only briefly discussed.

Chapter 1

1. For a detailed theoretical discussion see Chapter 4 of my doctoral thesis, in which I discuss what Althusser's return to Machiavelli contributes to the conception of revolutionary politics in the (post)Marxist theory (Kirn 2012a: 95–131).

2. Althusser adopted 'the standpoint of reproduction', 'which is the standpoint of the class struggle as an overall process [*proces d'ensemble*], not a sum of confrontations that are punctual or limited to this or that 'sphere' (the economy, politics, ideology); and as a *historical process*, not *isolated* episodes of repression or revolt' (Althusser 2014: 220).

3. Regarding the significance of Machiavelli for early Althusser, see also Terray (1996). For a sound historical-political overview of the struggles in Europe during this period, see Mastnak (2001); for Florence and Italy, see especially N. Rubinstein (1994: 30–65).

4. Katja Kolšek (2013) has already brought to attention the double understanding of the rupture of 'verità effetuale dela cosa'. Kolšek explores the philosophical void and the aleatory moment within historical science, which introduces the Hegelian dialectic and its causality of expressive totality. In this text we are more interested in the transition into the political void and the registration of its political materiality.

5. Althusser defines the void with a minimal distinction between the theoretical and political practice (2006: 113–14).

6. Hannah Arendt also explored the Kantian self-foundation gesture and the contingency of politics in her comments on Machiavelli (Arendt, 1958). The

differences between Arendt's and Althusser's understanding of politics are considerable, and they become totally incompatible with regard to the points of separation between the private and the public and in regard to Arendt's central assumption about the privileged position of politics in which politics is seen as public and supposedly separated from the 'social'. Althusser, on the other hand, insists on Marx's thesis of the politicisation of 'social' and revolutionary experiences that have strong consequences for the whole society. Revolutionary events politicise all spheres of human activity, which thus become a public matter.

7. See Kirn (2013); Morfino (2013); Badiou (2005).

8. Karl Marx and Friedrich Engels (MECW 1975–2005, vol. 5: 8–11). This is also one of the key guidelines of Marx's Theses on Feuerbach, especially the 2nd, 3rd, 4th, and, naturally, the 11th thesis, which reveal the idealism of those positions that focus only on the changes of ideas rather than material circumstances. For an excellent conceptual presentation, see Debenjak (2008); Labica (1987); Macherey (2008).

9. One of the best criticisms of the position of the abstract that lacks the organisational potential and capacity was written by Lukács in his studies of Lenin (1971).

10. Althusser relativised the separation of theory and practice with the concept of 'theoretical practice' (Althusser 2005).

11. The most consistent development of this thesis was accomplished by Alain Badiou (2005), a former student of Althusser. Despite some reservations I will employ some of Badiou's elaborations on the politics of the 'event', which in Althusser's terms would be identical to 'encounter'.

12. The post-Gramscian theory of hegemony is supported by many post-colonial and emancipation theoreticians who build upon the joint works of Laclau and Mouffe (1985). The side of the 'pure politics' of the event is upheld, for example, by Badiou (2005) and Rancière (1999).

13. If we insist that revolutions are political overthrows that change merely the political leadership, we quickly return to the pre-modern understanding of revolutions as cyclical phenomena (*revolvere*).

14. As Toscano points out, many leftist theories are mistaken as regards their evolutionary concept of transition on the one hand and the direct leap into communism on the other. Toscano demonstrates that Balibar was one of the few who considered a theory of transition that did not stem from catastrophism or an evolutionary movement through stages.

15. Although Marx wrote very little about socialism and communism, his analyses of the concrete situations in the case of the Paris Commune clearly show that he did not find any guaranties within the revolutionary politics that a revolution would change the world forever.

16. Buck-Morss (2002). I will return to the issue of productivity in socialism in the subsequent chapters of the book, in which I will analyse the market reforms and Yugoslav socialism.

17. For the most detailed history of the concept of rupture through Machiavelli, see Lahtinen (2009).

18. We should mention that in his early period, Althusser identified with the line that supported the idea of revolutions as pure and irreversible ruptures. The concept of the 'epistemological rupture', which Althusser adopted from Bachelard, is based on the thesis that after the discovery of the new theoretical continent (e.g. the science of the class struggle, the science of the subconscious), the ultimate separation between science and ideology occurs. The epistemological rupture sets a strict division and triggers effects that are supposed to be exclusively intra-scientific. If we apply this to the political reality, the epistemological rupture would separate the communist revolution and movement from the bourgeois revolutions and political forms irreversibly, thus irrevocably cutting the umbilical cord between politics and ideology.

19. Antonio Negri explored this differentiation between the 'constitutive' and 'constituted power' while interpreting Machiavelli in his text *Insurgencies* (1999). If the latter appears as a consolidated power, the former is the one that the revolutionary 'tradition' relied upon in its future struggles.

20. For Machiavelli's theory of revolution, see Kirn (2012: 124–31).

21. In Machiavelli's times, fortune was defined as fate and depicted as a female figure that supposedly ran our lives and brought about catastrophes. *Virtù*, however, was mainly viewed through a moral optics and defined as a moral obligation by humanists. Machiavelli abandoned these two concepts or, rather, remade them completely: fortune was thus no longer an objective and unchangeable destiny of an act (criticism of the cyclicity of history and Polybius), while the prince's *virtù* became a political ability, capable of controlling destiny. For more on this issue see Kirn (2012: 111–120) and Lahtinen (2009).

22. Particularly in the text *Reply to John Lewis* (1976). Althusser here argued in favour of the people's masses: 'Something can rise and develop in the union of the people of France, something that has been destroyed by Stalinist practices but which is at the heart of the Marxist and Leninist tradition: something that concerns the relation between the Party and the masses. *Return the word to the masses* that make history, be at the service not only of the masses (a slogan that could also sound reactionary), but *listen to their voices*, to study and comprehend their aspirations and contradictions, their aspirations in their contradictions, be able to pay attention to the imagination and creativity of the masses'. (Althusser, 1977: 11). Althusser by no means answers the questions as to how exactly the Party is supposed to listen to the masses, how it should cooperate with them more closely, or how to act in the historical moments in which the masses themselves are divided, for example during civil wars.

23. According to Rancière (1999), the politics of rupture involves a rupture with the police order in particular. It intervenes with the logic of the existing counting, making those who have been inaudible, invisible, or structurally excluded from the 'police' order visible and audible. True politics bores into the 'distribution of the sensible' and thus begins a new logic of counting, which asserts the egalitarian maxim and includes everything, even the 'parts

of no-part'. This universal principle of politics stops at the point where the new logic of counting produces new miscounts and when politics gives birth to a new police order. With its eternal reoccurrence, the police prevented Rancière from deliberating on the transition or on the long-term effects of politics.

24. In this sense, Heinrich's interpretation (2012) of the contingency of the revolution agrees in its entirety with Althusser's critique of vulgar Marxism (2005).

25. I am referring to the interpretations that are nowadays based on Schmitt (1996), which established the political field in the context of the opposition between enemies and friends. I shall return to this subject in the following section.

26. The discussion on universalism has been well developed, among others, by Butler (1997); Rancière (1999); Badiou (2005), and the volume from Žižek, Butler, and Laclau (2000).

27. It is inappropriate for the discussion on the (lack of the) political justification for terror to end too quickly with the criticism of violence. I shall revisit this issue at a later point.

28. Althusser (2006) insists on the differentiation between taking over the state power (Lenin) and state apparatus (Stalin): between the apparatus and the machine.

29. Claude Lefort also focuses on this. According to him, the main characteristic of any democratic government – in comparison with totalitarian ones – is to preserve the 'empty space of power' (Lefort, 1988).

30. Rancière (1999) and Badiou (2005) offer an extremely interesting politicisation of what was otherwise the legal and initially liberal principle of equality as the core of any emancipatory politics.

31. Althusser (1999: 79).

32. Let us merely refer to a few excellent studies on space and strategic stakes with regard to both the emancipatory politics and the understanding of the conjunction of the authorities and capitalism. For example, see Foucault (2004); Harvey (2001); Hardt and Negri (2009); Lefebvre (1970); Sassen (1996).

33. In this sense, Althusser looked to the Italian theoretician Antonio Gramsci, who had, in Althusser's opinion, paved the way for the thematisation of the superstructure. See Gramsci (1957). The anarchistic tradition, some of the postoperaists (Negri and Hardt, 2009), and the popular theory by Holloway (2002) all discuss the strategic mistake of the Communist Parties that merely took over the state governments. The mere takeover of power leads merely to the stifling of the revolution and the wish to change the world. The focus should therefore be on changing the world without any (state) governments. Badiou (2005) developed the internal critique of the 'Party-state' from another perspective. He sees any state as an opponent of the procedure of truth and the event that cannot be represented. Politics should be taken away from the state. This is the point of controversy between socialism and communism.

34. Rancière wrote an exceedingly important critique of Negri's concept of the 'multitude' (Rancière 2002).

35. See Hooker (2009: 210–11); Aureli (2011); Agamben (1998). Žižek (2011) comes up with similar interpretations with a more Leninist emphasis.

36. Che Guevara (2002), who defines the partisan army as the 'armed vanguard of the people' and thus criticises the established model of the contemporaneous socialist politics (the Party – the working class), is one of the vital theoretical references.

37. Schmitt (2004: 38).

38. Toscano (2008: 417–33).

39. Within Schmitt's strict legal frame the partisans were not officially recognised either by the occupying forces or by the Allies, except when they represented the old government. In this sense, the Allies – by waiting for recognition of the Yugoslav partisans – legitimised, in accordance with the legal logic, the Nazi terror against 'the bandits', whom the fascists failed to treat as regular prisoners of war or as a part of the anti-fascist coalition.

40. The fact that Giorgio Agamben, one of the main supporters of Schmitt today, never discussed the partisan figure, is extremely telling. Agamben (1998) constructs his theory of sovereign authority through the figures of the extraordinary sovereign on the one hand and the 'homo sacer' on the other. According to the logic of sovereignty, 'homo sacer' is subjected to the mechanism of 'inclusive exclusion' and represents the most internal element of the sovereign order (a sovereign may designate anyone as an exception) and consequently also the most external element (which can be killed rather than sacrificed). Due to his insistence on desubjectification and a more passive moment of politics, Agamben does not thematise the partisans, as the latter drives the logic of sovereignty beyond its limits. See also Hallward's critique of Agamben (Hallward 2005: 237–44).

41. Schmitt is not interested in the experiences of the anti-colonial movement or the Non-Aligned Movement. Moreover, he cynically equals these movements with 'zones of neutrality' that promote 'planetary liberalism'.

42. Schmitt suspends the antagonism and makes the conflict practically eternal through the optics of the division into friends and enemies, which, after all, results in the depoliticisation of Schmitt's theory.

43. Toscano (2008: 425).

44. Let me mention the example of the Lithuanian partisans, who, between the end of World War II and 1956, fought against the Soviet army and remained dedicated to the telluric moment. The Soviet liberation, which came at a price in the East, should by no means be idealised. However, at the same time we should be aware that during the war, a part of the Lithuanian military formations collaborated with the German Nazis. If we could conditionally say that the Lithuanian partisans fought against the Soviet imperialism, this does not absolve them of their wartime collaboration, and their struggle by no means qualifies among the revolutionary transformations of social relations.

45. On 'subjective violence', see Balibar (2002); Žižek (2008). Should religious

foundations be established instead of national ones, a resistance can also turn into religious fundamentalism, which excludes anyone who does not belong to the correct religion.

46. Toscano (2010) advocates an attack against the dominant clichés about fanaticism in politics and the appropriation of militant subjectivities in order to argue in favour of the current emancipatory policies.

47. If we are more concise, Schmitt's reference to the telluric is largely based on Fichte's interpretation of Machiavelli, while the import of Machiavelli into the German context is closely related to the genesis of nationalism. Schmitt's demand for a German Machiavelli calls not only for a unified Germany, but also for a colonialist expansion of the Reich (Schmitt 2004: 74).

Chapter 2

1. On the Banat Republic see Radonić (1919), while Titl (1970) wrote an in-depth study of the Prekmurje region, which describes the local revolutionary forces, ethnic, and religious groups, and the various takeovers of power in 1919. These territories – disputed by Romania, Hungary, and the Kingdom of SHS – were annexed to the Kingdom of SHS in accordance with the 1921 Treaty of Trianon.

2. See Banac (1984), Čalić (2010).

3. The extreme national divisions were further exacerbated by the socio-economic situation, as the bourgeois parties and monarchists supported the unitarian concept of the constitution; Banac (1984: 226–48). See also Lampe (2000).

4. Centrih (2011). Centrih presents a sound summary of the conflicts between the factions (112–33).

5. Ibid., 112.

6. Magaš (1993: 23–7).

7. For more details on the Yugoslav concentration camps that emerged during the 1930s, see *Opća enciklopedija JLZ 4* (1978: 500–504).

8. The historian Ivo Banac emphasised the ambivalent position of the CPY that oscillated between national unity and Marxist internationalism (Banac 1984: 328–29). According to Banac, in the beginning of the 1920s, 'communist leaders were overconfident of their ability to ride the continental red wave', which is the reason why they did not include the national question in the political agenda. This criticism of the Yugoslav communists is appropriate to some extent, but it has to be noted that in the Soviet Union, Lenin's advocacy of the nations' right to self-determination already existed at the time. It differed greatly from Woodrow Wilson's principle, as the national struggle was included into the broader anti-imperialist and revolutionary struggle. It also supported the smaller nations in their struggle against the oppression by larger nations.

9. Dedijer (1980). According to some estimates, at least 200 CPY leaders died in Moscow. This political vacuum facilitated Tito's rise. He was officially recognised by the Comintern a year later, following Dimitrov's intervention.

10. Magaš (1993: 27–8).
11. See Beevor (2006).
12. For further details, see Tomasevich (2001: 233–303).
13. Tomasevich documented the dimensions of the destruction of the Jewish and Roma communities in Yugoslavia. The majority of the Yugoslav Jewish community was annihilated in the concentration camps. It is important to mention – irrespective of the discourse of the Holocaust, where Jews are merely passive victims – that some Jewish people had been members of the communist organisations and their leaderships since the end of the 1930s. Many of them joined the People's Liberation Struggle because of the terror suffered during World War II (ibid., 605–607; Romano 1980).
14. The recent wars in the post-Yugoslav context rekindled extreme nationalist imageries. New nationalists assumed the rhetoric and insignia of the local collaborators in World War II.
15. As Dežulović pointed out, the Chetniks even joined forces with the Ustashe in Dalmatia and Bosnia, where they would help with destroying partisan units and executing activists of the Young Communist League of Yugoslavia and the Women's Anti-Fascist Front (Dežulović 2013).
16. The fourth and fifth enemy offensives (Case White, 20 January–20 March 1943 and Case Black, 15 May–16 June 1943, respectively) confirmed the decisiveness and resilience of the anti-fascist partisan struggle – a fact also noted by the British Military Mission visiting the Supreme Headquarters of the National Liberation Army at the time (see the memoirs of Deakin, one of the members of the mission, 1973). The British Mission was instituted in mid-1943 and became increasingly disappointed in Mihailović's Chetniks, who kept delaying political action against the Nazis and instead fought the partisans (Petranović 1988: 241–43).
17. Rudi Omota, an activist within the Liberation Front, filmed the anti-communist manifestations, held by the local collaborators in Ljubljana in 1944. This material was later used at the post-war trials.

Chapter 3

1. Slovenian language distinguishes between 'people' (ljudstvo) and 'nation' (narod), even though in the political and theoretical texts these two concepts are used interchangeably and should be interpreted with regard to the specific context. For more information on the historical development of the concepts of the nation, nationality, and ethnicity in the Yugoslav space see Banac 1984: 23–7). Banac states that nationalism is a modern concept and places the development of the national awareness in the late nineteenth century. Nevertheless, occasionally his thesis transforms into emphasising the nationalist ideology as an eternal and ahistorical formation. In Slovenia an excellent study on this was written by Jernej Kosi (2013). Unlike Banac, Karl Deutsch offers a more precise definition of nationalities as groups of people on the path towards their political, economic and cultural autonomy (Deutsch, 1996). During World War II, a variety of terms were used in the

context of the partisan struggle, with the exception of the French version of *the nation* or the unitarian *Yugoslav nation* (jugoslovanska nacija), which had an exceedingly negative connotation from the time of the Kingdom of Yugoslavia. See also Woodward's critique of ethno-centrism (2003).

2. At this point my observations are based on the discussion on the alternative concept of 'the people', examined by Jacques Rancière (1999) who attempted to keep a critical distance towards the substantialisation of the people into a nation, as well as towards certain necessary results of the popular sovereignty in a nation-state. In Chapter 1, I pointed out how the partisan rupture and its subjective figure (the partisans/revolutionary people) subverted the retrospective nationalist readings that offer merely a perspective of the national statehood.

3. Pupovac (2006: 16).

4. Badiou (2005: 1–10) works on the understanding of the partisan uprisings in France in terms of a 'political event' that went beyond the situation.

5. Already in the 1960s the more critical artists started focusing on the mythicisation of the partisan struggle, which impoverished the understanding of the complexity of the PLS and tied it to the Party's teleology. In this regard we should mention the new political aesthetics of the modernist monuments to revolution (Karge, 2010; Kirn, 2012) as well as the so-called 'Black Wave' films. For further reading on the alternative commemoration of the partisan rupture see Kirn (forthcoming, Chapter 3).

6. Komelj was right in his assessment that the PLS also took place in the perspective of the 'ultimate fight', which was supposed to put an end to all (imperialist) wars.

7. The Yugoslav partisans co-organised the partisan actions in Bulgaria, Albania, Austria, and Italy. The attempt to establish a partisan movement, tasked with coordinating the antifascists in the Balkans, was prevented by the British Allies. Following World War II, it was Yugoslavia that helped the Greek partisans in their civil war, up until the international isolation of Yugoslavia in 1948 (Karamanić 2009). Svetozar Tempo Vukmanović, who was in charge of the Balkan coordination, discussed these issues in great detail in his memoirs (1982). See also Petranović (1991).

8. See Manucci's text (2003) on the Garibaldi Division.

9. Partisans were not a Yugoslav invention. Etymologically speaking, the word 'partisan' comes from the Latin word *pars* (part), and its first use can be tracked back to 1555 (in French). In the modern sense of the word, partisans appeared for the first time during Napoleon's invasion of Spain, when the local guerrilla fighters fought the occupying forces. The twentieth century saw a proliferation of guerrilla struggles, related to the fight against local/ regional dictatorships or to the struggle against fascism, imperialism, and colonialism.

10. In order to underline the differences, I would like to quote the oath of the Slovenian collaborators, the Home Guard, who took a collective oath under the SS command on Adolf Hitler's birthday, on 20 April 1944: 'I swear by almighty God that I will be loyal, brave and obedient to my superiors, that

I will stand in common struggle with the German armed forces, which are commanded by the leader of the Greater Germany, the SS troops and the police against bandits and communism and their allies. I will carry out this duty conscientiously in the name of my Slovenian homeland as a part of free Europe. In this struggle I am prepared to sacrifice my life. So help me God!' (from *Slovenec*, 21 April 1944). This oath originated in a clear conservative ideology and also disclosed – in the purest way possible – the moral and political hypocrisy of local collaborationism. As if the Nazi Germany envisioned a Slovenian homeland in 'free Europe'. In reality, Slovenians were forcefully exiled, tortured, executed, and sent to concentration camps during the wartime years; as the resistance movements were deemed as banditry, and, as such, their members were summarily executed.

11. Nine fundamental points of the Liberation Front were adopted, the first seven of which were adopted at the 4th session of the Supreme Plenum of the Liberation Front on 1 November 1941. The analysis of the Assembly of all People's Liberation Struggle Committee deputies in Kočevje between 1 and 3 October 1943 also attested to the duality of the social revolution (Kristan, 1973: 600–609). This duality had been at work from the very beginning, but in 1943 it incorporated the masses and attained a broader Yugoslav dimension.

12. After the war, the status of the national hero cities was given to the following cities: Drvar, Prilep, Cetinje, Belgrade, Zagreb, Ljubljana, Novi Sad, and Priština.

13. For an overview of the illegal network, see the edited volume by Repe and Pirjevec (2008).

14. The monograph *Ilegalčki* describes the activities involved in the organised care for the children of partisan parents, who were provided with temporary shelter and food while their parents were away fighting or incarcerated. See Štrajnar and Velagić, 2004.

15. Komelj (2008) described the operations of the Liberation Front, which started to carry out numerous actions early on, which was why the Italian authorities turned the entire city into one of the largest 'concentration camps'. They surrounded Ljubljana with barbed wire, bunkers, and machine gun posts with the intention of isolating the passages and destroying the organisational core of the Liberation Front. Despite the fact that many activists had to leave the city, the anti-fascist organisation remained in operation and its agents could be found in the highest offices within the police force.

16. Komelj established that the influence of the PLS was much more significant in the countryside.

17. Female fighters and the youth made a significant contribution to this process. They were tireless in their efforts of organising the learning, cultural, political and economic life. See interviews with female partisans, edited by Daško Milinović and Zoran Petakov (2010); a great study was written by Jančar-Webster (1990); and, more recently, a collective of female researchers and artists from Bosnia and Herzegovina created an excellent online archive

and collected materials on the legacy of women in the antifascist struggle (Okić and Dugandžić, 2018).

18. At this time the Chetniks and the partisans still occasionally worked together, but towards the end of the German offensive this cooperation was terminated (Roberts 1973).

19. More surprisingly, Stalin made several demands for Tito's partisans to cooperate with the Chetniks and renounce the revolutionary struggle in the liberated territories. For more information on the complex and ambivalent relations between the partisans and Allies see Bilandžić (1978); Kardelj (1980).

20. As a sphere of interest Yugoslavia was divided equally (50–50) between Great Britain and the Soviet Union. Greece, for example, was 90 per cent British and 10 per cent Soviet, which had tragic consequences once World War II finished. These imperialist divisions often took place without any involvement of the local resistance movements (Fejto 1952: 25), which is why the thesis of the anti-imperialist war within the context of World War II is valid. See Gluckstein (2012); Mandel (2013).

21. Nešović and Pagon (1973).

22. The AVNOJ Declaration opens with the following sentence: 'On the basis of every nation's right to self-determination, including the right to secession or unification with other nations, and in accordance with the true disposition of all Yugoslav nations, expressed during the three-year joint People's Liberation Struggle that forged an indivisible brotherhood of all nations of Yugoslavia, the Anti-Fascist Council for the National Liberation of Yugoslavia hereby issues the following Decree' (Nešović and Pagon, 1973: 238).

23. With one important exception, as the question of Albanians in Kosovo was already a pressing issue during the war. The Albanian anti-fascist activists and partisans were leaning towards the idea of merging with Albania, while the Communist Party of Yugoslavia tried to postpone this issue until after the war. Kosovo was also the only area in which armed resistance took place after the partisans had already liberated it: in February 1945. The Kosovo question remained at the core of the dispute between the Communist Party of Yugoslavia and the Communist Party of Albania, see Magaš (1993: 33–4). Regardless of the political and revolutionary nature of project Yugoslavia, which was open to all nationalities, we cannot ignore the culturological and symbolic restriction of the very name *Yugoslavia*, which refers to the place and adherence of all South Slavs.

24. A year later the King of Yugoslavia and a part of the government-in-exile publicly supported the partisan struggle, calling upon the population to join the PLS. The Allies, especially Churchill, strove to ensure that the partisan leadership formed as broad a government as possible, which would include a part of the government-in-exile and pave the way for the general transition to the new Yugoslavia. On 8 March 1945 Tito and Šubašić signed an agreement that appeased the British and formally brought together all political forces. This was a compromise with a calculation that the British forces would refrain from interfering in the internal matters of Yugoslavia after the war.

25. This angered Stalin, who demanded that Tito call off the temporary revolutionary government (Ramet 2006: 157–9). Naturally, AVNOJ and the Supreme Headquarters refused to abolish this founding act, and a year later, during the liberation of Belgrade and parts of Vojvodina, the Red Army requested permission to carry out joint military operations. Even though the Yugoslav Resistance Movement received material aid from the Allies, we could state that it managed to defeat the Nazi occupiers with its own forces. In Europe, the Albanian resistance and the Greek People's Liberation Army, ELAS, were the only resistance movements to manage the same.

26. For valuable elaborations and a critique of liberal subjectivity and the state see Balibar (2002).

27. At the end of the war the Yugoslav partisan forces consisted of almost a million fighting men and women, making them the largest resistance army of World War II. Besides the Ukrainian partisans and the Polish Resistance Army, the Yugoslav partisan army was the most numerous also in the absolute sense.

28. It was in this sense that Althusser criticised the representatives of the social contract and their categories most resolutely, as they already a priori represented a precisely defined and specific political system (Althusser, 2006).

29. The recently published archive on the Women's Anti-Fascist Front was collected by Okić and Dugandžić (2018).

30. In his memoirs, Suvin briefly described the activities of the Young Communist League of Yugoslavia (Suvin, 2010: 86–95).

31. However, this did not prevent the AFŽ from becoming a political organisation that kept operating in socialist Yugoslavia until 1953, when the Communist Party abolished it during the consolidation of the state and the process of re-traditionalising the private sphere. For further (also critical) information see also Jovanović (2014) and Chiara Bonfiglioli (2012), who develop an interesting comparative study of the left-wing feminist movements in Yugoslavia and Italy in the post-war era.

32. Komelj (2008) dedicated an excellent study to this topic, rethinking the dimensions of partisan art as an integral part of the political rupture. Komelj speaks about the rupture of political as well as aesthetic dimensions, breaking away from the preconceived role of the autonomy of art in the bourgeois society. A mass cultural explosion took place in times of war, for example, more than 12.000 poems were written solely in Slovenia (Paternu, 1987). In my article I tried to analyse the extraordinary conceptual achievements and thematisation of the revolutionary temporality in certain key poems written within the PLS (Kirn, 2014).

33. The scope and dynamics of the cultural activities throughout Yugoslavia has yet to be described, as Komelj focused predominantly on the Slovenian language area.

34. A good example of this can be found in the first printed collection of partisan songs, called 'Antifascist Songs', printed on 7 November 1941 in the first liberated territory, the Republic of Užice. This songbook was a mix

of popular, folk, and international revolutionary songs as well as new local partisan poems and songs that were popular during the first months of the resistance. More on this in Kirn (forthcoming).

35. See previous sections of this chapter, which detail the inventiveness and extensive social and cultural practices of the new people's government.

36. During the time of the Republic of Užice, the partisans took over an arms factory. For a more general and historical description of the Užice operation, see Tomasevich (2001).

37. In 1931, Pope Pius XI published the encyclical *Quadragesimo anno*. In it, he attacked communism and argued for private property that, however, had to be at least partly regulated. He also argued for the principle of subsidiarity, which could compete against different types of social organisation. This encyclical resounded strongly in certain parts of the Kingdom of Yugoslavia.

38. The intergenerational and reciprocal gift economies were conceptualised by Marcel Mauss (1966). To take the partisan side means to be ready to 'sacrifice oneself' and believe in a different world in the future, which will symbolically and – one could add – physically restore the belief in the world and justify the sacrifices made throughout the war.

39. The AVNOJ Declaration introduced a decree on the confiscation of the occupiers' and German collaborators' property (Nešović and Pagon, 1973).

40. Jovanović (2014) highlighted the multiplicity as well as the political character of the demands and topics, contributed by women during the struggle.

41. Žilnik's film *Uprising in Jazak* (1973) is one of the most authentic documents, presenting interviews with the rural men and women from Vojvodina who supported the partisans in their struggle, donated cattle and crops, concealed weapons, and provided them with shelter. These unsung and often overlooked heroes of the war actually represented the backbone of the partisan struggle and the military formations (see Kirn, forthcoming).

42. Mikuž (1969) also explains how the Liberation Front's associates in the Province of Ljubljana managed to con the Italian authorities and deprive them of a considerable sum of money through a fictitious transaction. Following the capitulation of Italy, the partisan forces also confiscated a vast amount of weapons and used them to arm more than 80,000 new fighting men and women.

43. Mikuž (1969) mentions a few incidents in the Gorenjska region, but also underlines that punishment would be immediately imposed upon anyone who would confiscate property without justification.

44. Fascism did not disappear with the end of World War II, as it persisted in Spain (1936–75), Portugal (1932–74), as well as in Greece after the end of the civil war (especially the military junta period 1967–74). Furthermore, many colonial forces would keep supporting genocidal regimes and wars against the anti-colonial movements well into the second half of the twentieth century. See Landa (2009) and Losurdo (2011). I shall revisit this subject in the chapter 5 on the Non-Aligned Movement.

45. The best critical volume that analyses the magnitude and relevance of Bleiburg for the national revisionism in the post-Yugoslav context was edited

by Brentin and Pavlaković (2018), and is a result of a long-term cooperation between the University of Rijeka and the University of Graz.

46. For detailed numbers, see Ramet (2006: 160–62).

47. Tomasevich (2001).

48. Some war criminals were captured much later, for example the Chetnik leader Draža Mihailović, who was apprehended on 13 March 1946; at the trial, he was found guilty of multiple crimes (Roberts, 1973: 307).

49. *Jugoslavija u ratu* (1991) is an openly revisionist documentary, however it appropriately outlines the partisan strategies of handling war prisoners. The prisoners were either convicted of national treason by the people's courts, exchanged for captured partisans, encouraged to join the partisans in their fight (many collaborators were forcefully mobilised), or released after a while, since the partisan units were mobile and lacked the infrastructure to incarcerate and sustain the prisoners. The way in which the partisans handled the prisoners and the wounded also helped them gain people's sympathies and support.

50. In 2018, the Ustashe and other fascist symbols were formally forbidden at Bleiburg. However, they are still displayed by certain individuals, or hidden beneath their clothes. See a short TV report by the Austrian public television: https://www.youtube.com/watch?v=B_88PDnjyBw.

51. For more on this subject see Kirn (2019).

52. I wrote about the specifics of the Slovenian national reconciliation and the fascist politics of memory in the case of monuments and the discourse of the so-called new historians. See Kirn (2012; 2019). The Ustashe and the Chetniks have become national heroes. Meanwhile, in Slovenia the governing ideology of 'national reconciliation' denied any differences between the Home Guard and the partisans, thereby redeeming everyone and finally resolving the Slovenian nation's trauma.

53. The number of victims in Yugoslavia was high in terms of the percentage of the population – almost 7 per cent of the population died as a result of the war. Independent research has shown that more than one million people perished and 670,000 emigrated, which, alongside the additional demographic loss of 326,000 people, amounts to almost two million people. Of these, 446,000 people fell in the battlefields, while 581,000 civilians died as a result of military and Nazi terror. If we compare these numbers with, for example, the 417,000 military and 1,700 civil casualties in the USA, the gravity of the situation becomes immediately clear.

Chapter 4

1. The negotiations with Stalin during and after the war are described by Edvard Kardelj, the most important communist ideologue, who was close to Tito, and a foreign minister of the new Yugoslavia (1980).

2. There is some good literature on the splits within the Greek Resistance during World War II, which already pointed in the direction of a Civil War (Sarafis, 1980).

3. For further details on the struggles within the Communist Party of Greece, see also articles under the topic 'Greek Civil War' in the Marxist Internet Archive.

4. The end of World War II and the new Cold War map played strongly into the imaginary of anticolonial struggles and subsequent alignments within and beyond the Iron Curtain. For more on this see Chapter 5.

5. In 1943, the Yugoslav partisan leadership sent Svetozar Vukomanović – Tempo as an emissary to the Bulgarian, Greek, and Albanian Parties with the task of discussing the military and political coordination of the revolutionary struggle in the Balkans. As a form of concrete collaboration, Tempo proposed the introduction of a united *Balkan General Staff* – a military body that would coordinate the joint army operations. This initiative was blocked after it received a negative response from the London authorities (Karamanić 2009: 338–9).

6. In the Yugoslav reality, the autonomous region of Kosovo and the question of the Albanian nation remained an extremely sensitive issue that was never completely resolved. For details on how the question was instrumentalised by newly nationalised political elites in the late 1980s see Chapter 13.

7. 'The striving of the Balkan peoples towards national liberation from under foreign domination in conjunction with the class struggle against capitalist exploitation and economic colonisation. The central aim of this political orientation was to establish a new political unity: a common federal republic that would unite the Balkan Peninsula on the basis of internationalism, political solidarity and economic equality' (Karamanić, 2009: 337). See also Petranović (1991).

8. According to Kardelj, who held talks with Stalin in Moscow in 1948, these were the worst negotiations in his life (1980: 111–20).

9. Later the Soviet Union retained strict control over the various revolutionary uprisings in Eastern Europe: East Germany (1953), Hungary (1956), Czechoslovakia (1968). The signifier 'Tito' has a specific history, for this empty signifier was intended to be revisionist, compromising with the West, self-isolating, betraying the socialist cause, and so forth. It served as an instrument to discipline and purge the spreading 'Titoist' elements (Garde 2000: 91–2).

10. A. Rubinstein (1970: 14). The Yugoslav liberation struggle had a strong legacy of self-reliance, which can be compared to the Chinese experience. In 1945 Mao stated: 'We stand for self-reliance. We hope for foreign aid, but cannot be dependent on it; we depend on our own efforts, on the creative power of the army and the entire people'. (1965: 241).

11. See Samary (1988: 75–6) and Kardelj (1980: 101–105).

12. At the same time Yugoslavia applied a similar procedure and pressure on Albania, which was at the time highly influenced by Yugoslav politics (see also Lee 1983, 84–6; Prifti 1978).

13. Recently Želimir Žilnik made a film about the woman who carried this letter (*One Woman, One Century,* 2011).

14. It is symptomatic that Goli Otok has not become a famous 'realm of memory' during the past few decades. This is not because the ideological climate

during the transition period was not staunchly anti-communist, but because the main victims of this camp were hard-core communists and partisans. Why should one remember communists/Stalinists, who do obviously not fit into the dominant commemoration of national heroes and (cultural) dissidents?

15. See: Suvin (2011: 10–11).

Chapter 5

1. See Healey's description of the formation of the Cominform (1948); for the minutes of the meetings and resolutions see Procacci (1994).

2. For the best study of the split's economic implications, see Marjanović et al. 1973.

3. I will return to the failure of collectivisation policy in Yugoslavia in Chapter 8. Collectivisation took place at the same time as the launch of the industrialisation campaign within the first five-year plan. The most detailed study on the history of agricultural development in Yugoslavia was carried out by Šuvar (1988), who believed that the major causes for the failure of collectivisation lay in the absence of an economic and cultural perspective for the peasants in the light of major changes; there was a weak development of productive forces and a meagre introduction of machinery and scientific procedures into agriculture (ibid. 156–7). To my knowledge there is no serious analytical study of the collectivisation campaign and the resistance shown by peasants, the majority of whom had already begun to move to the new industrial centres.

4. Césare Aimé (1950) wrote one of the first texts about the French context soon after World War II; his text openly addressed the hypocrisy and the colonial politics of the West. This was an important opening for Fanon (1952) and the entire wave of anti-colonial struggles that were emerging at the time.

5. On the demythologisation of the Western modernisation narrative see Said (1979).

6. For the world-system perspective and the politico-economic relation between the centre and the periphery see Wallerstein (1979); for a different view on the same topic see Frank (2002).

7. This is linked to the traumatic dissolution of Yugoslavia that was seen as one of the driving forces of the NAM and the historically problematic attitude of non-interference in domestic issues at all costs. Respecting the sovereignty could lead to indirectly tolerating genocide – what is to be done in such a situation? NAM clearly did not give a full answer, or rather failed in this respect.

8. The two-camp model was the dominant geopolitical framework for thinking and acting within the international arena. The USSR's foreign policies – even if in terms of military bases and interventions, smaller – used similar strategies to the US, and at times even pursued anti-communist policies. Prashad believed that the 'USSR'S commissars reached arrangements with the bourgeois forces within the postcolonial states at the expense of the local

Communists' (2007: 97). Toscano noted that Mao's China played an important role 'in the subjective perception and the objective unfolding of the Cold War', which hugely complicates this question. Through the vicissitudes of the Non-Aligned Movement, the Sino–Soviet split and the later rapprochement with the US, it disturbed the tidy teleology of a convergence between two camps (2008: 418).

9. The Southeast Asia Treaty Organisation was an initiative carried out by former/existing colonial powers France and Great Britain who were joined by Pakistan, The Philippines, Thailand, New Zealand, and Australia, while the Baghdad treaty saw the formation of the Central Treaty Organisation in which Great Britain and the US were joined by Iran, Iraq, Pakistan, and Turkey.

10. For details on the Bandung conference see Prashad (2007: 31–51) and Rubinstein (1970: 62–75).

11. Prashad (2007: 95).

12. The historical importance was strengthened by the fact that earlier that year the Soviet Union's president Nikita Khrushchev visited Yugoslavia and asked to reconcile with Yugoslavia following the split with Stalin in 1948. This signalled the rising importance of Yugoslavia's role as a bridge between the East and the West.

13. See also Frick's edited volume (2003) that brings together not only major visual markers – posters and magazines of the tricontinental movement – but also a few important analyses.

14. Smolej argued that 'coexistence should replace the blocs, as the division of the world into blocs is contrary to the idea of coexistence' (1961: 315).

15. One should ask if this moral approach to international relations does not simply reproduce the opposition between cynics (use of brutal force), realists, and idealists who strive to supplement the order with morality (humanism)?

16. Today, or at least following the failure to stop the war in Iraq, the peace or anti-war movement has seen a major decline, and has become almost absent from the various discussions and organisations. Despite the mass mobilisation and successful campaigns that attacked the US hegemony, the US nevertheless led the war against fictive weapons of mass destruction even if they were unsuccessful. In the years that followed the major capitalist crisis of 2007, it seemed that the systemic proliferation of both global war against terror and the certain revival of Cold War geopolitics with superpowers China and Russia challenging the falling hegemonic power of the USA has been on the surge. We need to urgently rethink and redeploy the legacy of peace and anti-war movements.

17. Rubinstein (1970: 23). Perhaps one of the most provoking thoughts articulated during the Korean War, was presented by Kardelj, at the time Yugoslavia's foreign minister: 'Peace cannot be preserved by means of a crusade against socialism or against the strivings of peoples towards freedom and independence. On the contrary, peace can be preserved only by combating domination and aggression wherever they appear, regardless of the chief political and ideological slogan behind which they conceal themselves'. (1950: 72).

18. See Prashad (2007: 103–104).
19. Kardelj (1960). This thesis runs very close to Che Guevara's claim for a peaceful coexistence, which does not include the coexistence between the exploiter and the exploited, between the oppressors and the oppressed (Prashad, 2007: 104). For the left-leaning NAM states the discussion of peace was linked to the issue of justice from the very beginning. For a more critical view on the Yugoslav position see Stubbs (2019).
20. See Campbell (1967: 38–40).

Chapter 6

1. For the most detailed analysis of historical data and the system on Goli Otok see Previšić (2015).
2. The term 'self-management' has been long established in the literature on socialist Yugoslavia, however, there are also other competing terms when discussing workers struggles and organisation, such as 'self-government' or 'self-organisation'. The etymological roots of the word *autogestión* lie in Greek and Latin and Marcelo Vieta orients us towards draws on Farmer's argument: to define it as 'one can conceptualise it as 'self-gestation' – which entails activity to self-create, self-control, self-provide, and, ultimately, self-produce; in other words, to practice *autogestión* means to be self-reliant. The term 'self-management' is arguably the inadequate but well-accepted English translation of the French and Spanish word 'autogestión', which has a Greek and Latin etymology (Farmer 1979). The word auto comes from the Greek 'autós' (self, same). Gestión comes from the Latin 'gestio' (managing), which in turn comes from 'gerere' (to bear, carry, manage) (ibid.). More evocatively and literally, one can conceptualize autogestión as 'self-gestation' – self-creation, self-control, and self-provision; in other words, to be self-reliant and self-determining. In this etymology there are deep connections, in practice and in theory, with proposals for the self-determination of working lives that resonate across social anarchist and libertarian socialist economics. Taken together, auto-gestión – self-management– alludes to a processual movement of self-creation, self-conception, and self-definition. It is pregnant with ethico-political relevance for the struggle for freedom from hierarchical and autocratic systems of control and exploitation, drawing on the ancient philosophical notion of potentiality – an evolution into something other than what one is in the now. (2014: 783).
3. The entire text of this law can be found in Horvat (1975: 256–8).
4. Yugoslav communists turned to Marx and Engels, especially their political texts (*The Gotha Programme, The Communist Manifesto,* and *The Paris Commune*) and to Lenin's *State and Revolution* (1972). They sought to tackle the major obstacles for any emerging revolutionary power that would respond to the centralisation and bureaucratisation on the one hand, and the empowerment of the working people on the other. For philosophical influences see Marković (1975 vol. I: 327–50).
5. For an interesting note on the 7th Congress of the League of Communists

of Yugoslavia see Centrih's elaboration of the Yugoslav example as a special contribution to 'socialism as a global system' (2011: 55–62).

6. This differentiation between Yugoslav and Soviet socialism has to be analysed beyond the ideological discussion about the deviations and revisionisms that reduce matters to Titoism and Stalinism.

Chapter 7

1. Many ideologemes that defined Yugoslavia negatively as an 'artificial entity' or a 'prison of nations' were intertwined with the orientalist views that saw the Balkans as a 'powder keg'. One of the more famous representatives of this position was Kaplan (2005), who became the key reference for the American president (Bill Clinton) and other Western diplomats. For example, Kaplan defended the thesis that the Balkan conflict stemmed from the eternal and ancient hatred between the ethnic and religious groups. The thesis on the eternal character of ethno-nationalism became omnipresent. Susan Woodward was one of the first to reject it resolutely and in a well-argued manner (2003: 73–92).

2. Repe (1992) and Balažic (1994) are two representatives of a more liberal orientation. A descriptive overview of the various actors during the times of the Committee for the Protection of Human Rights and the turn towards nationalism (Žerdin, 1997) is also available. In a thematic issue of the *Borec* magazine (2008), dedicated to this topic, Močnik explored various representatives of the Slovenian nationalist revisionism.

3. Althusser (2006) develops a concept of history as an encounter of atoms, where contingency takes precedence over teleology or the inevitability of encounter.

4. In his analysis of capitalist production, Marx demonstrated that the tendency is to be understood as a movement of contradictions. One of the key characteristics of capitalist reproduction is the point of unity between two contradictory tendencies, i.e. the tendency of the rate of profit to fall and the tendency of the surplus value to increase. For a further theoretic analysis of tendencies, see Lipietz (1993).

5. Bettelheim's theory of transition is predominantly based on the history of the Soviet Union (1975: 13–30). Regardless of his sound foundations, in the final instance, Bettelheim still settles for the primacy of the productive forces, which is in direct opposition of Althusser's insistence on the primacy of productive relations.

6. Mira Bogdanović recently wrote an excellent critical study (2014) on the phenomenon and conversion of Djilas. She also pointed out the present-day liberal appropriation of Djilas.

7. See especially the introductory methodological chapter in Suvin (2014). An excellent critique of this approach was also published by Kerševan (1985).

8. Despite the tendencies that the governing classes should attain autonomy and privileges in the name of the workers, which were present in certain periods, these social differences were related more closely to the status and

political power rather than to the position in the production process.

9. Real socialism has been criticised by the leftist theoretical field at least since the 1950s, for example by the group *Socialisme ou Barbarie* in France; in the United States in the collection of essays written by C.L.R. James, Grace Lee and Pierre Chaulieu (1958). In a short section of his otherwise thorough study David McNally (1993) even stated that Yugoslavia was a Stalinist formation that practiced state capitalism. Criticism was expressed from the anarcho-syndicalist as well as Trotskyist positions, in Yugoslavia, the representatives of a more Trotskyist orientation included Igor Bavčar, Srečo Kirn, and Bojan Korsika (1985), and nowadays also Vladimir Unkovski-Korica (2016). The critique of real socialism from a more 'generous' perspective has recently been given by Michael Lebowitz (2012) and Darko Suvin (2016).

10. Even if the leaders of the CPY partly supported the integration into the global market in their discussions, this represented only one aspect of the ideological struggle. In the reality of political economy, it is impossible to talk about an immediate integration into the global market, as Yugoslavia was isolated at the time and had troubles receiving credits. The actual integration into the global financial flows did not occur until a decade later.

11. As a result of the abandonment of collectivisation, the new economic policy was introduced in the countryside by the end of the 1940s. This made it possible for farmers to keep a part of their private or at least extended personal property in agriculture, and they were also aided by the existence of the retail trade. However, the process of socialisation continued during the 1950s, and housing was nationalised as late as 1958 (Horvat 1976: 6–9). Had private property in fact existed, this would have implied that factories could have been closed down easily, workers let go, machinery sold, and the surplus value used freely. Yet, none of this was true.

12. Johanna Bockman (2011) drew attention to the socialist theoretical origins of neoliberalism. Bockman turns around the prevailing perspective, which claims that neoliberalism defeated the socialist and Keynesian theories, and demonstrates the opposite – that a kind of synthesis between the neo-classicist and socialist theories occurred due to the economic experience of market socialism (not only in Yugoslavia) and the scientific exchange between economists.

13. Althusser (1970) was extremely averse to 'historicism', while C. Bettelheim did exactly this in his long-term studies on the Soviet Union and its transitions: he presented a rigorous conceptualisation of modalities and ownership changes in the socialist social formation.

14. It would be possible to argue that numerous transitional socialist elements are also present in the welfarist, yet capitalist states in the West. This is partly true, and it demonstrates the important achievements in the history of workers' movements, which influenced the constitution of a more socialised capital and social protection mechanisms of the working class. One should take notice of the specific post-war situation when the spread of communism at home and abroad was restrained by giving concessions to the workers.

15. Kržan established four criteria for the (un)successfulness of the socialist

economy: the abolition of capitalist exploitation; the decrease in the developmental differences between the republics and provinces; the reduction of the developmental lag in comparison with the developed countries; and the assurance of political independence. These four indicators assumed a negative trend in the mid-1960s, and the self-management system was no longer capable of solving the problems on its own (Kržan 2013).

16. This division is used by Branka Brborić-Likić (2003); see also Kržan (2013) and Mihajlević (2018).

Chapter 8

1. Sundhaussen (2012) gives a very good description of the 'primary accumulation' process.

2. Unkovski-Korica (2016) brings attention to the documents attesting to the leadership's discussions indicating its openness to the idea of a global market. However, Woodward's thesis (1995a) is more precise. In her thesis she states that Yugoslav development oscillated between two models, the so-called Slovenian export model (capital intense) and the Bosnian or Foča model (the military-industrial complex). The Yugoslav development policy was adjusted in view of the international crises, the favourability of lending, and the lending capacity (1995). This is the so-called 'external explanation' model, which, does not account for all of the contradictions that kept occurring within the self-management system and socialist development.

3. The most precise critical and Marxist study of this period was written by Samary (1988). See also Suvin's recent study (2016), which combines a sociological analysis with utopian Marxist philosophy in relation to various periods within socialist Yugoslavia.

4. In an unpublished text, Močnik stated that in 1952 'the workers' collectives managed approximately one third of the generated value'; by 1962 the ratio of 'self-management and the state changed in favour of the workers' control, amounting to 57.7% / 42.3% and this kept increasing until the 1980s'.

5. Even in the long-term perspective, the annual economic growth of industrial production between 1952 and 1969 was still impressive, at approximately 10.5%, which resulted in Yugoslavia being officially ranked the fifth highest in economic growth in the world. The national income in view of industry vs agriculture ranged as follows: in 1947, the proportion was 18% vs 42.6%, by 1972 it had changed to 38.1% vs 18.8%. Between 1953 and 1969, the GDP increased by 259%, which amounts to an average annual rise of 6.1%. In 1953 the GDP per capita amounted to US$300, and by 1971 this had risen to US$800 (Bilandžić, 1980: 386–94).

6. Dejan Jović established that between 1950 and 1959, Yugoslavia received approximately US$1.5 billion in economic aid as well as US$724 million in military aid (Jović, 2009: 85). At the beginning of the 1950s, almost half of the Yugoslav trade deficit was covered by this aid (Denitch 1990: 137).

7. See also Horvat (1976: 5–12); Samary (1988). On the topic of socialist modernisation and urbanisation, see the excellent collection of scientific

texts edited by Mrduljaš and Kulić (2012).

8. This did not have merely positive effects, and by the end of the 1960s, unemployment represented an increasingly pressing social problem (Woodward, 1995a). She correctly assessed that this topic had not been focused on either by the originators of the socialist policies or by the critical theorists. I will return to this question later.

9. The table is summarised from Lampe (2000: 295).

10. Kornai wrote on this topic extensively. Lebowitz (2012) underlines one of the main reasons for this situation: the measuring of political power manifested itself in companies (and managers) bending and manipulating the information, as they preferred to retain some of the goods and materials in their warehouses so that they could ensure they would meet their own work quotas.

11. The thesis that the workers' collectives were introduced in order to settle the score with the strong trade unions that protected the workers and enabled workplace mobility is not entirely correct. The following finding is much more astute: in the key moments towards the end of the 1940s, the managers were aware that they required strong support from the people after the dispute with Stalin (cf. Woodward, 1995b: 261).

12. From private correspondence with Rastko Močnik, (still) unpublished text.

13. The Goli Otok prison was a re-education camp. In the early 1950s, the majority of those who were sent to this island were accused of being 'Stalinists'. Ironically, the solution – getting rid of Stalinists – was implemented in a Stalinist manner. Previšić (2015) documented that approximately 15,000 prisoners were sent to Goli Otok between 1948 and 1956, and that approximately 400 of them died (2015: 190). From the perspective of the culture of memory, it is not a coincidence that almost nobody is interested in commemorating a place where mostly partisans, hardcore communists, and actual Stalinists served their sentence.

14. Foucauldian interpretations of real socialisms with regard to the Yugoslav example are practically non-existent. See the excellent study by Eyal (2003).

15. From private correspondence with Rastko Močnik, his unpublished text.

16. Katja Praznik (2013) sums up the most important changes within the socialist cultural system and infrastructure.

17. From private correspondence with Rastko Močnik, his unpublished text.

18. The film and music industry represented a good example. I wrote in greater detail on this topic in the article (Kirn 2014: 62–80).

19. Local self-imposed contributions depended on referendums, and after their successful implementation, the inhabitants of certain municipalities were obligated to donate a specific percentage of their income. Significant parts of the social infrastructure were constructed by means of local self-imposed contributions, for example nursery schools, community health centres, etc. Cf. Močnik, unpublished text.

20. The social self-management model was importantly upgraded in the middle of the 1970s. At that point, the so-called Self-Management Interest Associations were established in order to promote the plurality of self-management

interests. The main task of the Self-Management Interest Associations was to ensure public services. They also operated as an intermediary between the larger social systems, in close cooperation with the League of Communists, the Socialist Alliance of Working People, and the Socialist Youth League. See also Močnik (2010a: 139–56).

21. Many transition experts reproach the Yugoslav self-management system for not developing democratic institutions with general elections every four years. See Dyker and Vejvoda (1994: 6). This reproach is clearly valid, as democratic general elections did not exist in Yugoslavia, in light of its single party system. However, these critics tend to ignore the fact that the Party as such was not a homogenous subject. Instead, exceedingly opposing opinions and outlooks on the development were shaped at the level of the individual republics and the federation. Furthermore, the critics failed to note that the political participation on other levels – from companies and municipalities to consumer and cultural self-management organisations that made up the delegate system of representation – had existed in Yugoslavia from as early as the end of the 1950s. And these levels had elections – and we can even claim that the amount of political decision-making at the time exceeded that of a liberal representative democracy. The reproach that the highest positions in the republican and federal political apparatus were always taken by candidates who were 'vetted' by the League of Communists is partially true. However, once again, this did not involve the Central Committee of the LCY, but rather the central committees of the Leagues of Communists of the individual republics. If we measured and compared the (in)direct influence of the inhabitants of municipalities and workers in the current and former political system, we would arrive to different conclusions from those drawn by the present-day advocates of the transition.

22. See also Močnik (2010).

23. This republican and confederate character of Yugoslavia, apparent from the 1960s onwards, should be emphasised whenever we come across the populist interpretations arguing in favour of the thesis that the republics did not possess any autonomy, as they had allegedly been dominated by the malevolent centre (Belgrade) from the very beginning.

24. On the problematic consolidation and neutralisation of the feminist movement, see Čakardić (2012).

25. Horvat carried out a detailed analysis of the various measures and agencies with a protectionist agenda. In particular, the mechanisms involved significant import taxes and export subsidies (see ibid., 196).

Chapter 9

1. The main goal of this reform was to liberalise the prices. According to Bockman, by the beginning of the 1960s, 'the Yugoslavs would abolish central planning, introduce commercial banking to allow for enterprise-driven investment, and open their economy to the world market. As a result, the Yugoslavs created an innovative form of socialism' (Bockman 2011: 80).

Real commercial banking was not introduced until after the 1965 market reform. Furthermore, the process of introducing the logic of capital into enterprises and labour market intensified in the 1965–72 phase.

2. This is Susan Woodward's approach (1995a), which is by the date the most detailed study of the (un)employment in Yugoslavia.

3. For a general discussion of the 1961 reform, see Bilandžić (1980: 297–310); Horvat (1976: 22–5). The purpose of this act was to increase the flexibility of prices and establish the market productivity mechanisms.

4. Smaller companies were not given easy access to loans, and they prioritised higher salaries rather than employing additional staff. Larger companies had other issues, as they had easier access to loans in the new banks, where they kept their deposits (Kržan, 2013). Nevertheless, they preferred merging with other large companies rather than employing new workers. As Kržan correctly pointed out, the employment and unemployment rates varied through different regions and sectors.

5. The loan and monetary policy as well as the import and export policy remained in the hands of the federal institutions.

6. Depoliticisation occurred not only as a result of the limited access to the actual decision-making institutions, but also because of the time shortage. Instead of holding continuous meetings, a circle of experts was created at a more systemic level, and they started to direct the development of companies and banks. For the workers' participation issues, see the sociological studies that measured the efficiency and level of happiness in companies (Županov, 1967).

7. Post-communism and the strong tendency to restore capitalism is one of the key subjects of Buden (2009).

8. The division of time periods here is predominantly based on Brborić-Likić (2002: 88).

Chapter 10

1. Katelenac (2013) claims that private property did in fact exist in Yugoslavia. This is only partly true in restrained segments of agriculture, while within the general economy, private property was only restored towards the end of the 1980s. For details regarding this footnote, see Geoffroy (2006).

2. Svetozar Vukmanović – Tempo provides an excellent description as to how the workers could set their wages at the time (1982: 369–70).

3. Various official ideologues acknowledged this position, but claimed that this was a secondary fact, regardless of the certain conflicts that exhibited the class nature. According to Kardelj, the main issues were to be found in the political formation of the new bureaucratic class as well as in the social differences that appeared within the working class (1979: 124).

4. Recently, the approach of state capitalism and the direct application of Marx's concept of capital in the Yugoslav case has been studied by Katalenac (2013), Živković (2015), as well as Unkovski-Korica (2016). The authors of the book *Kapital in delo v SFRJ* also partly adhere to this theory.

5. Kardelj claimed that commodity production and the market were not the sources of inequality or capitalist relations, while the authors of *Kapital in delo v SFRJ* responded that individual commodities were seamlessly linked to the free engagement of the labour force. As the latter could assert itself only on the basis of an unequal distribution of production circumstances, it remained rooted in the asymmetrical relationship between capital and labour. The analysis of the class domination of capital over labour is best suited for the period of the market reform and from the mid-1980s onwards, but it can by no means be applied without a more precise analysis of the logic of representation and the macroeconomic regulation in various periods (Bavčar et al.,1985: 10–35).

6. For now, the contradiction and opposition to all other workers and industries will be excluded from this incongruity.

7. Among other things, this led to the accumulation of personal property within the ruling class and certain other 'non-socialist' moments (Samary 1988: 170–89).

8. From personal correspondence with Rastko Močnik, unpublished text.

9. There are plenty of topics that deserve a more extensive analysis. For example, the issue of women's labour and the domination over women in the general reproductive regime is even more neglected, however, this has been recently correctly underlined by certain Marxist feminists, for example Ankica Čakardić, Dora Levačić, Lilijana Burcar, and others.

10. In the 1980s, an important paper was written by Tonči Kuzmanić (1988). He brought to attention the rich history of the miners' struggles throughout the twentieth century, focusing in particular on the so-called Labin Commune of 1921 as the first 'self-management cell' and, of course, on the strike over several weeks in 1987.

11. In Kirn (2017), I developed a detailed analysis of this film and of the insights for class analysis.

12. Jovanov explored the most viewpoints from the 7th session of the LCY in 1969, and concluded the that the authorities could no longer ignore the scale of strikes. On 15 December 1969, the Presidency of the LCY published the tasks for the communists involved in the self-management solutions that would tackle the conflicts better.

13. Unkovski-Korica (2016) claims that the workers' councils represented direct competition to the trade unions, which had been well organised ever since World War II. Later, especially in the 1970s and less so during the 1980s, they would occasionally function as an extension of the socialist authorities and an apparatus for disciplining the workers.

14. For further information on the workers' uprising and strike action in Maribor in 1988, see Kirn (2014).

15. I am inclined to agree with Žižek's argument that the general characteristic of the socialist authorities lay in their dedication to the project of enlightenment, which manifested itself in the strong belief in the convincing nature of progressive ideas and the pedagogic model of government (Žižek, 2011). A strong belief that the future would remember this period for its artworks

rather than for its political congresses and minutes indeed existed, which is why the (Party) investments and interventions in cultural activities were an important part of the disciplinary authorities. For further information on these strategies and an example of the so-called 'Black Wave', see Buden (2008); Kirn (2017).

16. This thesis can encourage the association that I have all those groups in mind that either did not correspond to the prevalent canon of ideological figures or remained somewhere in between – for example, Albanians and the Roma in Kosovo, both of whom were considered second-rate citizens in Yugoslavia at the time. This sort of conceptualisation would probably apply in the case of the Roma people (certain aspects of their everyday life have even worsened after the dissolution of Yugoslavia). However, in the case of the Kosovo Albanians, this categorisation all too quickly leads to the currently prevailing model of 'ethnic identification', which claims that Yugoslavia was a 'prison of nations'. In the words of Jović, the model of 'brotherhood and unity' was replaced by the model (Kardelj's) that culminated in the 1974 Constitution of the Socialist Federal Republic of Yugoslavia already by the end of the 1960s and which set out the ethnic criterion as one of the most relevant aspects of political adherence. See Jović (2009: 62–82). The Kosovo Albanians were, however, recognised as an ethnic group. In their autonomous region (which was gradually becoming a republic), they had their own political representation, university, and cultural institutions, where the Albanian language was used. Regardless of the long history of tensions between the individual Yugoslav nations, it was the unequal economic development within Yugoslavia that was much more problematic than the cultural moment.

17. Marx explained this excellently in the first part of *Capital*: 'The law, finally, that always equilibrates the relative surplus population, or industrial reserve army, to the extent and energy of accumulation, this law rivets the labourer to capital more firmly than the wedges of Vulcan did Prometheus to the rock. It establishes an accumulation of misery, corresponding with accumulation of capital. Accumulation of wealth at one pole is, therefore, at the same time, accumulation of misery, agony of toil, slavery, ignorance, brutality, mental degradation, at the opposite pole, i.e., on the side of the class that produces its own product in the form of capital' (MECW: vol. 24: 315).

18. Film producers and other filmmakers would thus sign contracts for particular film projects, while the authors of the films would, besides investing their labour, often request additional loans from the banks. Any additional earnings depended on the success of the film – i.e., on the box office sales in the domestic and international market as well as on any awards received at film festivals. For further details on the financing of the Yugoslav film industry, see Kirn (2014).

19. Between 1950 and 1960 the unemployment rate ranged between 5 and 6 per cent however, in the 1960s it reached 10 per cent. By the 1980s this problem had become acute: without taking into account the so-called *Gastarbeiters* (roughly one million migrant workers who worked in Western Europe), the unemployment rate came close to 17.5 per cent towards the end of the 1980s (Woodward 1995a: 191).

Chapter 11

1. Here, the possibility of drawing credit lines from the regional banks has to be taken into account; the Ljubljanska banka, for example, had conducted business with foreign banking institutions since 1967.
2. See also Suvin (2014: 232–42).
3. For one of the first theoretical outlines of the relationship between the centre and the periphery and the global system and Yugoslav economy, see Kirn (1982: 51–3).
4. Catherine Samary also points out that the workers' councils could not influence the crediting and the banks' decisions. Credit committees were composed of expert groups that oversaw the circulation of monetary capital. See Samary (1988: 197).
5. Extensive infrastructure and tourism projects were undoubtedly linked to the opening towards the West. This, however, cannot be described as 'Coca-Cola socialism'. If we focus merely on the development of tourist facilities, we can see that many projects were oriented towards a specific socialist modernisation that sustained the agricultural and other industrial areas (and activities) as well as the late modernist architectural orientation. Instead of turning tourism into a private consumer complex, this modernisation policy created numerous open and public spaces, designed for socialising and artistic activities. The public and educational aspects of the construction of tourist facilities cannot simply be equated with consumerism.
6. In 1955 the inflation rate was 4% and this figure did not change considerably over the following years. See Samary (1988: 187–9). Inflation started rising more substantially by the end of the 1960s.
7. The trade with OECD countries grew from 47% in 1965 to as much as 62% in 1970. As opposed to the trade deficit with the West, the trade balance with Eastern and Non-Aligned Countries was more favourable. Prior to 1965, the trade with the Council for Mutual Economic Assistance (the Comecon) was also slightly more substantial. The trade with the Comecon (36%) dwindled to 25% in 1970, while the trade with the Non-Aligned remained at the same level in this period – at approximately 15% of the total trade. The trade balance with the Eastern and Non-Aligned economies was positive for Yugoslavia. For statistical details, see Samary (1988). For an overview on state borrowing, see Živković (2015).
8. External debt started to increase once US aid had ended and Yugoslavia started opening up towards the West. However, the change was not that substantial: in 1964, for example, Yugoslavia only had a $US2.7 billion debt, while in 1971, its debt was within the range of the current austerity policies and represented approximately 30% of Yugoslavia's GDP. The less successful indicator was hidden in the structure of this debt, as the key creditor was the World Bank with approximately 40% of the total Yugoslav debt, followed by the Western countries, while the Eastern countries represented a mere 14% (Suvin 2014).

9. Horvat criticised this credit policy, which led to the dissolution of Yugoslavia; however, in the 1960s, he represented the line that supported the market reform and economic efficiency together with a cautious balance between the market and the plan.

10. Vučetić recently wrote a book about 'Coca-Cola Socialism' (2012), which transferred the paradigm of Americanisation/consumerism into the Yugoslav context rather uncritically. Even though the book contains valuable data, one should also read a sound critique of her position by Kršić (2013).

11. Woodward (1995b) attributed the greatest share of answerability to the World Bank and IMF, who mercilessly introduced austerity policies during a severe economic crisis. The urgency of the further liberalisation of prices and trade, as well as institutional reforms that would introduce monetary discipline, strict public finance control, and even a possible dismissal of workers in the public sector – all of this turned into a new standard in the beginning of the 1980s.

12. Such liberal reforms closely resembled the neoliberal autocratic economic model, which was already being tested in Chile at the time. See also Klein (2008), and Bockman (2011).

13. Catherine Samary researched the phenomenon of 'mixed companies', which were supposed to be managed jointly with foreign capital (1988: 201–207). Although loose legislation enabled partial tax avoidance, these companies never really took off. This part of the reforms thus mainly demonstrates the ideological shift within the legal-political structure of self-management.

14. Woodward thoroughly analysed the crucial economic positions assumed by the economists and politicians at the end of the 1970s and during the 1980s. She concluded that the Keynesians and the neoliberals represented two different poles in this strategic conflict. The Keynesians and the representatives of the federation (the federal bureaucracy) who cooperated with the IMF were on one side; while the liberals (technocrats), who represented the specific interests of the wealthier republics and small companies, were on the other side.

15. The comparison between Slovenia as the wealthiest republic and Kosovo as the poorest province reveals that, in 1947, the Slovenian economy represented 153 units of the average value in the Yugoslav economy, while Kosovo represented 50 units. In the 1960s, these differences started increasing and the Slovenian share amounted to as much as 177 in 1963, while Kosovo stagnated at 36 units of the average value. For a more detailed table of income and living standard indicators, see Bavčar et al. (1985: 64), where the slow increase of disparities in the 1960s, as well as their extensive growth in the 1970s and afterwards, are clearly demonstrated.

16. We could add that this was also true of the other underdeveloped republics.

17. Industrialisation was the sacred cow of Yugoslav development throughout the post-war period, right until the mid-1980s. Bavčar (1985).

18. For more detailed numbers, see Samary (1988: 167).

19. A lower level of agricultural population; an improvement in the infrastructure; the number of students at the University of Pristina increased by as much as 500% between 1964 and 1975.

20. The income per capita in Kosovo was decreasing in comparison with the Yugoslav average. In 1947, it amounted to 52%; in 1975 to 33%; and in 1979 it fell to 28% of the Yugoslav average. In the 1980s, the situation became unbearable, as strikes and police repression were on the rise (Kirn, 1982: 73–7).

Chapter 12

1. Močnik drew a pertinent line between the 'ruling ideology' and the 'ideology of the ruling class', which allowed for a more in-depth analysis of the ideological and state reproduction of the self-management system. (Močnik, 1985: 7–22).

2. For further theories on ideology, see Gillot (2013).

3. Althusser (1994: 253–314). Within the Yugoslav context, the most consistent critiques and theories of ideology were written by Rastko Močnik, Slavoj Žižek, and Mladen Dolar. If I were to generalise somewhat, I would say that these authors have pointed at the theoretical limitations of the prevailing Marxist schools (e.g. Praxis in Yugoslavia), while underlining, in the political perspective, a number of inconsistencies in the operation of the self-management system and the persistence of Stalinism as the ideology of the 'ruling class'.

4. See Lebowitz (2012).

5. Močnik claims that 'social management', 'a legal-political' category of self-management outside the enterprise, appears as an anticipation of what is currently called 'governance': the management of society by depoliticisation ..., while workers remain separated from intellectual capacities within the labour process' (Močnik, 2010b).

6. Suvin claims that the inequalities became much more frequent in the aftermath of the 1965 market reform and identified them on three different levels: high echelons, white collar workers – blue collar workers' (2014: 260–66).

7. See for example Kardelj (1978: 174).

8. In the Soviet Union, the figure of the shock worker (Stakhanovite) was at the forefront for a long time, as it had been promoted at least from the beginning of the 1930s onwards. In Yugoslavia this role was assumed by the miner Alija Sirotanović in 1949, when he and his eight comrades dug up 158 tonnes of coal in a single shift. It is noteworthy that this took place one year after the Cominform dispute. The fact that Sirotanović and his comrades represented the dominant ideological figure does not imply that all workers wished to achieve this ideal. On the contrary: numerous workers rejected such a figure due to the issue of labour discipline.

9. It should be underlined that any extensive study of the working-class figure should involve a long-term analysis of the everyday lives of workers and

migrant workers. This should also take into account their political, social, and cultural activities. This has not been achieved so far, but I nevertheless wish to point out an extremely interesting study from Rajković (2015) that focuses on the ethnography of the workers in the (old) Zastava factory in Kragujevac, which points out certain ambivalent perceptions of the role of workers in society at the time. This analysis is further complicated by the fact that several figures exist already within the working class: from the more militant figure of the agitator, shock worker, and (collective) work brigade to the self-management worker and consumer of social services.

10. For the entire televised speech with subtitles, see the Archive of the Museum of History of Yugoslavia, https://www.youtube.com/watch?v=Nne2feNUEu8.

11. For further information on the occupation of the University in Ljubljana and other related activities – such as the granting of autonomy, the emergence of Radio Študent (an important student radio station), and other cultural activities – see Baškovič et al. (1982).

12. In the subchapter on Makavejev, Boris Buden (2009) presents an excellent thesis in which he states that these alternative artists criticised post-communism rather than communism, which they actually wanted to get back on its feet.

13. See Kirn (2012).

14. The criticism of the worker figure can be found in the films created by the most important Black Wave directors – from Dušan Makavejev (*Man Is Not a Bird*, 1965), Živojin Pavlović (*When I Am Dead and Gone*, 1967), to Želimir Žilnik (*Early Works*, 1969). In these films the workers were portrayed in a negative way, sometimes bordering on the prevalent clichés that reflected the cultural and class racism and corresponded to the following model: because the workers were uncultivated and uneducated, they were easy prey for either the government's ideological apparatus or criminal associations. At least on the macro level, this model should be placed in parentheses, and many of these critical films should be interpreted in a more dialectical manner. In their works, the radical independent film directors attempted to demystify the self-management ideology and argue for a radical change of the existing relations (Buden 2008).

15. *Praxis* implies an integral realisation of man that transcends the objective material framework. In this regard, at least two contributions of the Praxis school should be pointed out for their role in developing this thesis further. The first one is a short article on the concept of estrangement and man by Gajo Petrović, one of the main representatives of this school (see Horvat et al., 363–6). The second example can be found in Tadić's concept of individual freedom that he seeks in the excess of Order (see ibid., 405–15). For a more detailed overview of the Praxis school, see Popov (2003).

16. Some representatives of the Praxis school became nationalists in the late 1980s, while others turned to a more left-liberal standpoint.

17. While Marx insisted on this radicalisation and realisation of the human essence during his early years, he would in his later years openly criticise the concept of human rights that became the cornerstone of the bourgeois law,

as it was 'blind' to the class relations within the sphere of exchange and the 'free contract'.

18. Stojanović places special emphasis on the discrepancy between the ideals and the socialist reality (in: Horvat et al., 467–78).

19. Kardelj also stopped mentioning the dictatorship of the proletariat at that time – in fact, he even had a few negative comments as regards this concept (ibid., 174). As Slobodan Stanković demonstrated, 'until now, the official Yugoslav theory has been announcing the workers' self-management system as a special form of dictatorship of the proletariat. This slogan has nevertheless been abandoned by certain pro-Soviet and even independent Communist Parties as well as by the Communist Party of the Soviet Union itself (in the draft of the new constitution). In Yugoslavia it has also been decided that this term is no longer needed. Thus, the term "self-management pluralism" is now preferred, which is evidently diametrically opposed to the "dictatorship of the proletariat"'. (Stanković 1977).

20. Repe (1992) provides a general overview of Slovenian liberalism within socialist Yugoslavia. My critique focuses on the central ideological position expressed in the conclusion of Repe's study, where the liberal perspective is the most visible: 'In the national sphere, Yugoslavia established an insurmountable framework for Slovenian liberalism ... "Liberalism" in Slovenia thus represented an important step on the historical path towards an independent, economically successful, socially secure, democratic, and globally open state' (ibid., 260). The fact that liberalism was an important factor in the ideological transformation is not at issue here. What is problematic, though, is that it was presented as a natural fact, which necessarily resulted in the formation of the Slovenian state. It is more pertinent to consider whether the supposed democratic transition was not in fact more successful because of the economic achievements that were a result of the past social labour and industrial politics of socialist Yugoslavia. Franček Drenovec (2013) points out the end of the success story very well: in the 1990s, the economic indicators revealed increasing class differences, poverty, and unemployment, all of which are normally omitted from the success story. The transition was not in the least democratic, and one of the criteria – openness to the world – can also imply greater dependence on the IMF and higher debts, leading to the exhaustion of the economy and the dismantling of social rights. The liberal suppositions are caught in a circular logic and come true, just like the conservative narration, in the story of the successful and independent Slovenia.

21. See Woodward (1995b).

22. The demand of the Croatian political leadership for a less centralised approach regarding the management of foreign currency, which originated mainly from tourism, may be a sound economic argument, however, it neglects the aspect of federal investments, joint debts, and efforts to construct the tourist infrastructure.

23. For a more detailed historical study, see Repe (1992).

24. Kirn's article (2012) focuses on this in particular.

25. Ustav SFRJ (1974: 499–503). These sections also emphasise the community of self-management interests.

26. Woodward's critique focuses on the ethno-nationalist paradigm: 'Ethnic differences, even substantial differences, do not set a society inexorably on a path toward war. Few states are free of the potential for animosity along ethnic, religious, racial, or communal lines. All countries have histories, even unresolved quarrels and unexpunged traumas, but they do not inevitably become the cause of war'. (Woodward, 1995b: 18).

27. Budding (1998) focused predominantly on the Serbian intelligentsia, while Wachtel (2002) analysed the media's influence. In Croatia, the rise of nationalism was excellently described by Klasić (2012).

28. Partisan film spectacles, such as for instance the *Battle of Neretva* directed by Veljko Bulajić (1969), were not merely a lucrative business: this film was also one of the major Yugoslav cultural export articles.

29. *The Man from the Oak Forest* (Popović, 1964) was one of the first films to depict Chetniks in a more complex, but also exotic manner. Its first public screening at the Pula film festival was followed by a brief silence and then a loud applause. For a more detailed contextual analysis, see Goulding (2002). This sort of a response is symptomatic and attests to the recognition of the courage to tackle a topic that was not supposed to be spoken about.

30. See the collection of texts *Albanians and Serbs* (1989), which focus on the history of Albanian–Serbian relations, especially the texts by Dimitrije Tucović, founder of the Serbian Social Democratic Party. See also Budding (1998), who analysed the role of the intellectuals and the ideological formation of the anti-Albanian sentiment in particular.

31. Such was the agreement between the linguists and cultural workers in 1954 in Novi Sad (Dragović-Sosso, 2002: 32).

32. *Matica Hrvatska* is the oldest independent Croatian national institution. Its main goals are to promote Croatian national and cultural identity in the fields of art, science, spiritual creativity, economy, and public life as well as to care for the social development of Croatia.

33. The phenomenon of the Yugoslav super-identity – people who would (super)ethnically declare themselves as Yugoslavs – was noticeable and was becoming stronger in all parts of the federation during the 1980s (Mrdjen, 2002). It involved the unfinished process of the Yugoslav project as well as the Yugoslav ideological apparatuses – from the institutions of the Yugoslav People's Army, Tito, sports games, as well as mixed marriages and other supranational institutions (Velikonja, 2009).

34. Tito brought together the communist politics, the masses, and the Party. However, at this point, Tito's name lost these emancipatory dimensions and he remained merely the master/statesman who maintained the relations of domination.

Chapter 13

1. In his early writings Marx developed his critique of the bourgeois society, which is best represented in the following texts: *On the Jewish Question, Con-*

tribution to the Critique of Hegel's Philosophy (1975: vol. 3), *The German Ideology* (MECW 1975–2010: vol. 5) and in certain passages of *Capital* (vol. 35).

2. This chapter focuses predominantly on the Slovenian 'civil society'. This does not mean that Slovenia was an exceptional case, but rather a representative of one of the 'extremes'. Slovenia enjoyed a relative economic privilege in comparison with the other regions: it had close to full employment and retained its economic growth despite the austerity measures; it also had significant political influence within the federal structures. For details on other regions and their civil society developments, see Buden (2009), while for a broader Yugoslav framework see Lazić (1994).

3. The demands for private property and a market economy circulated throughout the major magazines/journals/colloquia and were tested by the 'last' communist leadership (Ante Marković's federal government) as Yugoslavia was reaching its end. For a lucid analysis of the conditions and information on the economic programme, see Géraud-Legros (2006).

Conclusion

1. Identical political conclusions on the defeat of communism in Poland have been reached by Jan Sowa, see especially the section on 'so-called communists' (2012: 174-180).

Bibliography

Adamczak, Bini. 2007. *Gestern Morgen*. Berlin: Unrast Verlag.

Adamič, Louis. 1952. *The Eagle and the Roots*. New York: Doubleday.

Agamben, Giorgio. 1998. *Homo Sacer: Sovereign Power and Bare Life*. Stanford, California: Stanford University Press.

Alcoy, Philip. 2018. 'Yugoslav Students in the 1968 Wave of Revolt: An Interview with Dragomir Olujić'. Verso Books online: https://www.versobooks.com/blogs/3913-yugoslav-students-in-the-1968-wave-of-revolt-an-interview-with-dragomir-olujic (accessed 15 August 2019).

Althusser, Louis. 1971. *Lenin and Philosophy and Other Essays*. London: New Left Books.

——. 1976. *Elements of Self-Criticism*. London: New Left Books.

——. 1999. *Machiavelli and Us*. London: Verso.

——. 2003. *Humanist Controversy and Other Texts*. London: Verso,.

——. 2005. *For Marx*. London: Verso.

——. 2006. *Philosophy of the Encounter: Later Writings, 1978–1987*. London: Verso.

——. 2014. *On the Reproduction of Capitalism*. London: Verso.

Althusser, Louis and Étienne Balibar. 1970. *Reading Capital*. London: New Left Books.

Anderson, Benedict. 2010. *Imagined Communities*. London: Verso.

Arendt, Hannah. 1958. *The Human Condition*. Chicago: University of Chicago Press.

Arns, Inke. 2006. *Avantgarda v vzvratnem ogledalu* [Avant-garde in the Rear-window]. Ljubljana: Maska.

Arsenijević, Damir, and Nebojša Jovanović. 2007. 'Protiv konsocijacijskih teza Mirjane Kasapović'. [Against the Consociationist Theses of Mirjana Kasapović]. *Agregat* 5, 11–12: 22–27.

Aureli, Vittorio Pier. 2011. *Possibility of an Absolute Architecture*. Cambridge, Massachusetts: MIT Press.

Avbar, Alojz. 1971. *Zakaj je padla Španska republika?* [Why Did the Spanish Republic Fall?]. Ljubljana: Borec.

Badiou, Alain. 1998. *D'un désastre obscur: sur la fin de la vérité d'État*. La Tour d'Aigues: Éditions de l'Aub.

——. 2005. *Metapolitics*, London: Verso.

——. 2006. *L'être et l'événement. 2, Logiques des Mondes*. Paris: Seuil.

Bajt, Aleksander. 1975. 'Social Ownership-Collective and Individual'. In *Self-Governing Socialism: A Reader,* (151–63): vol. 2, (eds.) Branko Horvat et al. New York: International Arts and Sciences Press.

Bakarić, Vladimir. 1983. *Socijalistički samoupravni sistem i društvena reprodukcija* [Socialist Self-management System and Social Reproduction], 4 vols. Zagreb: Informator.

Balibar, Étienne. 1974. *Cinq études du matérialisme historique*. Paris: Maspero.

——. 2002. *Politics and the Other Scene*. London: Verso.

——. 2008. *Masses, Classes, Ideas: Studies on Politics and Philosophy Before and After Marx*. London: Routledge.

——. 2012. 'Lenin and Gandhi. A Missed Encounter?'. *Radical Philosophy* 172. Available online: https://www.radicalphilosophy.com/article/lenin-and-gandhi (accessed 15 August 2019).

Balibar, Etienne and Immanuel Wallerstein. 1991. *Race, Nation, Class: Ambiguous Identities*. London: Verso.

Banac, Ivo. 1984. *The National Question in Yugoslavia*. London: Cornell University Press.

Balažic, Milan. 2004. *Slovenska demokratična revolucija* [Slovenian Democratic Revolution]. Ljubljana: Liberalna akademija.

Bašković, Ciril et al. 1982. Študentsko gibanje 1968–1972 [The Student Movement 1968-1972]. Ljubljana: Krt.

Bavčar, Igor. 1982. 'Spremna beseda' [Foreword]. In Michael Mauke, *Marxova in Engelsova teorija razredov* [Marx and Engels' Theory of Classes]. Ljubljana: Krt.

——. 1985. 'Spremna beseda' [Foreword]. In Geoffrey Kay, *Razvitost in nerazvitost* [Development and Non-development]. Ljubljana: Krt.

Bavčar, Igor, Srečo Kirn in Bojan Korsika. *Kapital + Delo v SFRJ* [Capital and Work in the Socialist Federative Republic of Yugoslavia]. Ljubljana: Krt, 1985.

Beevor, Anthony. 2006. *The Battle for Spain*. London: Penguin Books.

Benjamin, Walter. 1968. *Illuminations*. New York: Harcourt, Brace & World.

——. 1974. 'The Paris of the Second Empire in Baudelaire'. In *Gesammelte Schriften*, ed. Hermann Schweppenhäuser and Rolf Tiedemann, vol. I. 3, pp. 1160–61. Frankfurt a. Main: Suhrkamp. (English translation https://anthropologicalmaterialism.hypotheses.org/2082, accessed 15 August 2019).

——. 2008. *The Work of Art in the Age of Mechanical Reproduction, and Other Writings on Media*. Cambridge, Massachusetts: Harvard University Press.

Bhattacharya, Tithi. 2017. *Social Reproduction Theory*. London: Pluto Press.

Bičanić, Rudolf. 2010. *Economic Policy in Socialist Yugoslavia*. Cambridge: Cambridge University Press.

Bilandžić, Dušan. 1973. *Ideje i praksa društvenog razvoja Jugoslavije 1945–1973* [Ideas and Practice of Social Development of Yugoslavia 1945–1973]. Belgrade: Komunist.

——. 1980. *Zgodovina Socialistične federativne republike Jugoslavije: glavni procesi* [History of the Socialist Federative Republic of Yugoslavia: Central Processes]. Ljubljana: Mladinska knjiga.

Black & Red Correspondents, 1968. 'Down with the Red Bourgeoisie of Yugoslavia'. In *Black & Red* 3. Available online: http://theanarchistlibrary.org/library/black-red-correspondents-down-with-the-red-bourgeoisie-of-yugoslavia (accessed 15 August 2019).

Bockman, Jochanna. 2011. *Markets in the Name of Socialism: The Left-Wing Origins of Neoliberalism*. Stanford: Stanford University Press.

Bogdanović, Mira. 2014. *Konstante konvertitstva* [Constants of Conversion]. Belgrade: Centar za libertarne studije.

Boltanski and Chiapello, 2007. *The New Spirit of Capitalism*. London: Verso.

Bonfiglioli, Chiara. 2012. *Revolutionary Networks: Women's Political and Social Activism in Cold War Italy and Yugoslavia (1945–1957)*. Utrecht: Utrecht University (Unpublished PhD dissertation).

Booker, Christopher. 1997. *A Looking-Glass Tragedy: The Controversy Over the Repatriations from Austria in 1945*. London: Gerald Duckworth & Co Ltd.

Bor, Matej. 1946. *Pesmi* [Poems]. Ljubljana: Slovenski knjižni zavod.

Boym, Svetlana. 2002. *The Future of Nostalgia*. New York: Basic Books.

Boynik, Sezgin. 2018. Introduction to *Coiled Verbal Spring: Devices of Lenin's Language* Helsinki: Rab-Rab Press.

Brborić-Likić, Branka. 2003. *Democratic Governance in the Transition from Yugoslav Self-Management to a Market Economy*. Uppsala: Uppsala Studies in Economic History 69.

Breznik, Maja. 1995. 'Solidarity or What We Were Fighting For'. In: Tomassi, N. and Heer, B. (eds), *Management Tools: A Workbook for Arts Professionals in East and Central Europe*. (73–9). New York: Arts International.

Buck-Morss, Susan. 2002. *Dreamworld and Catastrophe: The Passing of Mass Utopia in East and West*. Cambridge, Massachusetts: MIT Press.

——. 2009. *Hegel, Haiti and Universal History*. Pittsburgh: University of Pittsburgh Press.

Buden, Boris. 2003. 'Još o komunistićkim krvolocima, ili zašto smo se ono rastali?' [Again on Communist Hangmen, or Why we Broke up?]. *Prelom* 3, 5: 51–8.

——. 2007. 'The Post-Yugoslavian Condition of Institutional Critique: An Introduction. On Critique as Countercultural Translation'. *EIPCP online journal* 11: http://eipcp.net/transversal/0208/buden/en. accessed 15 August 2019.

——. 2008. 'Behind the Velvet Curtain. Remembering Dušan Makavejev's *W. R.: Mysteries of the Organism*'. *Afterall* 18. Online: https://www.afterall.org/journal/issue.18/behind.velvet.curtain.remembering.dusan.makavejevs, accessed 15 August 2019.

——. 2009. *Zone des Übergangs: vom Ende des Postkommunismus*. Frankfurt am Main: Suhrkamp.

Burčar, Lilijana. 2009. 'Izkrivljanje in degradacija samoupravnega socializma v imenu liberalnega feminizma in novodobnega "antifa"'[Distorting and Degrading of Self-management Socialism in the Name of Liberal Feminism and the New "Antifa"]. *Borec* 61, 657–61: 296–331.

Butler, Judith, Ernsto Laclau, and Slavoj Žižek (eds). 2000. *Contingency, Hegemony, Universality: Contemporary Dialogues on the Left*. London: Verso.

Campbell, John. 1967. *Tito's Separate Road: America and Yugoslavia in World Politics*. New York: Harper.

Centrih, Lev. 2008. 'O pomenu Komunistične partije Slovenije med drugo svetovno vojno in po njej' [On the Role of The Communist Party of Slovenia During and After WWII]. *Borec* 60, 648–91: 61–80.

——. 2011. *Marksistična formacija* [Marxist Formation]. Ljubljana: Založba cf/*.

——. 2013. 'The Socialist, Revolutionary and Antifascist Dimensions of the Liberation Front of the Slovenian Nation in Yugoslavia and Its Place in the History of Class Struggles'. Ljubljana: Prvomajska šola. Online: https://www.youtube.com/watch? v=aV9K8CP_6VU, accessed 15 August 2019.

——. 2015. 'The Road to Collapse: The Demise of the League of Communists of Yugoslavia'. *Research Paper Series of Rosa Luxemburg Stiftung Southeast Europe* No. 2, 2015. Belgrade: Rosa Luxembourg Stiftung.

Césaire, Aimé. 2000. *Discourse on Colonialism.* New York: Monthly Review Press.

Chin, Rita. 2009. *The Guest Worker Question in Postwar Germany.* Cambridge: Cambridge University Press.

Čakardić, Ankica, 'Ženski problem u političkoj ekonomiji – od jugoslavenskog samoupravljanja do mjeraštednji' [Problem of Women in Political Economy – From Yugoslav Self-management to Austerity Policies], *Gerusija.* Available online: http://gerusija.com/ankica-cakardic-zenski-problem-u-politickoj-ekonomiji-od-jugoslavenskog-samoupravljanja-do-mjera-stednji/#M9zGeYlwHbhWY6jR.99 (accessed 15 August 2019).

Čalić, Marie-Janine. 2010. *Geschichte Jugoslawiens im 20. Jahrhundert.* Munich: Beck.

Čolić, Milutin. 1981. 'Umetnici ,od volje' i vojnici revolucije'[Artists of 'Will' and Fighters of Revolution]. In Života Marković (ed.), *Užička Republika i Sjećanja* I, pp. 313–17. Belgrade. Titovo Užice: Narodni muzej.

Deakin, William. 1973. *The Embattled Mountain.* London: Oxford University Press.

Dean, Jodi. 2019. *Comrade.* London: Verso.

Debenjak, Bozidar. 2008. *O Spremembi Sveta.* [On the Change of World]. Ljubljana: zalozba Sophija.

Dedić, Nikola. 2016. '*Post-Yugoslav* Artistic Practices: Or, Art as …'. In: Beronja, Vlad and Vervaet, Stijn (eds), *Post-Yugoslav Constellations.* Berlin: De Gruyter: 169–90.

Dedijer, Vladimir. 1953. *Tito Speaks.* London: Weidenfeld & Nicolson/Orion.

——. 1980. *Novi prilozi za biografiju Josipa Broza Tita* [New Annexed Documents for Biography of Josip Broz Tito]. Zagreb: Mladost Zagreb.

Deleuze, Gilles and Felix Guattari. 1977. *Anti-Oedipus: Capitalism and Schizophrenia.* Minneapolis, Minnesota: University of Minnesota Press.

Denitch, Bogdan Denis. 1990. *Limits and Possibilities: The Crisis of Yugoslav Socialism and State Socialist Systems.* Minnesota: University of Minnesota Press.

Derrida, Jacques. 1995. 'Archive Fever: A Freudian Impression'. *Diacritics* 2, 25: 9–63.

Deutsch, Karl. 1996. *Nationalism and Social Communication.* Cambridge: Cambridge University Press.

Dežulović, Boris. 2013. 'Pismo čitateljima Blica i gledateljima serije Ravna Gora' [Letter to Readers of *Blic* and Spectators of Series Ravna Gora]. Available online: http://pescanik.net/2013/12/pismo-citateljima-blica-i-gledateljima-serije-ravna-gora, accessed 15 August 2019.

Dimitrijević, Branislav. 2009. 'Behind Skepticism Lies the Fire of a Revolutionary'. In Branka Ćurčić (ed.), *For an Idea – Against the Status Quo*, pp. 136–51. Novi Sad: Kuda org.

——. 2016. *Potrošeni socijalizam – Kultura, konzumerizam i društvena imaginacija u Jugoslaviji (1950-1974)* [Consumed Socialism – Culture, Consumerism, and Social Imagination in Yugoslavia]. Belgrade: Fabrika knjiga.

Dimitrov, Georgi. 1975. *The United Front*. San Francisco: Proletarian Publishers.

Djilas, Milovan. 1982. *The New Class: Analysis of the Communist System*. Boston: Mariner Books.

Dobnikar, M. (ed). 1985. *O ženski in ženskem gibanju*. [On Woman and the Woman's Movement]. Ljubljana: Krt.

Dolar, Mladen. 2015. 'Psychoanalysis in Power: On Fascism, Marxism and the Poster Scandal'. In Zdenka Badovinc (ed). *NSK from Kapital to Capital*. (50–66). Cambridge, Massachusetts: MIT Press.

Dolenc, Danijela and Mislav Žitko. 2013. 'Ostrom and Horvat: Identifying Principles of a Socialist Governmentality', *Group 22 Working Paper Series*. Available online: beyondostrom.blog.rosalux.de/files/2013/09/Dolenec-Zitko-Working-Paper-2013-1.pdf, accessed 15 August 2019.

Dragović-Sosso, Jasna. 2002. *Saviours of the Nation? Serbia's Intellectual Opposition and the Revival of Nationalism*. Montreal: McGill-Queen's University Press.

Drenovec, Franček. 2013. *Kolaps elite* [Collapse of the Elite]. Ljubljana: založba cf/*.

Dugandžić, Andreja and Tijana Okić. 2016. *Between Myth and Forgetting*. Belgrade: RLS.

Duzinas, Costas and Slavoj Žižek (eds.). 2010. *The Idea of Communism*. London: Verso.

Dyker, David and Ivan Vejvoda (eds.). 1996. *Yugoslavia and After*. London: Routledge.

Epstein, Julius. 1973. *Operation Keelhaul*. Old Greenwich: Devin-Adair.

Eudes, Dominique. 1973. *The Kapetanios: Partisans and Civil War in Greece, 1943-1949*. New York: Monthly Review Press.

Eyal, Gil. 2003. *The Origins of Post-Communist Elites: From the Prague Spring to the Breakup of Czechoslovakia*. Minneapolis: University of Minnesota Press.

Fanon, Frantz. 1957. *Peau noire, masques blancs*. Paris: Seuil.

Federici, Silvia. 2012. *Revolution at Point Zero: Housework, Reproduction, and Feminist Struggle*. New York: PM Press.

Fejto, Francois. 1952. *L'ère de Staline 1945–1952*. Paris: Seuil.

Fink-Hafner, Danica, and Miro Haček. 2000. *Demokratični prehodi* 1, 2. [Democratic Transitions]. Ljubljana: Fakulteta za družbene vede.

Foucault, Michel. 2004. *Sécurité, Territoire, Population: Cours au Collège de France (1977–1978)*. Paris: Seuil/Gallimard.

Frick, Richard. 2003. *Das trikontinentale Solidaritätsplakat*. Bern: René Comedia-Verlag.

Fukuyama, Francis. 1992. *The End of History and the Last Man*. London: Penguin Books.

Gajić, Zoran and Željko, Popović (eds). 2011. *Kroz tranziciju* [Through Transition]. Novi Sad: Ako.

Garde, Paul. 2000, *Vie et mort de la Yougoslavie*. Paris: Fayard.

Gellner, Ernst. 2006. *Nations and Nationalism*. Oxford: Blackwell.

Géraud-Legros, Geoffroy. 2006. *Un point aveugle de la transition yougoslave: le programme Marković*. Paris: La Découverte.

Ghodsee, Kirsten. 2014. 'Tale of "Two Totalitarianisms": The Crisis of Capitalism and the Historical Memory of Communism'. *History of the Present: A Journal of Critical History* 4, 2: 115–42.

Gil, Eyal. *The Origins of Post-Communist Elites: From the Prague Spring to the Breakup of Czechoslovakia*. Minneapolis: University of Minnesota Press, 2003.

Gillot, Pascale. 'The Theory of Ideology and the Theory of the Unconscious'. In Sara Farris, Katja Diefenbach, Gal Kirn, and Peter Thomas (eds.), *Encountering Althusser*. (289–306) London: Continuum, 2013.

Gluckstein, Donny. 2012. *A People's History of Second World War*. London: Pluto Press.

Goldstein, Ivo. 2005. *Josip Broz Tito – između skrupuloznog historiografskog istraživanja i političke manipulacije*. [Josip Broz Tito – Between Scrupulous Historiographical Research and Political Manipulation]. Zagreb: Dijalog povjesničara – istoričara.

Gramsci, Antonio. 1971. *Selections from the Prison Notebooks*. London: Lawrence & Wishart.

Gunder Frank, Andre. 2002. *ReOrient: Global Economy in the Asian Age*. Berkeley: University of California Press.

Guevara, Che. 2002. *Guerrilla Warfare*. Lanham: Rowman & Littlefield Publishers.

Gužvica, Stefan. Forthcoming. *Factional Struggles in the Communist Party of Yugoslavia during the Great Purge (1936–1940)*. Ljubljana: založba Sophia.

Habermas, Jürgen. 1973. *Theory and Practice*. Boston: Beacon Press.

Hajdini, Simon (ed). 2013. *Prvotna akumulacija med konceptom in zgodovino* [Primitive Accumulation between Concept and History]. Ljubljana: Inštitut za delavske študije.

Hallward, Peter. 2005. 'Beyond salvage'. *South Atlantic Quarterly* 104, 2: 237–44.

Harman, Chris. 2004.'The Rise of Capitalism'. *International Socialism* 2, 102: 53–86.

Hardt, Michael and Negri, Antonio. 2000. *Empire*, Cambridge, Massachusetts: Harvard University Press.

——. 2009. *Commonwealth*. Cambridge, Massachusetts: Harvard University Press.

Harvey, David. 2001. *The Condition of Postmodernity: An Enquiry into the Origins of Cultural Change*. Oxford: Blackwell.

Heinrich, Michael. 2012. *An Introduction to the Three Volumes of Karl Marx's Capital*. New York: Monthly Review Press.

Ho Chi Minh. 1960–62. *Selected Works*. Hanoi: Foreign Languages Publishing House.

Hobsbawm, Eric and Terence Ranger (eds). 1988. *The Invention of Tradition*. Cambridge, New York; New Rochelle: Cambridge University Press.

Hobsbawm, Eric. 1992. *Nations and Nationalism Since 1780: Programme, Myth, Reality*. Cambridge: Cambridge University Press.

Holloway, John. 2002. *Change the World Without Taking Power: The Meaning of Revolution Today*. London: Pluto Press.

Hooker, William. 2009. *Carl Schmitt's International Thought: Order and Orientation*. Cambridge: Cambridge University Press.

Hornberger, Jacob. 1995. *Repatriation – The Dark Side of World War II*. Available online: https://www.fff.org/explore-freedom/article/repatriation-dark-side-world-war-ii-part-1/, accessed 15 August 2019.

Horvat, Branko. 1969. *Ogled o jugoslavenskom društvu* [Sketch of Yugoslav Society]. Mladost: Zagreb.

——. 1975. 'The Pricing Factors of Production'. In Branko Horvat et al (eds), *Self-Governing Socialism: A Reader,* II. (293–335). New York: International Arts and Sciences Press.

——. 1976. *The Yugoslav Economic System*. Armonk, NY: Sharpe.

——. 1983. *Political Economy of Socialism*. Armonk, NY: Sharpe.

Horvat, Srećko and Igor Štiks (eds.). 2014. *Welcome to the Desert of Post-Socialism: Radical Politics after Yugoslavia*. London: Verso.

Horvatinčić, Sanja. 2013. 'Prijedlog modela problemske analize spomeničke plastike iz razdoblja socijalizma' [Proposal of Modelling the Problem Analysis of Sculptural Plastic from Socialism]. *Radovi Instituta za povijest umjetnosti* 37: 217–28.

——. 2017. 'Memorials from the Socialist Era in Croatia – Typology Model'. Zadar University: Unpublished PhD dissertation.

Jalušić, Vlasta. 2002. *Kako smo hodile v feministično gimnazijo* [How We went to the Feminist Gymnasium]. Ljubljana: Založba.

James, C.L.R., Grace Lee and Pierre Chaulieu. 1958. *Facing Reality*. Detroit: Bewick Press.

Jameson, Fredric. 1982. *Political Unconscious*. Ithaca: Cornell University Press.

Jameson, Fredric. 1991. *Postmodernism, or, The Cultural Logic of Late Capitalism,* London: Verso.

Jančar-Webster, Barbara. 1990. *Women and Revolution in Yugoslavia, 1941–1945*. Denver: Arden.

Job, Cvijeto. 2002. *Yugoslavia's Ruin*. Lanham: Rowman & Littlefield.

Jovanov, Neca. 1979. *Radnički štrajkovi u SFRJ* [Workers' Strikes in the Socialist Federative Republic of Yugoslavia]. Belgrade: Zapis.

Jovanović, Andrea. 2014. 'The Yugoslav Antifascist Front of Women (AFŽ): Legacy, Lessons and Some Insights'. *Borec* 66: 712–14.

Jovanović, Nebojša. 2012. 'Futur Anterieur of Yugoslav Cinema, or Why Emir Kusturica's Legacy is Worth Fighting for'. In Daniel Šuber and Slobodan Karamanić (eds), *Retracing Images: Visual Cultures after Yugoslavia*, pp. 149–70. Leiden: Brill.

Jović, Dejan. 2009. *Withering Away of State*. West Lafayette: Purdue University Press.

——. 2010. 'Problems of the Early Post-Communist Transition Theory'. *Politička misao : časopis za politologiju* 47, 5: 44–68.

Jurišević, Fran. 1975. *Partizansko gospodarstvo na Primorskem* [The Partisan Economy in Primorska]. Koper: Lipa.

Kanzleiter, Boris. 2011. *1968 in Jugoslawien: Studentenproteste und kulturelle Avantgarde zwischen 1960 und 1975: Gespräche und Dokumente*. Berlin: Dietz.

Kaplan, Robert. 2005. *Balkan Ghosts*. London: Picador.

Karamanić, Slobodan. 'Kosovo after Yugoslavia'. *Prelom* 8, 5 (2006): 23–39.

——. 2009. 'Balkan Socialist Confederation 1910–1948'. In: Immanuel Ness (ed.), *International Encyclopaedia of Revolution and Protest*, pp. 337–9. Malden: Blackwell Publishing.

Kardelj, Edvard. 1937. *Razvoj slovenskega narodnega vprašanja* [Development of the Slovenian National Question]. Ljubljana: Naša založba.

——. 1960. *Socialism and War: A Survey of Chinese Criticism of the Policy of Peaceful Coexistence*. London: Metheun.

——. 1975. 'Samoupravljanje – ena izmed zakonitosti v razvoju socializma' [Self-management – One of the Laws in the Development of Socialism]. *Teorija in praksa* 12, 10: 947–54.

——. 1976. *Protislovja družbene lastnine v sodobni socialistični praksi* [Contradictions of Social Ownership in Contemporary Socialist Practice]. Ljubljana: DZS.

——. 1978. *Pravci razvoja političkog sistema socijalističkog samoupravljanja* [Directions in the Developments of the Political System of Socialist Self-management]. Belgrade: Komunist.

——. 1979. *Samoupravljanje* [Self-Management]. Ljubljana: DZS.

——. 1980. *Spomini* [Reminiscences]. Ljubljana: DZS.

——. 1981. *Nation and Socialism*. Belgrade: Socialist Thought and Practice.

Karge, Haike. 2010. *Steinerne Erinnerung—Versteinerte Erinnerung? Kriegsgedenken in Jugoslawien (1947–1970)*. Wiesbaden: Harrassowitz.

Katalenac, Juraj. 2013.'Yugoslav Self-Management: Capitalism Under the Red Banner'. *Insurgent Notes* 9. Available online: https://libcom.org/library/yugoslav-self-management-capitalism-under-red-banner-juraj-katalenac, accessed 15 August 2019.

Kerševan, Marko. 1980. *Razredna analiza in marksistična družbena teorija* [Class Analysis and Marxist Social Theory]. Ljubljana: Delavska enotnost.

Kerševan, Marko. 1985. 'K vprašanju razrednosti socialističnih družbenih sistemov' [On the Question of Class in Socialist Social Systems]. *Teorija in praksa* 22, 12: 1467–86.

Kidrič, Boris. 1948. *O izgradnji socialističke ekonomike FNRJ* [Lecture on V. Congress of Communist Party of Yugoslavia]. Belgrade: Borba.

——. 1987. *Zbrana dela* [Collected Works]. Ljubljana: DZS.

Kirn, Gal. 2010. 'From Partisan Primacy of Politics to Postfordist Tendency in Yugoslav Self-Management'. In Gal Kirn (ed.), *Postfordism and its Discontents* (253–305). Maastricht – Ljubljana: Jan van Eyck Academie – Mirovni inštitut.

———. 2011. 'Nacrt tranzicije u kapitalističkoj nacionalnoj državi kao projekat liberalno proljeća, odnosno killing us softly na slovenački način' [Sketch of Transition to the Capitalist National State as a Project of Liberal Spring, or How to Kill us Softly in the Slovenian Way]. In Zoran Gajić and Željko Popović (eds.), *Kroz Tranziciju*. (21–43). Novi Sad: AKU.

———. 2012a. *Conceptualisation of Politics and Reproduction in the Work of Louis Althusser: Case of Socialist Yugoslavia*. PhD dissertation. Nova Gorica: University of Novi Gorica.

———. 2012b. 'New Yugoslav Cinema: A Humanist Cinema? Not really'. In Gal Kirn, Dubravka Sekulić, and Žiga Testen (eds.), *Surfing the Black: Black Wave Cinema and its Transgressive Moments.*(10–46). Maastricht: Jan van Eyck Academy.

———. 2014. 'Multiple Temporalities of the Partisan Struggle: From Post-Yugoslav Nationalist Reconciliation Back to Partisan Poetry'. In Christoph Holzhey (ed.), *On the Critical Potential of Ir/Reversible Aspect-Seeing*. (163–90). Vienna–Berlin: Turia + Kant.

———. 2017. 'Critique of Transition Studies on Postsocialism, or How to Rethink and Reorient 1989? The Case of (Post)Socialist (Post)Yugoslavia'. In: Burchardt, Marian and Kirn (eds.), *Beyond Neoliberalism. Approaches to Social Inequality and Difference*. (43–68). London: Palgrave Macmillan.

———. 2019. 'Anti-totalitarian Monuments in Ljubljana and Brussels: From Nationalist Reconciliation to Open Rehabilitation of Fascism'. In Ahyan, Kaya and Cesari (eds.), *European Memory in Populism*. (47-69). London: Routledge.

———. Forthcoming. *Partisan Counter Archive*. Berlin: De Gruyter.

Kirn, Srečo. 1982. 'Razvoj Nerazvoja: Primer Kosova'[Development of Undevelopment. The Case of Kosovo]. ČKZ 51–2: 53–95.

Klasić, Hrvoje.2012. *Jugoslavija i svijet 1968* [Yugoslavia and world in 1968]. Zagreb: Naklada Ljevak.

Klein, Naomi. 2008. The *Shock Doctrine*. London: Penguin.

Kocbek, Edvard. 1982. *Listina: Dnevniški zapiski od 3. maja do 2. decembra 1943* [Diary from May 5 to December 2 1943]. Ljubljana: Slovenska Matica.

Kolšek, Katja. 2013. 'The Parallax Object of Althusser's Materialist Philosophy'. In Sara Farris, Katja Diefenbach, Gal Kirn, and Peter Thomas (eds), *Encountering Althusser*. (75–89). London: Continuum.

Komel, Mirt. 2011. 'The Yugoslav Wars as the Primordial Accumulation of Capital'. In: *Fast capitalism*, issue 8.1. Available online: https://www.uta.edu/huma/agger/fastcapitalism/8_1/komel8_1.html, accessed 15 August 2019.

Komelj, Miklavž. 2009. *Kako misliti partizansko umetnost?* (How to Think Partisan Art?). Ljubljana: Založba.

Koposov, Nikolay. 2017. *Memory Laws, Memory Wars: The Politics of the Past in Europe and Russia*. Cambridge: Cambridge University Press.

Kosi, Jernej. 2013. *Kako je nastal slovenski narod* [How Did the Slovenian Nation Come into Being?]. Ljubljana: Založba Sophia.

Kosi, Jernej and Lev Centrih. 2007. 'Med slovenskim narodnim vprašanjem in slovensko nacionalno zgodovino – komentarji k Slovenski novejši zgodovini' [Between the Slovenian National Question and National History – Comments on Slovenian Recent History]. *Zgodovina za vse: vse za zgodovino* 14, 1: 155–65.

Kostja, Vojin. 1981. 'Partizanska država'[Partisan state]. In *Užička Republika i Sječanja*, 1: 214–27. Titovo Užice: Narodni muzej.

Kouvelakis, Stathis. 2003. *Philosophy and Revolution: From Kant to Marx*. London: Verso.

Kovač, Bogomir. 1986. 'Družbenoekonomska kriza in mednacionalni odnosi v SFRJ' [Socioeconomic Crisis and Inter-ethnic Relations in Yugoslavia]. ČKZ 89–90: 3–36.

Kristan, Ivan. 1973. 'Kočevski zbor – rojstvo samostojne Slovenije' [Assembly of Kočevje – Birth of an Independent Slovenia]. *Teorija in praksa* 10, 7–8: 600–609.

Kršić, Dejan. 2013. 'Kokakola oportunizam'. Available online: http: //www. e-novine. com/kultura/kultura-tema/91023-Koka-kola-oportunizam.html, accessed 15 August 2019.

Kržan, Marko. 2013. 'Uspehi in neuspehi jugoslovanskega samoupravljanja' [Achievements and Failures of Yugoslav Self-management]. *Predavanje* 17. letnik IDŠ – *Socializem*. Ljubljana, 12 December.

Kuljić, Todor. 2010. *Umkämpfte Vergangenheiten. Die Kultur der Erinnerung im postjugoslawischen Raum* (Bonn: BpB).

Kuzmanić, Tonči. 1988. *Labinski štrajk* [Labin's Strike]. Ljubljana: Krt.

Labica, Georges. 2001. *L'expropriation originelle*. Paris: Les Nuits rouges.

Labica, Georges and Gérard Bensussan. 1999. *Dictionnaire critique du marxisme*. Paris: PUF.

Laclau, Ernesto. 2005. *On Populist Reason*. London: Verso.

Laclau, Ernesto, and Chantal Mouffe. 1985. *Hegemony and Socialist Strategy: Towards a Radical Democracy*. London: Verso.

Lahtinen, Mikko. 2009. Politics and Philosophy: Niccolò Machiavelli and Louis Althusser's Aleatory Materialism, Brill: HM book series.

Landa, Ishay. 2009. *The Apprentice's Sorcerer: Liberal Tradition and Fascism*. Leiden: Brill.

Lampe, John. 2000. *Yugoslavia as History: Twice There Was a Country*. Cambridge: Cambridge University Press.

Lampe, John et al (eds). 1990. *Yugoslav-American Economic Relations Since World War II*. Durham: Duke University Press.

Lampe, John. 2000. *Yugoslavia as History: Twice There Was a Country*. Cambridge: Cambridge University Press.

Lazić, Mladen. 1994. *Sistem i slom: Raspad socijalizma i struktura jugoslovenskog društva*. [System and Break: Break-up of Socialism and Structure of Yugoslav Society]. Belgrade: Filip Višnjić.

Lebowitz, Michael. 2010. *The Socialist Alternative*. New York: The Monthly Press.
——. 2012. *The Contradictions of Real Socialism*. New York: Monthly Review Press.

Lefebvre, Henri. 1970. *La révolution urbaine*, Paris: Gallimard.

Lefort, Claude. 1988. *Democracy and Political Theory*. Cambridge: Polity Press.

Lee, Michèle.1983 July–August. 'Kosovo between Yugoslavia and Albania'. *New Left Review* 1, 140: 62–91.

Lenin, Vladimir Ilič. 1972. *Marxism on the State*. Moscow: Progress Publishers.
——. 1977. *Izbrana dela* [Selected Works]. Ljubljana: Cankarjeva založba.

Lešaja, Ante. 2012. *Knjigocid: Uništavanje knjiga u Hrvatskoj 1990-ih*. [Book-ocide: Destruction of Books in Croatia in 1990s]. Zagreb: Srpsko narodno vijeće.

Lešnik, Doroteja and Grega Tomc. 1995. *Rdeče in črno: slovensko partizanstvo in domobranstvo* [Red and Black: Slovenian Partisans and Home-guards]. Ljubljana: ZIS.

Levine, Andrew. 1978. 'Robespierre: Critic of Rousseau'. *Canadian Journal of Philosophy* 8, 3: 543–57.

Levi, Pavle. 2007. *Disintegration in Frames*. Stanford: Stanford University Press.

Lipietz, Alain. 1993. 'From Althusserianism to "Regulation Theory"'. In Ann E. Kaplan and Michel Sprinker (eds.), *The Althusserian Legacy*. (99–138). London: Verso.

Losurdo, Dominico. 2015. *Revolution and War*, London: Verso.

Lovšin, Peter, Peter Mlakar, and Igor Vidmar (eds). 2002. *Punk je bil prej: 25 let punka pod Slovenci* [Punk was Before: 25 Years of Punk Under Slovenes]. Ljubljana: Cankarjeva založba in ROPOT.

Lukács, Georg. 1971. *History and Class Consciousness*. Cambridge, Massachusetts: MIT Press.

Lukič, Goran and Rastko Močnik. *Sindikalno gibanje odpira nove poglede* [Trade Union Movement Opening New Horizons]. Ljubljana: ZSSS, 2009.

Macherey, Pierre. 1999. *Histories de Dinosaur*. Paris: PUF.

Magaš, Branka. 1993. *The Destruction of Yugoslavia*. London: Verso.

Malečkar, Neža and Tomaž Mastnak (eds.). 1985. *Punk pod Slovenci*. [Punk Under Slovenes]. Ljubljana: KRT.

Mandel, Ernst. 2011. *The Meaning of the Second World War*. London: Verso.

Manucci, Lando. 2003. 'Divizija Garibaldi u Crnoj Gori' [Division of Garibaldi in Monte Negro]. Available online: http://www.montenegrina.net/pages/pages1/istorija/cg_u_2_svj_ratu/divizija_garibaldi_u_crnoj_gori_lando_manuci.html, accessed 15 August 2019.

Marković, Luka. 1978. *Klasna borba i koncepcije razvoja* [Class Struggle and Conceptions of Development]. Zagreb: Naprijed.

Marković, Mihailo. 1975. 'Philosophical Foundations of the Idea of Self-management'. In Branko Horvat et al. (eds.), *Self-Governing Socialism: A Reader* 1. (327–50). New York: International Arts and Sciences Press.

Marković, Mihailo and Gajo Petrović (eds.). 1979. *Praxis: Yugoslav Essays in the Philosophy and Methodology of the Social Sciences*. Dordrecht: D. Reidel.

Marx, Karl. 1985. *Grundrisse*. Cambridge, Massachusetts: Peter Smith Publishers.

Marx, Karl, and Friedrich Engels. 1975–2005. *Marx and Engels Collected Works* (MECW). New York: International Publishers.

Mastnak, Tomaž. 1982. *H kritiki stalinizma*. [On the Critique of Stalinism]. Ljubljana: Krt.

——. 1987. 'Totalitarizem od spodaj'. [Totalitarianism from Below]. *Družboslovne razprave* 4, 5: 91–8.

——. 1992. *Vzhodno od raja: civilna družba pod komunizmom in po njem* [East from Paradise: Civil Society Under Communism and After]. Ljubljana: Državna založba Slovenije.

——. 2005. 'The Reinvention of Civil Society: Through the Looking Glass of Democracy'. *European Journal of Sociology* 46, 2: 323–55. doi:10.1017/ S0003975605000111.

Mauke, Michael. 1982. *Marxova in Engelsova teorija razredov* [Marx and Engel's Theory of Classes]. Ljubljana: Krt.

Mauss, Marcel. 1966. *Essay on the Gift*. London: Lowe & Brydone.

Majewska, Ewa and Kuba Szreder. 2016. 'So Far, So Good: Contemporary Fascism, Weak Resistance, and Postartistic Practices in Today's Poland'. *e-flux Journal 76*. Available online: https://www.librarystack.org/e-flux-journal-76/?ref=unknown, accessed 15 August 2019.

McGregor, Sheila. 2002. 'Neither Washington nor Moscow'. *International Socialism* 2: 97.

McNally, David. 1993. *Against the Market*. London: Verso.

Mihajlević, Domagoj. 2017. *Goodbye to the Avant-garde – on the Ruins of Yugoslav Socialist Modernisation*. Belgrade: Rosa Luxembourg Foundation.

Mihajlović, Kosta. 1970. *Razvoj i životni standard regiona Jugoslavije* [Development and Life Standard in the Region of Yugoslavia]. Belgrade: Ekonomski institut.

Mikuž, Metod. 1969. *Slovensko partizansko gospodarstvo* [Slovenian Partisan Economics]. Ljubljana: Zavod Borec.

Miletić, Miloš and Mirjana Radovanović. 2017. 'Kulturna delatnost NOP-a: narodna/ revolucionarna' [Cultural Activities of People's Liberation Struggle: Popular/Revolutionary]. In Miletić, Miloš and Mirjana Radovanović (eds), *Lekcije o odbrani* [Lessons of Defense]. (129–55). Belgrade: KURS.

Milinović, Daško and Zoran Petakov (eds). 2010. *Partizanke: žene u NOB*. Novi Sad: Ako.

Minehan, Philip. 2011. *Civil War and World War in Europe: Spain, Yugoslavia, and Greece, 1936–1949*. London: Palgrave Macmillan.

Močnik, Rastko. 1985. 'Spremna beseda' [Foreword]. In Karl Marx, *Cenzura in svoboda tiska*, [Censorship and Freedom of the Press]. (7–22). Ljubljana: Krt.

——. 1995. *Extravagantia II: koliko fašizma?* [Extravaganza II: How Much Fascism?]. Ljubljana: ISH.

——. 1999. *3 teorije: ideologija, nacija, institucija* [3 Theories: Ideology, Nation, Institution]. Ljubljana: Založba.

——. 2003. 'Social change in the Balkans'. *Online Eurozine*: https://www.eurozine. com/social-change-in-the-balkans/, accessed 15 August 2019.

——. 2006. *Svetovno gospodarstvo in revolucionarna politika* [World Economy and Revolutionary Politics]. Ljubljana: založba.

——. 2008. 'Zgodovinopisje kot identitetna vednost: trije slovenski zgodovinarji o razbitju jugoslovanske federacije' [Historiography as Identity Knowledge: Three Historians on the Destruction of the Yugoslav Federation]. *Borec* 60: 648–51.

——. 2010a. 'Excess Memory', Available online: http://www.transeuropeennes.eu/ en/articles/202/Excess_Memory, accessed August 2017).

——. 2010b. 'Nismo krivi, ali smo odgovorni' (interview). [We are Not Guilty, but are Responsible]. *Up and Undergorund* 17/18: 139–56.

——. 2014. 'The Vagaries of the Expression "Civil Society": The Yugoslav Alternative'. *L'Internationale Online*: Available online: http://www. internationaleonline.org/research/real_democracy/6_the_vagaries_of_the_ expression_civil_society_the_yugoslav_alternative, accessed 15 August 2019.

—— 'Workers Self-Management in Yugoslavia – Possible Lessons for the Present', unpublished text.

Morfino, Vittorio. 2013. 'History as Permanent Revocation of the Accomplished Fact: Machiavelli in the Last Althusser'. In *Encountering Althusser*. (61–75). New York: Continuum.

Mouffe, Chantal (ed.). 1999. *The Challenge of Carl Schmitt*. London: Verso.

Mrđen, Snježana. 2002. 'Narodnost u popisima' [Nationality in Census]. Available online: http://www.doiserbia.nb.rs/img/doi/0038-982x/2002/0038-982X0201077M.pdf, accessible 15 August 2019.

Mrduljaš, Maroje and Vladimir Kulić (eds). 2012. *Unfinished Modernisations – Between Utopia and Pragmatism: Architecture and Urban Planning in Former Yugoslavia and its Successor States*. Zagreb: Udruženje hrvatskih arhitekata.

Mušić, Goran. 2011. 'Yugoslavia: Workers' Self-Management as State Paradigm'. In Immanuel Ness and Dario Azzelini (eds.). *Ours to Master and to Own: Workers' Control from the Commune to the Present*. Chicago: Haymarket Books, 2011.

Negri, Antonio. 1999. *Insurgencies: Constituent Power and the Modern State*. Minneapolis: University of Minnesota Press.

Negri, Antonio. 2008. *Goodbye Mr. Socialism*. New York: Seven Stories Press.

Nešović, Slobodan and Neda Pagon (eds). 1973. *Prvo in drugo zasedanje AVNOJ* [First and Second Meeting of Avnoj]. Ljubljana: Komunist.

Neumayer, Laure. 2018. *The Criminalisation of Communism in the European Political Space after the Cold War*. Milton Park: Routledge.

Nolte, Ernst. 1986. 'Vergangenheit, die nicht vergehen will: Eine Rede, die geschrieben, aber nicht mehr gehalten werden konnte'. *Frankfurter Allgemeine Zeitung*, Frankfurt, 6. 6. 1986.

Noys, Benjamin. 2010. 'The Arrow and the Compass', conference paper 'Waiting for the Political Moment' International Conference, Erasmus University, Rotterdam: https://www.academia.edu/247299/The_Arrow_and_the_ Compass, accessible 15 August 2019.

Obradović, Ana. 2018. *Disintegration of Yugoslavia and its Consequences on the Serbian Labour Market*. Cidade Universitária 'Zeferino Vaz': dissertation thesis.

Paternu, Boris et al. (eds). 1988. *Slovensko pesništvo upora* [Slovenian Poetry of Resistance]. Novo Mesto: Dolenjska založba.

Pavlaković, Vjeran. 2016. *Yugoslav Volunteers in the Spanish Civil War*. Research Paper Series of Rosa Luxemburg Stiftung Southeast Europe.4. Belgrade: Rosa Luxemburg Stiftung.

Pavlaković, Vjeran. 2018. 'Controversial Monuments'. In *Monuments and the Politics of Memory in Bosnia and Herzegovina and Croatia, Controversies*. Sarajevo: UDIK.

Petranović, Branko. 1988. *Istorija Jugoslavije 2: Narodnooslobodilacki Rat i Revolucija* [History of Yugoslavia 2: People's Liberation Struggle and Revolution]. Belgrade: Nolit.

——. 1991. *Balkanska federacija 1943–1948* [Balkan Federation 1943–1948]. Belgrade: Zaslon.

Petrović, Tanja. 2013. 'The Past That Binds us: Yugonostalgia as the Politics of the Future'. In Srdja Pavlović and Marko Živković (eds.). *Transcending Fratricide: Political Mythologies, Reconciliations, and the Uncertain Future in the Former Yugoslavia*. Baden–Baden: Nomos.

Pirjevec, Jože. 2011. *Tito in tovariši* [Tito and Comrades]. Ljubljana: Cankarjeva založba.

Pirjevec, Dušan and Repe, Božo (eds). 2008. *Resistance, Suffering, Hope: The Slovene Partisan Movement 1941-1945*. Ljubljana: National Committee of Union of Societies of Combatants of the Slovene National Liberation Struggle; Trieste: Založništvo Tržaškega tiska.

Plamenić, Darko. 1969. 'Belgrade Student Insurrection'. *New Left Review* (March–April) 54. Available online: https://newleftreview.org/issues/I54/articles/d-plamenic-the-belgrade-student-insurrection, accessed 15 August 2019.

Popov, Nebojša. *Sloboda i nasilje: Razgovor o časopisu Praxis i Korčulanskoj letnjoj školi* Freedom and Violence: Dialogue on the *Praxis* Journal and Korcula summer school]. Belgrade: Res Publica, 2003.

Potts, George. 1996. *The Development of the System of Representation of Yugoslavia with Special Reference to the Period Since 1974*. New York: University Press of America.

Procacci et al. (eds). 1994. *The Cominform: Minutes of the Three Conferences 1947/1948/1949*. Milan: Feltrinelli Editore.

Poulantzas, Nikos. 1978. *State, Power, Socialism*. London: New Left Books.

Prashad, Vijay. 2007. *The Darker Nations*. New York: The New Press.

Praznik, Katja. 2013. *Intelektualno gospostvo: sodobna umetnost med vzhodom in zahodom* [Intellectual Domination: Contemporary Area between East and West]. Unpublished PhD dissertation. Ljubljana: University of Ljubljana.

Prifti, Peter R. 1978. *Socialist Albania since 1944: Domestic and Foreign Developments*. London: MIT Press.

Prispevki za slovenski nacionalni program, 57 edition of Nova Revija. [Contributions for Slovenian National Programme]. Ljubljana: Cankarjeva založba, 1987.

Prunk, Janko. 2000, [2004]. *Zgodovina ideoloških spopadov med vojnama* [History of Ideological Struggle between the Wars]. Ljubljana: Društvo.

Przeworski, Adam. 1991. *Democracy and the Market,* Cambridge: Cambridge University Press.

Pučnik, Joze. 1987. 'Politični sistem civilne družbe' [Political System of Civil Society]. *Nova Revija* 57: 130–44.

Pupovac, Ozren. 2006. 'Projekt Jugoslavija: dialektika revolucije' [Project Yugoslavia: Dialectics of Revolution]. *Agregat* 4: 9–10.

——. 2008. *Post-Marxism and Post-Socialism*. Unpublished PhD dissertation. London: Open University.

——. 2010. 'Present Perfect, or the Time of Post-Socialism'. In WHW Collective (ed.), *Art Always Has its Consequences*. (107–13). Zagreb: WHW.

——. 2011. 'Lecture on the Concept of Praxis/humanism'. Korcula: organised by the Rosa Luxembourg Foundation.

Radojević-Kreinzer and Podvršič, Ana. 2018. 'Slovenačka omladina i neoliberalizacija Jugoslavije: od alternativnih pokreta do liberalnog trećeg bloka' [Slovenian Youth and the Neoliberalisation of Yugoslavia: From Alternative Movements to the Liberal Third Bloc]. Lecture at exhibition *Gradove smo vam podigli*, Belgrade.

Radonić, Jovan. 1919. *The Banat and Serbo-Roumanian frontier problem* Paris: Ligue des Universitaires Serbo-Croato-Slovènes.

Radonić, Ljiljana. 2009. 'Post-communist Invocation of Europe: Memorial Museums' Narratives and the Europeanization of Memory'. *National Identities* 19, 2: 269–88.

Rajković, Ivan. 2015. *Struggles for moral Ground: Problems with Work and Legitimacy in a Serbian Industrial Town*. Unpublished PhD dissertation. Manchester: Manchester University.

Rakita, Milan. 2011. 'Prilog kritici teorija modernizacije i tranzitologije u društvenim naukama' [Contribution to the Critique of Modernisation Theory and Transitology in the Social Sciences]. In Ana Veselinović et al. (eds.), *Izgubljeno u tranziciji*. (7–33). Belgrade: Rosa Luxembourg Foundation.

Ramet, P. Sabrina. 2005. *Thinking about Yugoslavia: Scholarly Debates About Yugoslav Breakup and the Wars in Bosnia and Kosovo*. New York: Cambridge University Press.

——. 2006. *The Three Yugoslavias: State-building and Legitimation, 1918–2003*. Bloomington: Indiana University Press.

Rancière, Jacques. 1999. *Disagreement: Politics and Philosophy*. Minneapolis: University of Minnesota Press.

——. 2002. 'Peuple ou multitude?'. *Multitudes online journal*. Available online: http://www.multitudes.net/Peuple-ou-multitudes/, accessed 15 August 2019.

Repe, Božo. 1992. *Liberalizem v Sloveniji*. [Liberalism in Slovenia]. Ljubljana: Borec.

Roberts, Walter. 1973. *Tito, Mihailović and the Allies 1941–1945*. New Brunswick: Rutgers University Press.

Romano, Jaša. 1980. *Jevreji Jugoslavije 1941–1945, žrtve genocida i učesnici NOR*. [Jews of Yugoslavia 1941–1945, Victims of Genocide and Participants in the People's Liberation Struggle]. Belgrade: Savez jevrejskih opština Jugoslavije.

Rubinstein, Alvin. 1970. *Yugoslavia and the Non-Aligned World*. Princeton: Princeton University Press.

Rubinstein, Nicolai 1994, 'Italian Political Thought, 1450-1530'. In Burns et al. (eds), *Political Thought*. (30–65). Cambridge: Cambridge University Press.

Rus, Veljko. 1988. 'Neekonomski vidiki lastništva'[Non-economic Aspects of Ownership]. *Družboslovne razprave* 6, 1: 5–22.

Rusinow, Dennison. 1977. *The Yugoslav Experiment 1948–1974*. London: Hurst, for the R. Institute for International Affairs.

Sabel, Charles, and David Stark. 1982. 'Planning, Politics and Shop-Floor Power: Hidden Forms of Bargaining in the Soviet Imposed State-Socialist Societies'. *Politics & Society* 11, 4: 439–75.

Said, Edward. 1978. *Orientalism*. New York: Pantheon.

Salecl, Renata. 1994. *The Spoils of Freedom: Psychoanalysis and Feminism after the Fall of Socialism*. London & New York: Routledge.

Samary, Catherine. 1988. *Le marché contre l'autogestion: l'expérience yougoslave*. Paris: Publisud, Montreuil.

Sarafis, Stefanos. 1980. *ELAS: Greek Resistance Army*. London: Merlin Press.

Sassen, Saskia. 1996. *Losing Control? Sovereignty in an Age of Globalization*. New York: Columbia University Press.

Schmitt, Carl. 1996. *The Concept of the Political*. Chicago: University of Chicago Press.

——. 2004. *The Theory of the Partisan*. Michigan: Michigan State University Press.

Schöpflin, George. 1993. *Politics in Eastern Europe 1945–1992*. Oxford and Cambridge; Massachusetts: Blackwell.

Sekulić, Dubravka. 2012. *Glotz nicht so romantisch!*. Maastricht: JvE Academy.

Serbian Academy of Arts and Sciences/SANU. 1986. 'Serbian Academy of Arts and Sciences (SANU) Memorandum, 1986'. *Making the History of 1989*, Item #674. Available online: https://chnm.gmu.edu/1989/items/show/674. Accessed 15 August 2019.

Smole, Jože. 1961. *Yugoslav Views of Coexistence*. Belgrade: Jugoslavija, 1961.

Solano, Wilebaldo. 1974. *The Spanish Revolution: The Life of Andreu Nin*. Leeds: Independent Labour Party.

Sowa, Jan. 2012. 'An Unexpected Twist in Ideology'. Praktyka Teoretyczna, 5 (152–80), Warsaw.

Stanković, Slobodan. 1977. 'Analysis of Edvard Kardelj and New Self-management (Relating to Articles from *Borba* in 1976/1977): online http://www.osaarchivum.org/files/holdings/300/8/3/text/82-4-92.shtml (accessed August 2017).

Stanojević, Miroslav. 1994. 'Changing Power Structures: Trade Unions, Privatisation and the End of Self-Management – The Slovenian Case'. *European Journal of Developmental Research* 6, 1: 164–74.

Stojaković, Krunoslav and Tomić, Đorđe. 2013. 'Aus der Geschichte der jugoslawischen Linken. Von den Anfängen im 19. Jahrhundert bis zum Ausbruch des Zweiten Weltkrieges – Desideratsskizzen'. In: Đorđe Tomić, Roland Zschächner, Mara Puškarević and Allegra Schneider (eds). '*Mythos Partizan*'. *(Dis-)Kontinuitäten der jugoslawischen Linken: Geschichte, Erinnerungen und Perspektiven*. (46–87). Münster: Unrast Verlag.

Stojanović, Branimir. 2003. 'Politika Partizana' [Politics of the Partisan]. *Prelom* 3, 5: 48–51.

Stubbs, Paul. 2019. 'Socialist Yugoslavia and the Antinomies of the Non-Aligned Movement'. *Lefteast* online journal: https://www.criticatac.ro/lefteast/yugoslavia-antinomies-non-aligned-movement/, accessed 15 August 2019.

Sundhaussen, Holm. 2012. *Jugoslawien und seine Nachfolgestaaten 1943–2011*. Weimar: Böhlau Verlag.

Suvin, Darko. 2010. 'Pogled unazad iz krize na komunizam i SFRJ' [Looking Back from Crisis to Communism and the Socialist Federative Republic of Yugoslavia]. *Up&Underground* 17–18: 86–95.

———. 2011. 'Ekonomsko-političke perspektive Borisa Kidriča' [Economic-political Perspectives of Boris Kidrič]. *Zarez* 308: 10–11.

———. 2014. *Samo jednom se ljubi: Radiografija SFR Jugoslavije* [You Love Just Once: Radiography of Socialist Federative Yugoslavia]. Belgrade: Rosa Luxembourg Foundation.

———. 2016. *Splendour, Misery, and Possibilities.* Leiden: Brill (HM Series).

Štrajnar, Milena, and Tanja Velagić (eds.). 2004. *Ilegalčki: vojna Ljubljana 1941–1945* [Illegal Kids: War in Ljubljana 1941–1945]. Ljubljana: Društvo ZAK.

Šuvar, Stipe. 1988. *Sociologija sela I, II* [Sociology of the Village]. Zagreb: Školska knjiga.

Tadić, Ljubomir. 1975. 'Order and Freedom'. In Branko Horvat (ed.), *Self-Governing Socialism: A Reader*, 1. (405–16). New York: International Arts and Sciences Press.

Tempo-Vukmanović, Svetozar. 1982. *Revolucija koja teće 1–4. Memoari* [Revolution in Flux, Reminiscences]. Zagreb: Globus.

Terray, Emmanuel, 1996: 'An Encounter: Althusser and Machiavelli'. In Antonio Callari and David Ruccio (eds), *Postmodern Materialism and the Future of Marxist Theory.* (257–77). London: Wesleyan University Press.

Tito, Josip Broz. 1955. *Tito Speaks in India and Burma.* New Delhi: Ananda Press.

———. 1966. *Tito: Selected Military Works.* Belgrade: Vojnoizdavčki Zavod.

Titl, Julij. 1970. *Murska republika 1919* [Mura's Republic 1919]. Murska Sobota: Pomurska založba.

Tomasevich, Jozo. 2001. *War and Revolution in Yugoslavia, 1941–1945: Occupation and Collaboration.* San Francisco: Stanford University Press.

Tomc, Gregor. 1987. 'Civilna družba pod slovenskim socializmom' [Civil Society Under Slovenian Socialism]. *Nova revija* 6, 57: 144–9.

Toscano, Alberto. 2008. 'Carl Schmitt in Beijing: Partisanship, Geopolitics and the Demolition of Eurocentric World'. *Postcolonial Studies* 11, 4: 417–33.

———. 2010. *Fanaticism: On the Uses of an Idea.* London: Verso.

———. 2013. 'Transition Deprogrammed'. Conference presentation at *Historical Materialism*, London, 2013. Available online: http://www.historicalmaterialism. org/conferences/annual10/submit/transition-deprogrammed (accessed May 2015).

Traverso, Enzo. 2017. 'Totalitarianism between History and Theory'. *History and Theory Journal*, Special Issue: Theorizing Histories of Violence. 97–118.

Trček, Tadej. 2016. *Mednarodni pravni vidik razpada SFRJ.*[International legal aspects of destruction of Yugoslavia]. Unpublished Dissertation. Ljubljana: University of Ljubljana, European Law Faculty.

UN General Assembly. 1950. *Fifth Session, Official records, Edvard Kardelj speech.*

Unkovski-Korica, Vladimir. 2011. *Workers' Self-management in the 'Yugoslav Road to Socialism': Market, Mobilisation and Political Conflict 1948–1962.* Unpublished PhD dissertation. London: London School of Economics.

———. 2014. 'Workers' Councils in the Service of the Market: New Archival Evidence on the Origins of Self-Management in Yugoslavia 1948–1950'. *Europe-Asia Studies* 66, 1: 108–34.

——. 2016. *The Economic Struggle for Power in Tito's Yugoslavia: From World War II to Non-Alignment*. London: I.B. Tauris.

Ustav SFRJ [Constitution of the Socialist Federal Republic of Yugoslavia]. 1974. Belgrade: Prosveta.

Velagić, Tanja et al. (ed.). 2009. 'Horizonti zgodovine: sečišča feminističnihbojev' [Horizons of History: Intersections of Feminist Struggles]. *Borec* 61: 657–61.

Velikonja, Mitja. 2009. *Titostalgia: A Study of Nostalgia for Josip Broz*, trans. Olga Vuković. Ljubljana: Peace Institute.

Vieta, Marcelo. 2014. 'The Stream of Self-Determination and Autogestión: Prefiguring Alternative Economic Realities'. *Ephemera* 14, 4: 781–809.

Villa G., Carlos. 2018. *Nova država za nov svetovni red* [New State for a New World Order] Ljubljana: zalozba.

Vittorelli, Natascha. 2015. 'With or Without Gun: Staging Female Partisans in Socialist Yugoslavia'. In Miranda Jakiša; Nikica Gilić (eds), *Partisans in Yugoslavia: Literature, Film and Visual Culture*. (117-136). Bielefeld: Transcript Verlag.

Veselinović, Ana et al. (eds). 2011. *Izgubljeno u tranziciji* [Lost in Transition] Belgrade: Rosa Luxembourg Foundation.

Vučetić, Radina. 2012. *Koka-kola socijalizam – Amerikanizacija jugoslovenske popularne kulture šezdesetih godina XX veka* [Coca-cola Socialism – The Americanisation of Yugoslav Popular Culture in the 1960s]. Belgrade: Službeni glasnik.

Wachtel, Andrew. 2002. *Making a Nation, Breaking a Nation: Literature and Cultural Politics in Yugoslavia*. Stanford: Stanford University Press.

Wallerstein, Immanuel. 1979. *The Capitalist World-Economy*. Cambridge: Cambridge University Press.

Williams, Raymond. 1961. *The Long Revolution*. Harmondsworth: Chatto & Windus.

——. 1989. *Resources of Hope*. London: Verso.

Woodhouse, Christopher. 2002. *The Struggle for Greece, 1941–1949*. London: Hurst & Co.

Woodward, Susan. 1995a. *Socialist Unemployment: The Political Economy of Yugoslavia 1945–1990*. Princeton: Princeton University Press.

——. 1995b. *Balkan Tragedy*. Washington: The Brookings Institution.

——. 2003. 'The Political Economy of Ethno-Nationalism in Yugoslavia'. *Socialist Register* 39: 73–92.

Tse-Tung, Mao. 1965. 'We Must Learn to do Economic Work'. In *Selected Works* 3. Peking: Foreign Language Press.

Zveza komunistov Jugoslavije, CK. 1969. *Naloge ZKJ v nadaljnji graditvi samoupravnih družbeno-ekonomskih odnosov: osnova za razpravo v pripravi na deveti 9. kongres ZKJ*. [Tasks of LCY in Future Building Of Self-Management Socioeconomic Relations: Preparatory Discussions for 9th Congress of the LCY]. Ljubljana: Komunist.

Žerdin, Ali. 1997. *Generali brez kape: čas Odbora za varstvo človekovih pravic*. [Generals Without Heats: Time of Committee For the Protection of Human Rights]. Ljubljana: Krtina.

Živković, Andreja. 2013. 'The Future Lasts a Long Time: A Short History of European Integration in the Ex-Yugoslavia'. Available online: http://www. criticatac.ro/lefteast/the-future-lasts-a-long-time-a-short-history-of-european-integration-in-the-ex-yugoslavia-2/, accessed 15 August 2019.

Živković, Andreja. 2015. 'From the Market ... To the Market: The Debt Economy after Yugoslavia'. In Srečko Horvat and Igor Štiks (eds), *Welcome to the Desert of Post-Socialism*. (27–38). London: Verso.

Žižek, Slavoj. 1989. *The Sublime Object of Ideology*. New York: Verso.

———. 1997. 'Multiculturalism, Or, the Cultural Logic of Multinational Capitalism'. *New Left Review*, September–October: 28–51.

———. 2000. *The Ticklish Subject: The Absent Centre of Political Ontology*. London: Verso.

———. 2001. *Did Somebody Say Totalitarianism? Five Interventions in the (Mis)Use of a Notation*. London: Verso.

———. 2006. *The Parallax View*. Cambridge, Massachusetts: MIT Press, 2006.

———. 2008a. *On Violence*. London: Profile Books.

———. 2008b. *In Defense of Lost Causes*. London: Verso.

———. 2011. *Living in the End Times*. London: Verso.

Županov, Josip. 1967. *O problemima upravljanja i rukovođenja u radnoj organizaciji* [The Problems of Management and Direction in the Organisation of Work]. Zagreb: Naše teme.

———. 1969. *Samoupravljanje i društvena moć* [Self-management and Social Power]. Zagreb: Naše teme.

Index

Močnik, Rastko 104–5, 117, 122–3,
  145–6, 160, 167, 197, 201, 249n4,
  257n1, 257n3, 257n5
modernisation 7, 8, 25, 102, 105, 129,
  172, 255n5
monarchy 37, 39, 56, 66, 72, 73, 218,
  239n24
monetary policy 164, 166–8
morality 22
motorway scandal 187–8
Mouffe, Chantal 24, 203
Mušić, Goran 121–2, 148, 151

Nasser, Gamal Abdel 90
nation-states
  capital accumulation in name of 8
  as hero of right-wing revisionism
    7–8
  revival of model of 194, 227
  'the people' and 236n1, 237n2
National Bank of Yugoslavia 127, 161
national liberalism 4
nationalisation, and transfer to society
  102, 104–5
nationalism
  during early Yugoslavia 191–3
  liberalism and 194–5
  neoliberalism and 5
  nostalgic critique of 11–13
  in political economy critiques 6–7
  research on 189–90
  rise of 205–15, 221–2; in Croatia
    192–3, 222; economic problems
    and 190, 191, 193; IMF funding
    allocation and 188; in Kosovo
    168, 191–2, 222–3; in Serbia
    206–7, 208, 210–12, 222; in
    Slovenia 206, 207–10, 213–14,
    222
  social contract, undermining of by
    175
  Yugoslav super-identity 260n33
Nazism, and colonialism 32–3 see also
  collaborators; fascism
NDH (Independent State of Croatia)
  43

negation 29
Negri, Antonio 232n19
Nehru, Jawaharlal 89–90
neoliberalism
  Bockman on 248n12
  as final stage of history 1
  IMF directives 164–5, 198, 225,
    256n11
  move towards 113, 224
  nationalism and 5
  rise of 9
  see also austerity; precarious work
New Collectivism poster 203–4
New Economic Policy (NEP) 248n11
Nolte, Ernst 9–10, 223
Non-Aligned Movement (NAM)
  88–93
North Macedonia 10
nostalgia 11–13
Nova Revija (magazine) 206, 207–8
Noys, Benjamin 36
NSK (Neue Slowenische Kunst) 203–4

Obodin 160
occupied Yugoslavia, collaborators
  in 43–6
October Revolution 37–8
Olujić-Oluja, Dragomir 178
Omota, Rudi 236n17
'one nation in one state' model 194,
  206, 213
overdetermination 20, 26–7
ownership rights 105

partisans
  definition 50–1, 237n9
  desubstantialisation of 48–54
  establishment of Yugoslavia by
    72–3
  number of 240n27
  oath of 51–2
  reproduction of 63–5, 238n14
  Schmitt on 32–6
  success of 240n25
Party of Democratic Renewal 212
Pavlaković, Vjeran 41–2